The first year of your marriage may not be the
most difficult, but it is the most important.

You're newlyweds, and this is the best time to do everything you can to ensure that your marriage can meet the challenges it will face. Cultivating good habits right away will prepare you for the years ahead.

With almost ninety years of marriage between them, Robert and Bobbie Wolgemuth and Mark and Susan DeVries will help guide you in successfully dealing with the life that happens after "I do."

In this unique flip-over format, the chapter topics are the same, but one half is written by Robert and Mark for the husband, and the other half is written by Susan and Bobbie for the wife. As a couple, you'll each read through your part of the book and "meet in the middle." Together, you'll learn how to have a great marriage that draws you closer to each other and to God.

Start reading, and make this first year together what it was meant to be: the most important year in your life.

Robert Wolgemuth has authored or coauthored more than twenty books, including *She Calls Me Daddy*, *The Most Important Place on Earth*, *Like the Shepherd*, and the notes to *The Devotional Bible for Dads*. Robert wrote this book with his wife of more than four decades, **Bobbie Wolgemuth**, who died of cancer in 2014. She was a Bible teacher and coauthor of several books, including the award-winning, bestselling series *Hymns for a Kid's Heart* with Joni Eareckson Tada.

Mark DeVries is the founder of Ministry Architects and the cofounder of Ministry Incubators and the Center for Youth Ministry Training. The author of twelve books, he served as a youth pastor for thirty-four years. **Susan DeVries** has made a career out of being a wife, mother, and supervising editor for Mark's writing. She has also partnered with Mark in providing premarital counseling and leading marriage retreats and classes for couples.

THE MOST
IMPORTANT YEAR IN A
MAN'S LIFE

WHAT EVERY GROOM

NEEDS TO KNOW

ROBERT WOLGEMUTH & MARK DEVRIES

*We dedicate these books to our "Upstream" Sunday school class
at the First Presbyterian Church of Orlando:
Singles, newly married, veterans—dear friends
And to you, the reader—
Our prayer is that you will find
ideas and encouragement
to make your marriage one of the great ones.*
—Robert & Bobbie Wolgemuth

CONTENTS

ACKNOWLEDGMENTS

These books have, in every sense, been a team effort. Of course, the starting lineup all-stars were Mark and Susan DeVries. For almost eighteen months our book-writing schedules included several multiple-day sessions, planning and outlining each chapter. Then, as the books took shape, countless phone conversations and e-mails were needed before all the "i's were dotted and the t's were crossed." Our deepest gratitude goes to Mark and Susan, not just for their partnership in this book, but for the indelible impact they've made on our family over the past twenty-five years.

When your children are small, you pray that God will send them a grown-up couple who will love them with no strings attached, another couple who will confirm your spiritual values, another couple to counsel them as they make life-altering decisions, another couple to advise them on their choices of mates, another couple to meet with them and their future spouses, and another couple to conduct their wedding ceremonies. In Mark and Susan DeVries, God has blessed us with *one* couple to do *every single one of these things*. Try as we might, we could never adequately express our deepest gratitude to these precious friends.

Once the four of us had finished the drafts of the manuscripts, we made copies and distributed them to a handful of wise—and honest—friends who would tell us the truth. We are so thankful to Asim and Colleen Ardaman, Jen Baxley, Jane Callahan, Jon and Angie Guillaume, Kevin Mercer, Sharon Merosi, David and Wynne McFarlin, Keith and Suzanne Rhodes, Jon and Missy Schrader, and Christopher and Julie Tassy.

In the middle of this book you'll find questions for personal reflection or group discussion. Lisa Guest helped us with these, and we're thankful to her. She came to us highly recommended, and now we know why.

Finally, our thanks goes to our literary agent, Ann Spangler; our Zondervan editor in chief, Sandy Vander Zicht—who hung in there with us when many mere mortals would have bailed out; substantive editors Lori VandenBosch and Dirk Buursma; and our friends in the Zondervan marketing and sales team.

We're very thankful to each of you.

Robert and Bobbie Wolgemuth
Orlando, Florida

INTRODUCTION

I t doesn't matter how you happened to get a copy of this book. It may have been a wedding gift to you and your bride; it may have been given to you by a friend, a minister, or a professional counselor. What matters, really, in the end is that you're here.

You may be eager to dive in and learn everything you can about having a great marriage. You may forego meals and sporting events until you get the whole way through because you're so excited. Or maybe not.

SOME PERSPECTIVE

When I opened the huge box I had just wrestled from the trunk of my car and set it on the garage floor, there was a piece of paper lying on top of all the unassembled pieces. "Warning: Improper Assembly May Cause Serious Injury" was printed on a piece of inescapable, iridescent lime-green paper.

My wife, Bobbie, and I had just bought one of those gigantic gas grills. I enjoyed barbecuing but decided that I had coaxed my last pile of smoldering charcoal briquettes. I needed gas!

The outside of the box had alerted me that there was "Some Assembly Required." But when I opened the crate and saw the lime-green warning, I became very serious about following the instructions. It was the words *may cause serious injury* that did it. Envisioning raw steaks on the grill and a well-done chef was not a pretty thing.

Your marriage license should have included a similar notice printed on loud paper: "Warning: Not Paying Attention to the *First Year of Marriage* May Result in Serious Lifelong Consequences—Unhappiness Like You Can't Imagine."

So you can think of this book as an assembly manual for your marriage—much easier to follow than the one included with the gas grill.

WHO ARE THESE PEOPLE AND WHAT ARE THEY TRYING TO DO?

These books are the result of the collaborative effort of two couples—Mark and Susan DeVries, and Bobbie and me, Robert Wolgemuth. Mark and Susan have been our close friends for many years. Our daughters, Missy and Julie, grew up with Mark and Susan, who were their youth leaders and mentors. Eventually our daughters both worked with them as volunteers in youth ministry.

As a pastor, Mark has counseled hundreds of engaged couples (sometimes with Susan, sometimes by himself), including our two daughters and their fiancés, Jon and Christopher. Seeing firsthand the effect of Mark and Susan's premarital counseling with our own children, we wanted to make these crucial insights available to others—people like you who may never have the chance to meet Mark and Susan.

Being a lay minister and Bible teacher for over thirty years has also allowed me to be involved with many couples who have dealt with marital challenges. And over the years I've come to a single conclusion: There is no more important human quest than building exceptional marriages. The principles you will soon read about were not learned in a classroom but through our own experience, particularly the multitude of mistakes we've made during the combined total of almost six decades of our own marriages.

The men's and the women's chapters have matching themes but contain quite different material. As we present this information, Mark and I are speaking on the "men's side," and Susan and Bobbie are speaking on the "women's side." For ease of reading, we have written each book in only one person's voice. In the men's book, you will hear my voice throughout, and in the women's book, your wife will hear Susan's. But Mark and Bobbie—whose voices you will not hear but whose names you will often see—have been at the heart of the development and the actual writing of both books from day one.

WHAT AM I SUPPOSED TO DO WITH THIS BOOK?

We want you to know from the outset that this is not a book to help you understand "the ordinary woman"—we realize that the woman you have married is not ordinary. This is a book to help you accomplish your mission of becoming an expert on how to bring happiness to just one woman and, in turn, enjoy the benefits of a great partnership.

Though different couples will approach these books in different ways, here's a process that can help you take what you are learning in these chapters and apply it to the end that you and your spouse will know and enjoy each other more:

Feel Free to Sneak: Once the first draft of the manuscript was complete, we presented copies to several volunteers from our *Upstream* Sunday school class for their reading and evaluation. We found that wives had a funny habit of reading the men's chapters. And every now and then, even the most reading-resistant man would snoop around in the women's chapters. That's good. Some of the best interaction you will experience will come when you and your wife read each other's chapters and then say, "That's me," or, "I'm not like that at all!"

Ask the Expert: There will likely be things you read about "women in general" that just aren't true about your wife. When you run across those things, ask your wife questions such as "Is this really what you think?" and "Is this true for you?"

Be the Expert: Even if you've only been married for a few weeks, your wife may already be struggling. Some researchers estimate that as many as 90 percent of brides experience some depression in their first year of marriage.[1] The more your bride has the chance to feel understood, to hear your reaction to what you're reading, the more quickly you'll see the fog of uncertainty lift.

Meet in the Middle: In the center of the book, we've provided a few questions that can help you review what you've read and jump-start your conversations about these chapters. You may want to make a date once a week or once a month with your wife to talk through what you've read, or perhaps you'll want to meet together with a few other couples.

A FEW MORE THINGS

The titles for these books are true for men and women who choose to marry. However, if the first year of marriage were the most important year in *every* man and *every* woman's life, people of no less stature than Jesus and Mother Teresa would have missed "the most important year" in their lives. Because you and I *have married* and because the first year of marriage *is* so critical in shaping our future, we are convinced that the titles *The Most Important Year in a Man's Life* and *The Most Important Year in a Woman's Life* best convey the heart of our message.

Some long-married couples who have reviewed these books have asked, "Is it too late for us to have the most important year?" If you and your wife are willing to wake up to your need to invest in your marriage in a whole new way, it is not too late. So whether you've been married for thirty days or for thirty years, we invite you to let this next year be *the most important year* of your life.

Just a final note: The stories you are about to read are true. In most cases, the names and the circumstances have been changed to mask the identity of those whose stories we are telling.

Robert Wolgemuth   *Mark DeVries*
Orlando, Florida   *Nashville, Tennessee*

1

THE MOST IMPORTANT YEAR: BRINGING HAPPINESS TO YOUR WIFE

If trying hard was the key to a healthy marriage, most couples would find themselves in the Healthy Marriage Hall of Fame.

JEFF VAN VONDEREN, *FAMILIES WHERE GRACE IS IN PLACE*

◆━◆▮◆━◆

The coach had seen enough. He called for a time-out and motioned his quarterback over to the sidelines. Something horrible was going on out there, and the quarterback needed to hear what the coach had to say. To ignore the issue would have spelled certain defeat, and this game was too precious to squander.

We've all seen these sideline conversations on television. Some quarterbacks are focused and listening carefully; some nervously glance back and forth while their coach gives instructions. Others almost seem cavalier, shrugging their shoulders. And when this happens, we see the coach's face become more intense, as if to say, "You listen to me, Buster! This whole game depends on it." We've even seen coaches grab their field commanders by the shoulders to make certain they don't miss anything.

How many weddings have you been to? A dozen? More?

And have you ever watched the groom's face? Does he remind you of the quarterback? Is he glancing left and right, even acting as though it's just another day? Or is he focused, listening to every word being said, as though his future depended on it?

Naturally, most grooms have a subtle first-night twinkle in their eye. That's to be expected. But what they may not know is that this night is the first night in the most important year of their lives.

If they fail to pay careful attention to what goes on over the next twelve months, the cost may be a lifetime of frustration and nonstop misery. But if they learn to do the right things and establish the right habits, the rewards will be measurable—and fantastic!

The goal of this book is, first of all, to get your focused attention. Then I'm going to do my best to convince you that the first year of your marriage *is*, in fact, the most important year in your life.

Making the Early Investment

Jerry set down his newspaper, swiveled his chair toward the window, and leaned back. "I'm a millionaire," he whispered. "A millionaire!" He closed his eyes and let it sink in.

Ten years earlier, one of Jerry's closest friends from graduate school had come with a proposal. Over breakfast, Clark Boyer had told Jerry about his idea for starting a house-call computer service business. "We're going to name it CompuCalls," Clark told him. "Today the computer business is where the automobile business was forty years ago— lots of hardware out there but not a lot of convenient, reliable service."

Jerry knew that Clark was above average in the intelligence department. But, even more important, Clark wasn't afraid of hard work. And CompuCalls was a solid idea.

"I need ten thousand dollars," Clark announced, just as breakfast arrived.

Jerry sat for a moment, staring at his bacon and eggs. Ten thousand dollars was a lot of money. He and Dianna had just bought their first home, and he still had a few payments left on his car loan. But Clark was his friend, and Jerry had this sense about the proposal. He wasn't a gambler by nature, but Jerry had confidence in Clark.

"As far as I'm concerned, you're on," Jerry said evenly. "Dianna knows you and trusts you. I'll check with her before I give you my final word, but I think she'll be on board, too," he added, a faint smile forming on his face. "I know you're going to make it work."

Over the next ten years Jerry watched Clark pour himself into his work. CompuCalls hired bright young graduates from their town's community college, and the company grew and thrived. Seven years into the business, Clark was given the "Young Entrepreneur of the Year" award, and several large computer sales companies had begun contacting him about a buyout. Clark kept Jerry informed about the offers.

Three years later, Jerry held the newspaper and read the headlines in the business section that made it official: "Boyer sells CompuCalls for Twelve Million."

Jerry's ten thousand dollars had bought him 15 percent of Clark's company, and now, after a decade, the investment was worth well over a million dollars.

Now here's an interesting question: What are the chances that the company that just bought CompuCalls will realize the same return on their investment that Jerry made?

Slim and none.

Why? One word: *timing*.

Jerry's investment came early in Clark's business plan. Ten years later the dividend opportunities just aren't the same. Ten years earlier, 15 percent of CompuCalls cost Jerry ten thousand dollars. Today it's costing someone $1.8 million, almost 200 times Jerry's investment. The new company will never get those multiples again.

Invest in the First Year

This is a book about the first year of marriage—the first year of *your* marriage. Let's pretend that you and I are having breakfast together, and just before you take your first bite of scrambled eggs I tell you about a great investment opportunity. "You've just gotten married. That's great. And if you do the right things now, I can guarantee a great return on your investment."

I've got your undivided attention.

"But if you decide not to make the investment," I add as a postscript, "your chances for a strong and satisfying marriage are going to be greatly reduced. And if your marriage fails, the consequences are going to be tragic—and expensive."

Then, as with any legitimate investment prospectus, I present you with a few convincing endorsements:

1. People with satisfying marriages live longer, enjoy better health, and report a much higher level of satisfaction about life in general.[2]
2. Married men report a deeper satisfaction about life in general than do single men. Forty percent of married couples say they are very happy, compared to 18 percent of those divorced and 22 percent of those never married or of unmarried couples living together.[3]

3. Despite the myths about the single life, married men enjoy much more frequent sex (almost twice as often) than single men.[4]

4. Even if you are a bottom-line kind of guy who likes to think in dollars and cents, check this out: Recent statistics show that the average married couple in their fifties has a net worth nearly five times that of the average divorced or single person.[5]

5. Divorce dramatically increases the likelihood of early death from strokes, hypertension, respiratory cancer, and intestinal cancer. Astonishingly, being a divorced nonsmoker is only slightly less dangerous than smoking a pack (or more) of cigarettes a day and staying married! (Should divorce summons papers come with the surgeon general's warning, too?)[6]

Research guarantees it: A satisfying marriage can bring you more happiness, more money, less sickness, and better sex. I think we've just redefined a no-brainer.

Pay Me Now or Pay Me Later

It's often assumed that marriages fail because of a lack of investment— time, effort, focus, and intentionality. That's true, but only partially.

Mark and I have talked with countless couples whose marriages are flailing—or failing. Many are more than willing to work at it, and work sacrificially. As a matter of fact, some of the guys we know who struggle in their marriages are investing exponentially *more* energy, anxiety, and money trying to keep their marriages alive than couples with healthy marriages will have to invest *during their entire lifetimes*.

The question must be asked: If these couples are working so hard, why are their marriages failing?

It's exactly what Jerry found out with his successful investment in CompuCalls. It's all about *good timing*. Failed marriages are not the result of the lack of investment but the lateness of that investment.

We've seen it happen over and over. Men have come to us for help only after their marriages are in deep trouble—in some cases, headed perilously toward divorce. A man may become motivated to work on his marriage when it's in critical condition. The work and the sacrifices he makes may be nothing short of heroic. But tragically, they come awfully late.

A DESPERATE SITUATION

He called to say that he had to talk—immediately! "Becky has left me. She won't even talk to me. What am I going to do?"

Bill was desperate. He knew he was about to lose the very thing that mattered to him the most—his family. Over coffee, Bill admitted that he had failed. Through tears he confessed that he had neglected his wife. And now she had moved out.

"I'll do anything," Bill vowed, his jaw set with determination. "I'll do anything to get her back."

Over the next months, Bill began the long, slow climb to rebuild Becky's trust. She was understandably skeptical. The emotional scars were too deep for a quick fix. Bill was beginning to realize that, after taking fifteen years to carelessly dismantle his marriage, it was unlikely that it could be rebuilt in a matter of months.

> I've never met a man who said, "I am choosing to invest poorly"—financially or in marriage. But many men simply do.

Can Bill's marriage be saved? Absolutely, particularly if he's willing to do the costly work he promised to do—work he should have done fifteen years before. But this kind of rebuilding can be exhausting. The challenge is often so demanding, so humbling, and so uncomfortable—and the progress so slow—that many men simply give up.

When Mark and I first talked about writing this book, we brought to mind guys like Bill. There have been times when it felt as though we were trying to stop a man in the middle of a free fall from a high cliff. It's been painful for us, but our discomfort has no comparison to the agony of these men.

I've never met a man who said, "I am choosing to invest poorly"—financially or in marriage. But many men simply do. Their minimal net worth has been the result of neglect. Sheer default.

Making careless investments comes easily; it takes intentional planning to invest wisely.

HOW DOES THIS HAPPEN?

Given the value of a great marriage, it doesn't make sense that men would scorn making a sound investment early on. However, so many make this mistake. I want to suggest two theories about why this happens:

The Conquest Phenomenon

Some men act as though their work is done the moment their bride says "I do." It's almost as though, on their wedding day, they take their to-do list and put a check mark next to "find a wife." Then, after the honeymoon, it's back to work—and back to that to-do list—with many more battles to win and more check marks to make.

Perhaps the most interesting part of this phenomenon in men is that, at the same moment they're feeling a sense of finality about their wedding-day accomplishment, their brides are seeing it as just the beginning.

Choosing Not to Choose

This book is based on a single foundational assumption: Your marriage and your life are going to be a hundred times more satisfying, more resilient, and more prosperous if you intentionally develop the right habits in the first year—when the investment is fairly "inexpensive."

If you undervalue this first year and develop bad habits, a solid marriage will be much more expensive to recover later on—or these habits may eventually destroy your marriage.

TIME-TESTED PRINCIPLES

As you and I begin to explore this first-year investment strategy, I want to unveil a treasure that is thousands of years old. Listen to this amazing piece of advice, tucked in the Old Testament between instructions on divorce and directions for the proper use of millstones when making a loan agreement (no kidding):

> If a man has recently married, he must not be sent to war or have any other duty laid on him. For one year he is to be free to stay at home and bring happiness to the wife he has married.
>
> DEUTERONOMY 24:5

Although the prospects of such a thing may sound hilarious or outrageous to you, there are some interesting investment principles buried here that you'll want to take seriously.

The Challenge Principle — "For one year"

Most guys love a contest. We gravitate toward the competitive. Well, here's a huge challenge: If you want to have a great marriage, don't do anything for a whole year except *learn to love your wife.*

I'm pretty sure I know what you're thinking. *C'mon, be reasonable. I've got work to do. If I were to take a whole year off, I'd be fired from my job—and that wouldn't be good for either of us.*

Don't worry. I'm not advocating unemployment. Just intentionality. Your job in your first year of marriage is to become an expert on one woman—your wife—and to learn, better than anyone else in the world, how to "bring her happiness." And the Old Testament advice is to take one year, ONE WHOLE YEAR. A weekend seminar or a great book about marriage will not be enough—not even the standard five-session premarital counseling commitment. There's no other way to say it: It's a big investment!

> Your job in your first year of marriage is to become an expert on *one* woman — your wife — and to learn how to "bring her happiness."

The ADD Principle — *"not be sent to war or have any other duty laid on him"*

Like folks who suffer from Attention Deficit Disorder (ADD), our problem often is our lack of focus. We're distracted by things our wives don't see—things they may not even care about.

Because you've checked "get married" off your list, you may be tempted to pay more attention to other unfinished things, such as going on to graduate school, landing a good job, or staying in shape physically. But now that you're married, your most important assignment *is* working on building this relationship with your wife.

The Reciprocity Principle — *"bring happiness to the wife he has married"*

Chalk it off to our humanness, but most of us have this backwards. We're eager for our wives to find ways to make *us* happy.

My friend Gary Smalley tells the story of the newlywed couple who moved into the house across the street from Hank and Edna. Soon Edna noticed that when the young groom came home from work each day, instead of pulling into the garage, he parked his car in the driveway and walked down the sidewalk to the front door.

She also noticed that he always had something in his hand—a wrapped gift, a bunch of flowers, or some other special item. He'd ring the doorbell, his wife would answer the door, he'd present the gift, and they'd embrace.

Edna couldn't help herself. One evening after dinner she told Hank all about the couple and what the young husband did each day.

"Why don't you start doing that, Hank?" she whined.

"Well," Hank stammered, "I guess I could." He took a deep breath. "I *could* do that—but I don't even *know* that lady."

Regardless, Edna had it right. It was Hank's job to remember what it was like when he was romancing her.

Early in our marriage my wife, Bobbie, said it to me this way: "I just want to know that, even though you're busy, once in a while you stop and think about me."

Okay, you might be thinking, *but what should my wife do for me?*

That's a fair question, but the answer is sobering. This Old Testament admonition says absolutely nothing about your wife's job. She's given no direction at all. But this is where the reciprocity part comes in. When you make her happiness your priority, your wife finds herself compelled to make *you* happy.

> When you make her happiness your priority, your wife finds herself compelled to make *you* happy.

Doing everything you can do during this first year to make your wife happy is not just an unselfish act of martyrdom. Having a contented wife will make an immense difference in your *own* happiness.

The book of Proverbs affirms this idea with a touch of humor—in fact, these exact words appear twice in Proverbs: "Better to live on a corner of the roof than share a house with a quarrelsome wife."[7]

Though it's not always the case, unhappy, nagging, contentious, quarrelsome wives are often married to overly busy, nonresponsive, preoccupied, self-absorbed husbands. And, by trial and error, these wives have learned that the only way to get their husbands' attention is to do something annoying.

Your challenge is to choose to pay more attention to your wife during this first year than you do to your neighbor's new car or to the NCAA Final Four on television. And when you make this investment during the first year, your marriage will be far more satisfying for the rest of your life. It'll be worth millions.

Before you turn the page, decide right now to make the next twelve months the most important year of your life.

2

NEEDS: THE YES
SPIRAL

◆◆◆◆◆

"Hi, honey, I'm home."

They're the same words you use each day when you come home, but this time the tone of your voice lets your bride know that it's been a rough one. Quitting your job is all you thought about the whole way home.

As you walk into the house, you're confronted by the aroma of something wonderful. Your wife hears your voice, and she hurries to meet you. Before you can put your computer case down, she wraps her arms around your neck and kisses you. She leans in and whispers something flirtatious about the surprise she has in store for you tonight. She pulls back and takes your computer case. Then she reaches up and loosens your tie.

"I've got just the thing for you," she says, leading you to your favorite chair. Next to the chair sits a frosted glass of your favorite beverage, today's newspaper, and the TV remote.

"You sit here and rest awhile," she says. "I'll get the rest of the dinner on the table."

◆◆◆◆◆

When this scenario is described to a roomful of couples, it doesn't take long for the men to begin groaning and laughing. "Yeah, right," they say. "Like that would ever happen in my house!" For most husbands, this kind of evening isn't something they'd ever expect. It's nothing they'd even dare to dream about.

But hold on. There *are* men who experience this—not every night, of course, but every once in a while. It's enough to make them shake their heads and wonder how they could have been so fortunate to have been given a wife like this. And "dumb luck" simply isn't the right answer.

> A husband finds great joy in bringing pleasure to his wife.

No, good things like this don't happen by pure chance. They happen when a couple chooses to cherish each other, finding fulfillment in meeting each other's needs in surprising and extravagant ways.

Now—a question for you: "What would make a woman treat her husband this way?"

You know the answer, don't you? A woman acts this way when her husband has gone first. Her lavishness is in direct response to his willingness to cherish her and to respond to her needs. In a healthy marriage, a husband finds great joy in bringing pleasure to his wife, and a wife delights in demonstrating her love in creative ways.

THE PROVERBS 31 *MAN!*

From time immemorial, people have challenged women with the description of the perfect wife—more like Wonder Woman—found in Proverbs 31. But when you take a good look at this ancient poem, there's a man hiding in there.

In fact, to understand the Middle Eastern culture in which this poem was composed, it would have been impossible for a married woman to experience this kind of success *without* a pretty unconventional—and terrific—husband!

Her Husband Has Full Confidence in Her (31:11)

Don't you love the sound of that? The Proverbs 31 man "has full confidence" in his wife. There's plenty of maturity—and balance—in their relationship. He doesn't treat his wife like a child, nor does he treat her like she's his mother. He encourages her specific gifts, and, like a plant living in a greenhouse, she blossoms in that environment.

This is a man who trusts his wife's judgment. He's not threatened by her success or by her busy life. This guy's wife manages her home and runs several businesses. And he gives her freedom to invest, freedom to manage the household, freedom to sell what she produces, and freedom to care for the poor and needy.

Over the years, my wife and I have observed this idea of mutual respect among married couples. We've seen couples where the husband is so domineering that his wife lives with fear that she'll make a mistake and her husband will discover it. She's terrorized by the specter of a bounced check or a dented fender. And we've seen couples where the wife is so independent that her husband has no idea what she's up to. Her friends, her daily activities, and her calendar are in a completely different sphere than his—and he's fine with it.

> He encourages her specific gifts, and, like a plant living in a greenhouse, she blossoms in that environment.

A Proverbs 31 husband has *full confidence* in his wife, and it's clear that he wouldn't be comfortable in either of the above scenarios.

Her Husband Is Respected at the City Gate, Where He Takes His Seat among the Elders of the Land (31:23)

A few questions to consider:

- Is this man respected among his peers because he has a wife who respects him? or
- Does her admiration raise him to higher levels of success and self-respect?
- Is this man's wife respectful of him because of his impeccable character? or
- Is his integrity tied to her high expectations of him?

The right answer to each of these questions: *Yes.*

Her Husband Praises Her (31:28)

The wife of the Proverbs 31 man immediately gains self-esteem from the sterling reputation of her husband. When she's seen with him in public, she swells with pride. His integrity automatically accrues to her! "[Her husband] praises her" (31:28). Few things are more motivating to a woman than words of sincere admiration coming from her husband. The Proverbs 31 man is liberal with these expressions.

Once again the chicken-and-egg question begs to be asked: "Which comes first—the praise or the success?" And once again, the answer is the same: *Yes.*

Because this woman is married to a man who believes in her and verbally honors her and celebrates her success, she grows in confidence and becomes increasingly competent—which produces more praise from her husband, which in turn enhances her achievements. When you meet this woman, you can tell that she's married to some kind of a great guy!

> When you meet this woman, you can tell that she's married to some kind of a great guy!

GETTING TO YES

Meeting each other's needs leads to an increasing comfort in conversation, which leads to more frequent opportunities for intimacy, which leads to more satisfaction, which leads to a greater motivation to meet each other's needs—and on and on it goes.

We call this the *Yes Spiral,* and it leads to outdoing each other in showing love. Here's how it works:

You: "Hi, sweetie, I'm home." No response from your wife, only the rattling of pans in the kitchen. "How 'bout a little welcome parade for the king of the castle?" The tone of your voice lets her know that you're just kidding.

Your Bride: "I'm sorry. I didn't hear you come in. I was just caught up in getting dinner ready." She comes over and wraps her arms around your waist. Looking up at you, she gives you a big kiss. "Hey, I hate to ask you to do this 'cause I know you just got home, but I'm in the middle of cooking and just realized I'm missing a couple different spices. I really need them for this recipe. Could you run out and get them for me?"

You: "Sure. What do I need to get?"

Your Bride: "You're the best. Here's the list."

You: "Oh, I almost forgot. While I'm out, would you call my parents and ask them when I can stop by their house and pick up that package?"

Your Bride: "Of course. I haven't talked to your mom in a couple days anyway."

You walk over to your wife and give her a hug.

Your Bride: "I love you so much."

You: "I'll get spices for you anytime."

Your Bride: "Hey, mister, if you hurry back, we can talk about some of my own secret spices." As you leave, she's shaking her head, smiling and saying quietly, "You amaze me."

A silly conversation? Maybe. But did you catch how many times you and your wife said yes to each other in this quick exchange?

1. She said yes to your nonverbal request for a warm greeting.
2. You said yes to her request to make a quick trip to the grocery store.
3. She said yes to your request to call your parents about the package.
4. You said yes by giving her a hug.
5. She said yes to any designs you may have had on being intimate tonight—and you didn't even have to ask.

With each affirmation—in words, actions, or attitudes—the view from your *Yes* ascent widens, and the two of you feel freer together, more willing to serve each other, more willing to creatively meet each other's needs.

But what if you and your wife chose another route:

You: "Hi, sweetie, I'm home." No response from your wife, only the rattling of pans in the kitchen. "How 'bout a little welcome parade for the king of the castle?" The tone of your voice contains just a hint of sarcasm.

Your Bride: "I'm sorry. I didn't hear you come in. I was just caught up in getting dinner ready." She stays in the kitchen and calls out to you from there. "Hey, I hate to ask you to do this 'cause I know you just got home, but I'm in the middle of cooking and just realized I'm missing a couple different spices. I really need them for this recipe. Could you run out and get them for me?"

You (thumbing through the mail): "Why didn't you get them when you were out? You just got groceries yesterday."

Your Bride: "I didn't realize this recipe called for them. I've had a few other things on my mind, you know." Her tone of voice has an edge. "Here's the list."

> *You:* "We'll just have to do without your little spices tonight. I'm not going out again. Not after the day I had. Hey, did you call my parents about when I'm supposed to stop by to pick up the package?"
>
> *Your Bride:* "You told me *you* were going to do it. I can't do *everything.* I have a job, too, you know."
>
> *You:* "Fine. I guess we won't pick it up. It doesn't matter to me anyway."
>
> *Your Bride:* "Excuse me. I need to go to the grocery store. Dinner will be a little late tonight." Her words are barely audible through her clenched teeth as she heads for the door—"You amaze me."

You can feel the tension, can't you? As you and your wife say no to each other's needs, each of you becomes less willing to say yes. The descending *No Spiral* becomes tighter and tighter. You feel trapped, less willing to give, and not at all interested in meeting each other's needs.

Consider the expenditure of energy in these two conversations. The first is smooth and effortless, though it takes a willingness at times to respond in ways that may feel less convenient. Not only do you love your wife more after this quick exchange, but you actually feel better about yourself. The second conversation—well, it is completely draining, leaving you feeling exhausted.

"Of Course I'd Die for Her, But . . ."

You may be thinking, *I understand about how conflict is more draining than peacefulness—but what if I don't feel like doing what my wife needs me to do?* So you take a deep breath and ask me the question you really don't want to ask: "Are you suggesting that I suck it up and go to the grocery store anyway, even though my heart's not in it?"

Yes, that's exactly what I'm suggesting.

The biblical mandate is perfectly clear: "Husbands, love your wives, just as Christ loved the church and gave himself up for her."[8] Love is always linked to *action,* even if we don't feel like it. Because you *say* you love your wife, your choice must always be to *do* things that please her, regardless of what may seem to be pure inconvenience.

In the *Yes Spiral* conversation, you demonstrated active love, and the feelings followed close behind. You felt great. But in the *No Spiral* conversation, you did exactly what you believed you had a right to do, exactly what you felt like doing. But by the time your wife stormed out of the house to get the spices, you were both tied up in knots. You were justified in claiming your right to unwind after a rough day, but you felt awful.

> Love is always linked to action, even if we don't feel like it.

Ask a man if he'd be willing to die for his wife, and it's very likely he'll say that he would. With visions of evil executioners offering the choice between our lives or our brides', we'd courageously give ourselves. "Take me instead," we'd say, with heroism oozing from every pore.

This kind of dying is the easy kind—quick, valiant, offering a clear choice between selfishness and sacrifice. But let's face it—it's highly unlikely that this will ever happen to us. "Laying down our lives" gets demonstrated in smaller and less visible or applaudable ways. You are charged with considering your wife's needs above your own. In this sense her request is more important than the fatigue you're feeling from a big day and your need to put your feet up. A *lot* more important!

"But what if meeting my wife's needs like this doesn't come naturally," you may argue. "Responding well to my wife's surprise requests is something I'm lousy at." Or how about this one? "My wife knows I don't do housework." Or this? "I'm just naturally a competitor, so showing consideration to other drivers on the highway just isn't who I am, even when my wife pleads with me to calm down."

Okay, so these things don't come naturally. Did learning to ride a bicycle come naturally, or did you have to work at it? How about swimming? Or learning to read? Or using a computer? Did these things come naturally, or did you *learn* them? And what did it take for these to become skills? That's easy to answer. You *wanted* to master them—and so you did.

WHAT DOES SHE NEED?

Late one evening a couple went for a walk around the neighborhood. They walked past two boys who were down on their knees under a streetlight. They were searching through the grass for something. Carefully they swept their hands back and forth.

"What's the matter?" the man said to the kids. "You boys lose something?"

"Yeah," one of the kids responded without looking up. "My friend lost his pocketknife."

"Did he lose it here?" the woman asked.

"No," said the boy, looking up at the woman. "He lost it down the street, but the light's a lot better here."

A silly joke, but it contains a powerful message: we do sometimes try to meet our wives' needs based on what might be convenient for us. But we're far away from finding what our wives are looking for. This may keep us busy, but it's not going to help us find the "lost pocketknife" that matters most to our wives.

So here's an idea. In order of importance, jot down five or six things you think your wife most wants from you. Be as general or as specific as you like. Then tell your wife what you're working on, and ask her to make her own list—without seeing yours. Then schedule an appointment with her to compare your lists. You may want to begin the conversation by telling her about the boys looking for the lost pocketknife in the wrong place. This will help her understand what you're up to.

Once you have her list, start doing the first thing she asks for, and let the fun begin.

WHAT DO I NEED?

Jeremy walked into Mark's office and plopped down on the overstuffed chair in the corner. Mark looked up from his work. Jeremy was clearly irritated.

"After a bad day," Jeremy began, "I need my wife to be there for me. But I have the hardest time putting anything in words. I want to tell Cindy what I need, but it's like my 'asker' is broken—so I pick a fight instead."

"Hey, thanks for being there for me," Jeremy would say sarcastically to Cindy, frustrated because she couldn't read his mind.

The evening was destined to be miserable for both Jeremy and Cindy.

"I've had enough of these tense evenings at home," Jeremy admitted. "What can I do?"

Okay, let me ask you: What would *you* say to Jeremy? How would you help him solve this problem?

We know that Cindy really *does* love Jeremy. But, on the days he needs her most, he doesn't give her much to work with, does he?

First of all, this couple needs a clean slate. And that can come only when Jeremy is courageous enough to admit that his sarcasm and fight-picking strategies are childish and not helpful. Next, Cindy needs a target—a clear picture of what her husband needs from her. Jeremy may simply want to reverse the exercise I suggested in the last section, only this time, the two of them list the things that Jeremy needs.

You may also want to take a look at the woman's side of the book—at the list of an expert's opinion of what most men need most from their wives (see pages 30–31). It may take some gut-level honesty to admit that you *need* your wife, and then a little more work to be honest about what your own needs are.

But if you want to actually find that pocketknife, you'll need to move to places where the search may not be as easy.

3

SPIRITUAL UNITY:
KEEPING YOUR HEAD
IN THE ONLY GAME
THAT MATTERS

Marriage for the Christian is a continuous sacrament, an act of praise and obedience, and a means of grace that is inherently every bit as "spiritual" as anything that goes on in a monastery, or in any church or mission field for that matter, and every bit as important (or more so) than any other "work" that one might do in the world.

MIKE MASON, *THE MYSTERY OF MARRIAGE*

Bobbie and I had been married for less than a year. She was trying to finish college and was holding a part-time job as a dental assistant. I was in youth work, making less than minimum wage. Early one afternoon we paid a visit to Bobbie's doctor and discovered that she—we, really—was pregnant.

I was excited about the baby, but the timing was a bit different from my original plan. Not only were we not in any kind of financial condition to add another person to our family, but I was still trying to figure out who *I* was and how I was going to be a good husband. I was also trying to figure out who this woman was, and now I was headed for fatherhood. "Overwhelmed?"—nice try, but it doesn't come close.

We drove home from the doctor's office with virtually no words exchanged. By the time I had unlocked our apartment door, emotion had completely swept over me. Tears were streaming down my face. We walked into the kitchen, and Bobbie pulled out a chair and sat down. I collapsed on the floor in front of her and buried my face in her knees. This was not normal behavior for me. Sobs came from some-where I had never visited before. Bobbie just sat there, probably won-dering who this man was and why he was crying so inconsolably.

> At that very moment, filled with sheer panic, I turned to *God* for help.

After a few minutes, I was able to speak. "I can't do this," was all I could say. "I can't do this."

Strange as it may sound to you, it was then that becoming a good husband and a good dad became achievable goals. Why? Because at that very moment, filled with sheer panic, I turned to *God* for help.

GETTING NAKED

Taking the initiative with regard to spiritual things in your marriage is not easy. It's going to take some honest effort. This is especially true if you can't remember ever seeing your parents express any sort of spiri-tual intimacy together.

For example, for many men there is the horror of an embarrassing "soul nakedness" that comes when they're called on to pray in public, much less one-on-one with their wives. Maybe you've seen an otherwise fearless man reduced to a quivering puddle of warm Jell-O simply by hearing the words, "Okay, Big John, why don't you close this meeting with prayer."

In many ways, you can judge the quality of a couple's intimacy by looking at the comfort level of their conversation in two areas: sex and spiritual things. Conversation about physical intimacy forces you to reveal hidden parts of your mind and your body; conversation about spiritual intimacy uncovers your soul.

Before going any further, let me tell you what I'm *not* talking about here. Spiritual intimacy is not about theological precision or agreeing to the same set of religious doctrines. It's not that these things don't matter. Surely they do. It's just that mere mutual assent to a set of ideas *about* God doesn't go far enough, either in your relationship with Jesus or in your relationship with your wife.

Both relationships require an additional step: an openhearted will-ingness to unveil the secret places, to explore each other's hearts with curiosity and pleasure, to disclose spiritual doubts and fears, and to celebrate new levels of understanding—and to do these things in the context of ordinary living.

"How 'bout that huge hawk up there," I may say to Bobbie as we're driving along the highway near our home. "Isn't God amazing?"

"Come, look at this rainbow," I've heard her call from the porch. These things thrill our eyes and lift our hearts.

We love music, especially old hymns and classical music. We also love jazz and some contemporary Christian music. In the car we'll sometimes stop talking and turn up a favorite, much-loved CD. I mean, *way* up. This music takes our spirits to another plane, and we go there together. Similarly, we rarely miss church, not because we feel guilty if we don't go but because we know that this experience of worship takes us into the presence of the living God. And when we've been with him, everything looks different.

> Conversation about physical intimacy forces you to reveal hidden parts of your mind and your body; conversation about spiritual intimacy uncovers your soul.

We have a retired friend. Not long ago he and his wife attended a marriage retreat. Even though they had passed their golden wedding anniversary a long time before, our friend and his wife were looking for ways to improve their marriage. The gentleman told us that he took pride in his depth of understanding of his wife and in building a successful marriage. (In fact, because they had done so well, this veteran couple had been asked to speak at several marriage retreats themselves.) But this weekend, as a participant, our friend saw something about his wife that he had never seen before.

On the retreat, one of the exercises required the wife to write down the most meaningful ways her husband showed love to her—and for him to do the same for her. With a disarming smile, our friend explained that, after decades of marriage, he expected no surprises from his wife's list. When his wife handed him her list, however, the first item *did* surprise him. He had expected her to say something about how much she appreciated his unsolicited help in cleaning the house, or perhaps how much she enjoyed their weekly date night. But number one on her list of the "most meaningful things my husband does to show me love" was this: when you pray with me and take the initiative about our spiritual life.

Our friend had always considered the carrying out of spiritual practices in his home to be a matter of duty. It had never occurred to him that these things were also a powerful way of *expressing love to his wife*. In her mind, it was number one.

BUT HOW?

You may have no trouble agreeing that these things are important, even *very* important. You know that your wife wants to know your heart, not just your mind and your body. You know that, as you explore spiritual things and place yourselves in God's presence together, good things will happen. But you're asking, "How do I *do* that?"

You may be encouraged to know that when a large number of Christian leaders were asked what they do in their own marriages to cultivate spiritual intimacy, their answers were completely unique. Almost every couple did something a little different.[9]

When Mark meets with couples before their weddings, he suggests the K.I.S.S. (keep it simple, stupid) approach to establishing a pattern for spiritual intimacy in marriage. He makes the simple suggestion that couples start with at least one regular habit: praying before meals, praying together at bedtime, attending church and Sunday school, or reading a devotional book together. Mark asks the groom and his bride to come up with some visible practice that will regularly remind them that theirs is a Christian marriage.

Look at the way the Old Testament describes spiritual intimacy: "Love the LORD your God with all your heart and with all your soul and with all your strength.... Talk about [these commandments] when you sit at home and when you walk along the road, when you lie down and when you get up."[10]

Love the LORD your God: Your proposal to the woman who is now your bride began with a learning and a longing and eventually progressed to a *decision*—"Will you marry me?" In the same way, your relationship with God begins with an understanding of who he is and the experience of a deep sense of lostness without him, and then progresses to a decision: "I want to follow you."

Talk about them when you sit at home: I've already mentioned our experiences of spotting a soaring hawk or a spectacular rainbow from the deck. Seeing these things and commenting, "Isn't God amazing?" reminds us that, by his voice alone, God created each of these wonderful things. There's no need to add anything to make it more "spiritual." There's no need to say, "You know, it's just like Rev. Jones said at the morning service."

Over the years, at special times or because of unusual situations we were facing, Bobbie and I have found time to pray out loud together before we go to sleep. There's nothing fancy about these prayers. They're simply a chance for the two of us to speak to our heavenly Father as though he's right there in the bedroom with us. Truth be told, he *is!*

Hinge Points and Prayer Hooks

Because they represent "corners" in their day, Mark and Susan refer to sitting down, getting up, or going to bed as "hinge points," the most natural arenas for making a spiritual connection. Susan may walk past Mark as they're crawling out of bed early in the morning, kiss him on the cheek, and say, "God is good." At night, Mark may reach across the bed and take Susan's hand before they fall asleep. "You want to pray tonight?" Mealtimes can be another hinge point for you and your wife. Pausing, holding hands, and saying a blessing is a natural hinge point.

There's no fanfare, no great preparation or training for this. But it *does* connect predictable moments in our walk with God, turning ordinary everyday things into spiritual things.

Bobbie and I have a similar thing we call "prayer hooks." These are familiar places, things, or situations we have intentionally connected to prayer. For example, when we're driving to church on Interstate 4 and begin slowing down for the Anderson Street exit, that's a prayer hook. So we pray (we keep going, with our eyes open) for the Sunday morning worship service and for Sunday school. We ask God to speak to us during this time in his house.

The first thing in the morning, when I turn on the lights in my office and see the green chair in the corner, that's a prayer hook. It's as though the chair is speaking to me and inviting me to kneel down and pray.

Some of my other prayer hooks are connected to some pretty mundane things, but they work. For example, when I use my ChapStick, I pray for my son-in-law Christopher, because he's a serious ChapStick user, too. When I take out the trash, I pray for my son-in-law Jon. He taught me to keep extra bags in the bottom of the trash container, so when I see the empty bags down there, I remember to pray for him. One time my friend Jake gave me one of those great trivia facts. He told me that monkeys peel bananas from the bottom because they're easier to open that way. So guess who I pray for every time I peel a banana from the bottom? There are more, but you get the idea.

These are the kinds of things the author of the Old Testament book of Deuteronomy had in mind. Spiritual intimacy with God simply means to include him in your day—especially in the little things.

BECOMING A FAITHFUL BRIDE

As you begin your life as a married man, it's interesting to note that one of the word pictures God uses in the Bible to describe your relationship with him is precisely what you've just experienced—marriage. But in this case *he's* the groom and *you're* his bride!

> As a bridegroom rejoices over his bride,
> so will your God rejoice over you.
>
> ISAIAH 62:5

Mother Teresa understood this. She had just finished teaching about God's standards for families when a man stood up and challenged her. "With all due respect, Mother Teresa," he said, "how can you—someone who has never been married—tell us about what kind of husbands and wives we're supposed to be?"

> Spiritual intimacy with God simply means to include him in your day— especially in the little things.

Unruffled by the man's abruptness, the tiny nun from Calcutta spoke—with a twinkle in her eye. "Sir, that's where you're wrong," she said. "I *am* married. And sometimes Jesus is very hard to live with!"

The man quietly sat down.

The question is clear: What can you learn from God's relationship with you, from the perfect Groom, about what it means to walk with your wife as *her* faithful groom? Here are some examples:

God Is Attentive

Can you imagine what it would be like to be married to someone who never stopped listening to you? Night or day, at a moment's notice—his ears are tuned to your every request. God is in constant communication with you. Sometimes this "communication" is without words. He's on call, just by his presence. Occasionally he "speaks" to you through circumstances, through books, or through the voices of people. And, of course, he speaks clearly when we read the Bible.

God's attentiveness is his full-time activity. Doesn't that sound great? Can you imagine how content your bride would be if she had a groom like that?

God Is Accountable

One of the great mysteries about God is that he is really *three* persons—Father, Son, and Holy Spirit. And these three operate in perfect sync. Nothing is done without each one's oversight and permission. With this Groom, there's perfect accountability.[11]

Even though Bobbie and I have lived in a number of cities throughout our marriage, I've done my best to be part of a group of Christian men—friends—with whom I can study, pray, and be honest about my defeats and victories. Mark has done the same. In fact, some groups get specific about keeping each other accountable in their marriages. In one such group, all the husbands made a pledge to follow this training plan. See what you think:

- I will pray for my wife at least once every day.
- I will pray with my wife at least once a week.
- I will do something every day to grow in my faith.
- I will agree to answer any question from anyone in this group and to give a full and honest answer. "I'd rather not talk about that right now" is not an acceptable response.
- If at any point this entire group agrees that I need to change a behavior they believe could be destructive to my marriage, my family, or my integrity, I agree to do everything in my power to make the change immediately.
- I will respond to my wife's expressed needs with a wholehearted, unqualified yes in my words, attitudes, and actions.

As you can tell, these guys are serious. Now, I have a question for you: Would your wife like to be the bride of a man like this?

God Is Humble

God visited the planet Earth in Jesus Christ. If ever there was anyone who had good reasons to strut, it was Jesus. Everything that was created—billions of galaxies, the nucleus of a carbon atom, a tree frog—came into existence at the mere sound of his voice. And with that same voice he holds all things together. But he refused to forcibly use his power. Instead, he laid it aside and took "the very nature of a servant."[12] He chose the way of humility.

> Arrogance is a strange disease. It makes everyone sick except the person who has it.

Arrogance is a strange disease. It makes everyone sick except the person who has it. I'm sure *you* don't have any interest in being married to someone like this. Neither does your bride. She'd probably rather be married to a man who tenderly served her than to a self-absorbed, swaggering fool. Probably.

God Has Integrity

How many lies does it take to make a man a liar? How many acts of unfaithfulness does it take to make a man a philanderer? How many things does a man need to steal before he is considered a thief? The answer to each of these questions is the same: *only one*. This is a cruel thing, but it's the truth.

The faithful groom has figured out how to take his passions, his character, his mind, and his activities and blend them into consistency. No single area of his life lags behind. A hidden camera would reveal no surprises. God *is* this kind of Groom, and we *know* how it feels to be the "bride" of such a Man.

GET IN THE GAME—SUCK IT UP AND GET IT DONE

Taylor and Laurie were thinking about getting married, but they didn't think they were ready. They wanted to see if they could build some spiritual unity first. They set out to do this by praying together and having a thirty-minute devotional time each week. After a few weeks, Taylor was about to scrap the whole idea. It just wasn't working. In his eagerness to do *something*, Taylor was taking a Bible story and expounding on it like a mini-sermon. Laurie wanted to have a good attitude, but she felt more like a third grader in Sunday school.

When Laurie confessed to Taylor how she felt about his "lectures," he could have thrown in the towel. But Taylor wasn't a quitter. And he did what you and I hate to do. He stopped and asked for directions from someone he trusted. And then he tried again, this time remembering the K.I.S.S. principle.

Taylor trimmed his thirty minute lesson to five minutes of reading verses from a psalm and then talking *with* Laurie about what it was saying to them. Occasionally, he would read from a devotional book, and again they'd discuss it together. Now, instead of Laurie feeling as though her fiancé had become an overnight clergyman, she discovered in Taylor a soul mate. A *spiritual* friend.

God never designed our marriages to be held together simply by sharing a street address or sex or sports or activities or even common beliefs. There is so much more to it than this. The often elusive quality of spiritual intimacy gives you and your bride a whole person-to-person union. It links you together with God and opens up a brand-new dimension to your marriage. Like hitting the "Surround Sound" button on your stereo, spiritual intimacy makes your marriage more magnificent than you could ever imagine.

It's exactly what you and your bride are looking for.

> The often elusive quality of spiritual intimacy gives you and your bride a whole person-to-person union.

4

FAMILY OF ORIGIN:
A RIVER RUNS
THROUGH IT

We say, "the two shall become one." That's fine, but the trouble is that six people marry and sometimes things get a little crowded around the house. There are two sets of parents and two children of the past.

DAVID SEAMANDS, *PUTTING AWAY CHILDISH THINGS*

I t was the longest, no-sleep trip I had ever taken. In 1973, fifteen high school boys and four leaders (I was one of them) borrowed a Winnebago and a pickup truck and drove nonstop from Chicago, Illinois, to Denver, Colorado. Then we boarded a school bus and drove nonstop to Ouray, Utah, where we put in for a white-water ride down the Green River.[13] The road trip from front to back—I drove most of it—took twenty-six hours, and we were all completely exhausted.

Just before we climbed aboard the largest rubber rafts any of us had ever seen, the guide talked us through the dangers of the trip we were about to take. "Inattentive" wouldn't come close to describing his listeners, who were yawning and slouching from road fatigue. He told us about the power of the current on top of the river and down below. He told us that there *would* be times when some of us would go for "unintentional swims." And he told us what to do and what not to do when it happened.

"Keep your legs up," he said. "If you drive them down, your feet can get caught under a rock, and you could be killed." His bluntness lifted some sleepy eyelids. Then he said something like this: "The river looks dangerous enough. But the danger you can see doesn't compare to what's happening below—just beneath the surface."

Over the next four days, the admonitions of the guide proved true. Many of us became "unintentional swimmers." Some of the biggest boys—football players and wrestlers—who thought the guide was exaggerating about the power of the currents below discovered that his warnings were completely true.

> "The river looks dangerous enough. But the danger you can see doesn't compare to what's happening below—just beneath the surface."

The most memorable moment occurred late one afternoon as our raft went straight into a frothing, raging "hole." In an instant, Bill Jackson, perhaps the most athletic boy on the trip, went airborne like a guided missile—from the front of the raft all the way to about fifteen feet behind us, landing with a huge splash. During the next few minutes of watery violence, we grabbed the ropes and hunkered down, hoping to avoid the same fate. Jax kept his legs up and rode it out with us, looking more like a cork than a boy. By nightfall we were able to joke about it, but when it was happening, there was nothing to laugh about.

Thankfully, we all made it to the end of the line safely. Some of us had cuts and bruises as trophies, but we made it nonetheless.

Marriage Currents

Marriage is like a white-water run in a river raft. We ride along, experiencing new adventures at every turn. But the things we bring to our marriage from the family in which we grew up are like the powerful currents beneath. There are times when we enjoy the currents above that shoot us along the river. But there are also times when the currents below become destructive danger zones—especially if they sneak up on us and surprise us.

When Bobbie and I were first married, our lives were filled with unexpected things about the way her family did things compared to mine. One night, after we had finished dinner, Bobbie offered to get me a bowl of ice cream.

"Sure," I said, "that would be great."

In a few minutes, she set a bowl of ice cream in front of me. I mean she brought me a BOWL of ice cream. "This would feed a family of six," I said, not realizing how thoughtless and condescending it sounded.

Bobbie wasn't amused.

I had grown up in a home where frugality and restraint were sacramental. Even though we were fourth-generation American Germans, that sober-minded, desks-in-straight-rows, no-running-in-the-hallways structure was tattooed to our chromosomes. When my mother put ice cream in front of us, it was a small single scoop. If we had been perfect children and Dad was out of town, maybe a scoop and a half. Bobbie's family, on the other hand, knew nothing of such culinary restraint. So to Bobbie, a BOWL of ice cream was perfectly normal.

> The things we bring to our marriage from the family in which we grew up are like the powerful currents beneath.

And there's the most important word in this chapter: *Normal.*

What was *normal* for Bobbie was *not* a scoop. A bowl of ice cream was a BOWL of ice cream. That was normal. My *normal* was something else. And I brought plenty of my own undercurrents to our marriage.

My dad didn't pay much attention to the neighbors. He wasn't rude or unkind to them. It's just that he didn't go out of his way to speak with them or get to know them. Participating in neighborhood parties would have ranked just below gargling with gasoline on his list of enjoyable activities. To me, *normal* was my dad, committed to spending time with his own family but coming and going with a wave and a hello to the neighbors—nothing more than that.

The first time I visited Bobbie's home in Virginia, she was in the kitchen, putting the finishing touches on a beautiful birthday cake. Although it was fairly early in our relationship, we were definitely boyfriend and girlfriend—an item, so to speak.

"Who's that for?" I asked.

"General Illig," she replied with delight.

"Who's General Illig?" I asked, trying not to sound jealous.

"He's our next-door neighbor," she answered.

I remember being completely shocked. *I'm sure he's a nice guy, but why would you waste a perfectly good cake on a neighbor?*

To me, *normal* would have been not even knowing *when* the neighbor's birthday was. What's more, *normal* wouldn't have included buying a birthday card if I *had* known. And it certainly wouldn't have included making a birthday cake—from scratch, no less! What was normal to Bobbie looked like a complete waste of time and energy to me. A good neighbor is a guy who isn't a bother, who keeps his house painted, his lawn mowed, and his weeds to a minimum. Period.

Now, here's something very important about this "normal" issue. Most of the *normals* that you and I bring to our marriages are amoral—neither good nor bad, neither right nor wrong. They're simply the things we were accustomed to as we were growing up—the things we didn't question because it was all we knew. It's a safe bet that most of your *normals* are different from your bride's *normals*.

Someone has suggested that everyone enters marriage with his or her own "ten commandments" about what's normal. But the only time these commandments are identified is when the spouse breaks one of them. Until then, they are only subconscious.

Both of our daughters and their fiancés did their premarital work with Mark and Susan. And Julie and Missy have both told us that, without question, the most productive (and most unsettling) premarital exercise they did centered around this topic of *normal*.

By making use of a genogram—a special family-tree diagram that begins with the grandparents—Mark and Susan are able to sift through the information to discover patterns of *normal*. They ask such questions as, "What would a child growing up in this system have learned about what a normal husband looks like? A normal wife? What does a normal marriage look like? Normal conflict? Normal spiritual life?"

Making Your Own Genogram

To do your own genogram, you and your bride can start by each drawing a family tree that looks something like this:

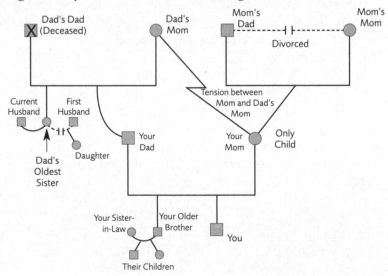

When Mark and Susan complete their work on the genogram with a couple, they ask the bride or groom to give them a brief description of each person in his or her own genogram. These descriptions can vary widely from very specific comments—"president of IBM," "lifetime homemaker," or "serving time"—to more general words such as "nurturer," "strict," or "a jerk." As couples share this information, Mark urges them to say the first things that come to their minds, not to think too long about their answers. Their honest and immediate responses will always provide the best clues to each one's sense of *normal*.

Once these initial descriptive notes are obtained, Mark asks for more information about parents and grandparents—always asking three questions:

- What can you tell us about their marriage?
- What can you tell us about how they dealt with conflict?
- What can you tell us about their spiritual life?

Mark and Susan also ask the bride and groom if there are any models of great marriages in their family systems. Then they ask about any tension between people within each of their families. From this information, Mark writes a "Normal Report," which gives the bride and groom a picture of what a typical person growing up in his or her family would see as normal. This report answers five questions:

1. What would someone growing up in this family system see as a normal husband?
2. What would someone growing up in this family system see as a normal wife?
3. What would someone growing up in this family system see as a normal marriage?
4. What would someone growing up in this family system see as a normal way to deal with conflict?
5. What would someone growing up in this family system see as a normal spiritual life for a married couple?

As Mark and Susan talk couples through the answers to these questions, the response is amazing. The vast majority of couples really get it. They leave this session with their eyes wide open, seeing their need to enter marriage prepared to do more than "what comes naturally."

Note this, too: Though there's much to be gained by working through a genogram with trained counselors, you can make some fascinating discoveries identifying your *normals* using the same process on your own.

SAMPLE "TEN COMMANDMENTS" OF *NORMAL*

After you construct your genogram, it might be helpful to make up a pretend list of "ten commandments." To get you started, here's a list of "commandments" that we've observed. How many would you identify as normal for you?

1. Married women only work until babies are born. Then they stay at home.
2. The fun of Christmas morning is sleeping late.
3. Sex is never to be discussed.
4. The fun of Christmas morning is waking up early and getting completely dressed for a big family breakfast.
5. Two people who really love each other should never argue.
6. No home is complete without a cat.
7. There's no room for childish silliness.
8. Men always do the driving.
9. Two people who really love each other have plenty of arguments.
10. Husbands always plan the vacations.
11. Two children—max.
12. Being late is cute.
13. Men do not need to engage in deep conversation. It's not natural.
14. Being on time is critical.
15. Men always initiate sex.
16. Women whose husbands don't engage in deep conversation are free to tell their friends about it.
17. Life is fun.
18. How many children a couple has is up to God.
19. Kitchen cabinet doors are a nuisance, which is why they should be left open.
20. Women hide their purchases from their husbands.
21. Men don't do housework.
22. Alcohol, in any form, is a bad idea.
23. Except for anger, men do not show their emotions.

24. The house should always be immaculate.
25. Cars are to be idolized and should never be dirty.
26. Dinner isn't dinner without a glass of wine. Football isn't football without a beer.
27. Cars are transportation. Period.
28. Saying a prayer before a meal is a nonnegotiable. Even at McDonald's.
29. Husbands write the checks.
30. Men should volunteer to do housework without being asked.
31. A man should always hold the door for his wife.
32. Sandwiches are always made with white bread.
33. Wives do the books.
34. It's not necessary to say a blessing before every meal. God knows we're thankful.
35. Sitting quietly and reading a book is a complete waste of time.
36. A woman should never make more money than her husband.
37. No home is complete without a dog—a really big dog.
38. A hot breakfast will only be possible if you put a lighted match to your cornflakes.
39. A loving husband should be blind to his wife's weight gain. Anything else is conditional love.
40. Watching sports on television is a complete waste of time.
41. Wives are responsible for the warmth and tenderness in the relationship.
42. In-laws are never to be consulted.
43. A basketball goal in the driveway is standard equipment for every house.
44. Screaming is always a bad idea. We never raise our voices. We never yell.
45. Women should be willing to move to follow their husbands' careers.
46. Men do yard work.
47. Couples should never borrow money from their parents.
48. Holding the door for a woman is chauvinistic.
49. Gaining weight is a sure sign that you no longer care about your spouse.
50. You're married for life, so you never need to talk about it.

You may want to take out a piece of paper and write down some of your *normals* that didn't make it onto this list. And go ahead—jot down some of your wife's *normals,* too.

OWNING YOUR UNSPOKEN RULES

The more you're aware of these unspoken rules—your own *normals*— the more you can own them. Instead of putting moral values on them and shaming your wife if she doesn't abide by them as well, you can simply recognize them as what you're familiar with because you learned it as you were growing up.

> The more you're aware of these unspoken rules— your own *normals*— the more you can own them.

Often when counselors confront clients about their patterns of *normal,* they're met with skepticism. "That may have been a *normal* in my family," counselees argue, "but it certainly doesn't affect me." Yet, if truth be told, it does. Consider these sobering—even frightening—facts about these patterns:

The Patterns Often Don't Show Up Until a Husband and Wife Begin to Establish Their Own *System*

Because these hidden rules about what's normal are often invisible to the person who holds them, they often don't reveal themselves before a couple gets married and begins to establish their own home.

During my engagement I owned a car that had a slight steering-wheel pull to the right. And because the available strength in my right arm was greater than the strength in my wallet, I chose to live with it. After a while, I no longer noticed it. When we got married, Bobbie used my car one time because hers was in the shop. "Your car nearly put me in the ditch," she exclaimed when she got back to our apartment. "I could have been killed!" (As I recall, I told her that I had forgotten about it—which until that moment was true—and made some quip about her overreacting.)

Normal was my car pulling to the right, and until Bobbie's *normal* of driving a perfectly safe car encountered mine, I hadn't thought twice about my *normal.*

These Patterns Show Up Most When We Are Experiencing Stress

For many couples, their marriage produces emotional anxiety soon after the honeymoon is over. Loneliness, depression, and frustration over a surprising lack of communication can sneak up on a bride or groom long before all the wedding thank-you notes are written. Because of this stress, you or your wife may drop your guard and expose your *normals* in no time at all.

One evening I was on a church bus filled with kids. We were headed for an outing—bowling, miniature golf, something like that. The driver slammed on the brakes to avoid a car that had illegally sped through an intersection. A teenage boy named Bubba (I'm not kidding), who was standing in the aisle, was caught off guard and found himself sprawled out on the floor. On his way down he let out an expletive at a smoke-alarm decibel. The bus went immediately silent. Bubba looked up. "I don't know where *that* came from," he said sheepishly.

Like you and me, Bubba had patterns of *normal* he could maintain under controlled circumstances and different patterns he expressed while under stress. He may not have known "where that came from," but you and I have a good idea.

Reading Your Genogram Is Like Reading Your X Ray— It's the Truth

When Mark interprets genograms for couples in counseling, he often says, "I'm just reading your X ray." And just like an X ray, the genogram may show a problem that has no visible symptoms.

One of my closest friends recently went in for his annual physical. One of his blood enzymes indicated the possibility of cancer. Further tests confirmed a diagnosis of leukemia. When he told me the story, I asked if he had experienced any symptoms, any pain, any discomfort at all.

> Not having symptoms can be misleading.

"None," he said. "Nothing at all."

But my friend believed the report, and he's in the process of a rigorous procedure to treat it. Not having symptoms can be misleading.

Sometimes We Identify Patterns by Reacting against Them

We are not destined to repeat the *normal* of our family system—but it is possible to wear ourselves out trying to be as *unlike* the inherited pattern as we can.

Mark has told me that, in his family, men tend toward intensity and seriousness. As he became aware of that *normal,* he determined that he would be different. He would be happy, *no matter what!* He spent many of his early years pushing himself to be happy, trying to make everyone around him happy as well. Thinking that he was declaring his independence from his family system, Mark came to find out that he was still being controlled by it.

Couples Seldom Fight About What They Are Fighting About

You may think that you and your bride are having a conflict about money or sex or in-laws or schedules or any one of a number of hot topics. But almost all conflicts in marriage—especially those that become destructive—come from something other than the issue that started them. More often than not, these fights come from a clash of your *normal*—and hers.

The value of beginning the work of defining the *normals* of your own family system early in your marriage is that by knowing them you'll be able to prevent sparks from igniting into an explosion. To avoid a disaster, here's something to consider saying: "You know what? The reason I said that to you was because, when I grew up, this wasn't our *normal.* What you did wasn't bad; it's only that it was unfamiliar to me."

Can you imagine what this could do to quell the battle about to begin?

Cautious Is Better Than Casual

The secret to interpreting your genogram is to focus on potential trouble spots—on places where the undercurrents are moving in conflicting and potentially destructive directions. A smart river guide before a white-water trip isn't going to spend a lot of time talking about the smooth water downstream. He or she will focus on the danger zones.

> Being prepared can turn danger into adventure.

The purpose of identifying these patterns of *normal* in your marriage is to prepare yourself for the places where you will face the greatest challenges. Actually, being prepared can turn danger into adventure.

What you need to hear is, "This *might* happen" or, "This *could* be a problem you'll have to deal with." In many cases, the potential problem area will not become a problem at all—and the couple will be pleasantly surprised. It's better to be cautious than casual. A stern warning about danger that never materializes is far better than nonchalantly discussing how wonderful the smooth water will be—and far better than being overwhelmed by the rapids.

WORKING ON, NOT JUST IN

When I started my own business in 1986, my business partner and I became acquainted with a book titled *The E-Myth,* written by Michael Gerber. The book gave some great advice—the most helpful of which was never to just work *in* our business. He urged readers not to let the pressures of marketing their product and making payroll distract them from time spent working *on* their business.

This meant that my partner, Mike Hyatt, and I needed to sit down every once in a while and ask the tough questions about where the business was going. It wasn't enough to have a "productive week" or even a "successful month." We had to make sure that our decisions and our activities were moving us in a direction consistent with our vision. We forced ourselves to stop and talk *about* our business, not just get caught up in the work from day to day.

> Are we doing the hard work of working *on* our marriages and not just living *in* them?

Sometimes these conversations started disagreements between Mike and me about such things as hiring a person to fill a spot—or continuing to do double-duty ourselves. "Couldn't you have just left well enough alone?" someone may have asked. "You know, let sleeping dogs lie?"

You and I are faced with identical situations in our marriages. There are plenty of day-to-day activities to accomplish, plenty to keep us busy. But are we doing the hard work of working *on* our marriages and not just living *in* them?

Mark and I have met thousands of couples. Most of these couples will make it all the way down the river. Many will actually enjoy the ride. But you and your bride don't just want to finish; you want to flourish. You want yours to be an outstanding marriage. The difference between the good ones and the great ones is this fact alone: Everyone works *in* a marriage, but only a few work *on* their marriages. Yours can be one of the great ones.

Enjoy the ride.

ROLES: WHEN YOU'RE TRYING TO DECIDE WHO WILL BE ON TOP

No marriage can succeed unless it is permeated, saturated, with this spirit of acquiescence, of continual giving in, of gracious and willing compliance.

MIKE MASON, *THE MYSTERY OF MARRIAGE*

I have always been drawn to team sports. Every man has his own assignment, and if he executes well, the team's chances for success skyrocket. There are few opportunities for the middle linebacker to carry the ball or for the quarterback to intercept a pass. These guys have the responsibilities of their specific positions, and so that's what they do. The same is true in hockey, basketball, soccer, and baseball.

Marriage is *not* a team sport. Your assignment today may be your wife's assignment tomorrow. Her task tomorrow may be yours the next day. Given the *normal* you grew up with—your parents' and grandparents' roles may have been quite fixed—this may be a huge adjustment for you.

Fifty years ago, when a man came home from work, he sat down and waited for the little lady to fix dinner. Now, when you get home and there's no dinner cooking in the oven (your wife may still be at work), you go to the freezer, the refrigerator, or, if you're really cool, the recipe book, and you whip something up for the two of you.

You no longer hustle past a pile of laundry, hoping that someday it'll magically disappear. No, you separate the whites from the darks, and toss a load into the washing machine, along with a dash of detergent.

Your marriage is not football or hockey or basketball or soccer. Your marriage is more like a two-person sailing expedition. Your goal is to

> Your marriage is more like a two-person sailing expedition.

get from here to there, and whatever jobs need to get done will get done by whomever happens to have the time to do them. There's no "hey, bailing water isn't my job—I man the rudder." Can you imagine?

THREE ROLES EVERY WIFE NEEDS HER HUSBAND TO PLAY

The roles you play in your marriage are far more important—more strategic—than going down two checklists: roles you take and roles your wife takes. And your roles are not just about what you do around the house. It's clearly about *who* you are.

You Are a Leader

Your chest may have swelled when you read these words: "You are a leader." *A leader?* you might think to yourself. *Now you're talking. It's about time I get the role I deserve around here.*

The leadership I'm talking about isn't the kind of leadership you may be accustomed to seeing. This leadership is a different sort altogether. Why? Because games of intimidation, power, control, and manipulation are utterly ineffective in marriage. A leader who demands that he be taken seriously simply on the basis of his position of leadership is a miserable leader.

Your first exposure to a man assuming leadership in marriage was your own dad. If he was a perfect example, you're blessed. All you have to do now is follow in his footsteps. If not, you're going to have to look elsewhere for a model.

Your parents' generation gave them husband prototypes like Ward Cleaver, whose voice, when he spoke to June, never reached a decibel higher than the sound of a marshmallow dropping on the floor. Ward was a really, really nice guy. Then there was Archie Bunker, who rarely spoke to Edith in anything lower than a shout—and regardless of the volume, his voice was *always* filled with condescension and biting sarcasm.

More contemporary examples include guys like Al Bundy and Homer Simpson, whose "leadership" was known only to them. They lived in their own little fantasy lands of power. But to Peggy Bundy, Marge Simpson, and the rest of their families, these guys were losers—the targets of well-earned ridicule and countless jokes. Or there's Raymond Barone—more interested in his own comfort and in keeping the peace than in effectively leading and loving his family.

But there are other examples—Jesus Christ, for instance. The apostle Paul wrote this enduring description:

> Do nothing out of selfish ambition or vain conceit, but in humility consider others better than yourselves. Each of you should look not only to your own interests, but also to the interests of others.
>
> Your attitude should be the same as that of Christ Jesus:
>
> Who, being in very nature God,
>   did not consider equality with God something to
>   be grasped,
> but made himself nothing,
>   taking the very nature of a servant,
>   being made in human likeness.
> And being found in appearance as a man,
>   he humbled himself
>   and became obedient to death—
>   even death on a cross.
>
> PHILIPPIANS 2:3–8

Jesus was God. He had more power than any man who ever walked the earth's surface, yet his life was a flawless example of the kind of leadership you need to take with your wife. In fact, Jesus commanded it:

> You know that the rulers of the Gentiles lord it over them, and their high officials exercise authority over them. *Not so with you.* Instead, whoever wants to become great among you *must* be your servant, and whoever wants to be first *must* be your slave—just as the Son of Man did not come to be served, but to serve, and to give his life as a ransom for many.
>
> MATTHEW 20:25–28, italics mine

Servanthood is the heart of leadership in your marriage.

Husbands who demand that their wives submit to them have missed the point of leadership altogether. They are like the cartoon king who stomps around the castle screaming, "*I'm* in charge around here!" Men who act this way are only revealing their own insecurity. They're afraid that if they don't make angry demands, no one will follow them.

Servanthood is the heart of leadership in your marriage.

"Not so with you," Jesus said.

Your most important role is to love your bride as Jesus loved his followers. And how did he do that? By serving. Sacrificing himself. Giving up his rights as the leader. Dying. God's word to us is this: "Husbands, love your wives, just as Christ loved the church and gave himself up for her."[14]

Here's what this kind of leadership might look like in your marriage:

- You and your wife are on your way to dinner. You've not discussed this with your bride, but you're headed for your favorite Mexican place. All day long you've had visions of cheese enchiladas dancing in your head. And this restaurant makes the best enchiladas this side of Tijuana. You turn to your wife, hoping for the "right" answer to the following question: "What sounds good to you tonight?"

  "It's funny," she says. "I've been craving Italian food since breakfast."

  Where do you go to dinner?

- You're backing out of the garage when your wife says something about its condition. This isn't the first time she's asked you to clean it out. You know she's right; it *is* a mess—but the first thing that flashes into your mind is the condition of her sink and vanity in the bathroom.

  What do you say?

Ironically, being a leader in your marriage *is* about you being first. It's about being the first to adjust in order to demonstrate love for your wife. It means being the first in serving, the first in forgiving, and the first in yielding your conveniences. (Something to ponder: Military officers are the first ones up in the morning and the last ones to bed at night.)

Being a leader in your marriage *is* about you being first.

Christian Leadership Concepts (CLC) is an increasingly popular Bible study program for men. Founded by Hal Haddon, a Nashville businessman, this two-year course includes a unit that helps men understand their role as spiritual leaders in their homes. The wives of the men in this course love it when their husbands are going through this section. Why? Is it because their husbands come home and start telling them how they need to get with the program? Of course not. Women love this component because their husbands start loving them in the same radical and sacrificial way that Jesus does.

When Mike Hyatt and I were drawing up the corporate documents for Wolgemuth & Hyatt Publishers, we decided—at the strong advice of our attorney—to make the ownership of the company 51/49 percent and not 50/50. Because I was a little older and had a few more years of publishing experience under my belt, Mike suggested that I take the larger share of ownership. I agreed. But at that moment—I'll never forget it—I made a quiet resolution never to put myself in a position of lording my 51 percent over the 49 percent my business partner held. My job was to cover some of the more cumbersome tasks of the business and to help him develop his skills and gifts. I never told him about this decision. My success was going to show up as his success.

You're the leader—a 51 percent "owner"—in your marriage. That's your role. It's what your wife would choose. Now your most important task should be crystal clear.

You Are a Warrior

When I was a little boy, my parents had a strict "no guns" policy. You never saw my brothers or me with toy-gun holsters hanging from our belts. But what my father and mother didn't realize was that we could make do with a banana, a stick, a pencil, a telephone, a piece of uncooked spaghetti, a sleeping cat, a young sibling, a finger, a stuffed animal—you get the idea.

Aggression is indelibly inscribed into every man. We love to conquer. This desire to do battle comes in different forms. We can spend our lives productively performing our way up the corporate ladder, battling an opponent in the courtroom, winning a local tennis tournament, or combating disease in the operating room. But men who don't give voice to their warrior role in healthy ways will, more often than not, find themselves fighting the wrong battles.

> Men who don't give voice to their warrior role in healthy ways will find themselves fighting the wrong battles.

Misguided Battles

- Kimberly walked into the counselor's office and began to unpack her story of loneliness and frustration. Even though she had only been married for a few months, she wept as she talked about how Ryan spends two to three hours a day in the gym but not a fraction of that time working on his marriage.
- Will thinks nothing of investing fifteen hours a week and thousands of dollars a year on his golf game. Betty is angry and confused when Will tells her that they just can't afford a date night—dinner and a movie—every week.
- Mitch would rather volunteer at church than spend time with his wife, Cindy. In fact, instead of treating his wife to breakfast in bed on their anniversary, he shows up at church to flip pancakes at the weekly prayer breakfast.

These warriors are fighting the wrong battles. And even though they didn't set out to destroy their marriages with "friendly fire," it's exactly what they're doing. Kimberly, Betty, and Cindy long for husbands who are strong enough to keep their promises and valiant enough to battle against those habits and attitudes that threaten to destroy their marriages.

You and I come from a long line of strong men who go lifeless in the face of threats to our marriages. This is a tradition that goes all the way back to Adam. Often in Bible studies on the first chapters of Genesis, some guy will quip that it was Eve who gave in to temptation and ate the forbidden fruit. But take a closer look. Where was Adam when the serpent was wooing Eve? He was likely right there next to her. And what did he do when she was beginning to cave in to Satan's lie? Nothing. A classic prototype of the passive man, Adam stood quietly by. When he could have fought for her and defended her against what they both knew was wrong, his lips turned to stone.

> You and I come from a long line of strong men who go lifeless in the face of threats to our marriages.

We were made for more than this. Your bride may not be a damsel to rescue from a prison tower, but that doesn't mean that there *isn't* a battle to be fought and won on her behalf. This struggle is even more challenging than sculpting your stomach, lowering your handicap, or feeding breakfast to the men at church. And it's more rewarding than any of these things.

You Are a Lover

Living in Central Florida means being surrounded by a lot of people who speak a language other than English—mostly Spanish. It can be pretty frustrating—for them and me—trying to figure out what each of us is saying.

Sometimes my words to my wife are misunderstood. It's almost as though I'm using the wrong dialect. We need to work on our "love language."[15] I think my love for her is best expressed one way—gifts, trips, shopping sprees—but she sees it completely differently. My love for her is most powerfully expressed when I give her time, tenderness, and my undivided attention—when I determine to be a vital part of our two-person "sailing expedition."

Patrick Morley, best-selling author of *The Man in the Mirror,* tells of his quest to learn his wife's love language. One evening, after dinner, instead of excusing himself to finish the newspaper, Patrick tried Patsy's "vernacular." He thanked her for the delicious dinner, stood up, and began to clear the table. Then he offered to put the leftovers into the refrigerator and didn't leave the kitchen until everything was cleaned up and put away. Patrick didn't make any grand announcements about what he was doing. He simply worked alongside his wife, continuing their dinner conversation until the work was done.

> The way I keep score of what counts and the way my bride keeps score are vastly different.

The next night he did exactly what he had done the night before, again with no fanfare. For two weeks Patrick did this. Neither one of them said anything about it. One morning as Patrick walked into the bathroom to shave, there on his mirror was a yellow Post-it note: "Patrick, thanks for being my best friend. Love, Patsy." Patrick had learned to speak her language—and adopted the habit of sharing the kitchen duty.

Several years ago, Bobbie began to use an expression when I'd do something she appreciated. "That counts," she'd say with a smile. As I look back on the things that earned this response, I've discovered something interesting about being a lover. The way I keep score of what counts and the way my bride keeps score are vastly different.

As a man, the way I calculate value goes something like this:

- take out the trash—.05 points
- early morning conversation over a cup of coffee—6 points
- dinner and a movie—50 points
- flowers for a birthday or anniversary—125 points
- a weekend at the Ritz in Naples—2,000 points
- jewelry—one point for every dollar spent

Bobbie does appreciate all these things—like I said, they "count." But Bobbie's scoring system works like this:

- take out the trash—1 point
- early morning conversation over a cup of coffee—1 point
- dinner and a movie—1 point
- flowers for a birthday or anniversary—1 point
- a weekend at the Ritz in Naples—1 point
- jewelry—1 point, regardless of the cost

Just the other day I heard about a husband who learned about this point system the hard way. Early one morning, as he was running out the door to work—earlier than usual—his wife stopped him to ask why they weren't having their usual morning cup of coffee together. He told her of a project he hadn't been able to finish the night before and the urgency of getting it done before an important meeting at 9:00 A.M.

"But we *always* start our day together," she said.

"Look," he said, "you and I are going to have a great getaway weekend soon. We'll get caught up then."

The husband thought that a weekend rendezvous at a fabulous hotel—six weeks down the road—would compensate for a missed conversation today. That's because his scoring system was calibrated incorrectly.

This was the reality:

- weekend getaway at a beach resort—1 point
- fifteen minutes of conversation with my wife before going to work—1 point

Becoming Fluent

After ten years of marriage and three kids, best-selling author John Ortberg tells how he discovered a nuance of the love language of his wife,

Nancy. At bedtime John took over the job of bathing the children. Not only was this a genuine convenience for a very tired mom, but Nancy confessed that watching her husband lean over the tub and scrub the children was a real turn-on for her.

"My kids," John said with a big smile, "were the cleanest kids in the neighborhood."

If you and I are going to be great lovers, the most powerful demonstration of that love will always be in our ability to communicate love in the language our wives understand—both big and little expressions. And once we learn how our brides tally the results, we can begin to keep score the way they do.

Being a charming sexual partner is only a very small part of being a lover who knows how to satisfy his wife. For her to believe that she's married to a great lover, your wife needs to be *known* by you.[16] You must become fluent in her distinct language. Created in the image of God as she is, your wife—like God—loves to be pursued, to be delighted in, to be sought after. She longs to know that she is captivating, cherished, and chosen, not just that you consider her to be "a trooper" or "solid" or "hardworking." And she looks uniquely and exclusively to you to *know* her in this way.

> Being a charming sexual partner is only a very small part of being a lover who knows how to satisfy his wife.

You *can* do this, sailor!

6

TALK: CONVERSATIONAL FOREPLAY

The key to reviving or divorce-proofing a relationship is not in how you handle disagreements but in how you are with each other when you're not fighting. Once the marriage gets "set" at a certain degree of positivity, it will take far more negativity to harm your relationship than if your "set point" were lower.

JOHN GOTTMAN, *THE SEVEN PRINCIPLES FOR MAKING MARRIAGE WORK*

O ne day Allen Lange drove to the airfield after lunch to take a quick spin in his airplane. Walking around the Cessna 182 to unfasten the tie-downs, Allen carefully examined the airplane. Even though he was only eighteen years old, no one would ever accuse him of being sloppy about safety.

With everything in order—including the fuel tanks topped off—Allen crawled into the cockpit, fastened his seat belt, slipped his headset over his ears, and pulled the choke. "Ignition," he whispered, turning the key.

In less than three minutes the tower cleared Allen Lange's plane for takeoff. Gathering speed, he lifted from the runway. It was a perfect day to fly. He was less than ten minutes from the airfield when a loud, popping sound came from the instrument panel directly in front of him. Smoke came pouring from somewhere behind the panel, just above his knees. Allen instinctively cracked open his window to let the smoke exit and turned the plane toward home.

Reaching up to the radio controls, Allen called to the tower: "Cessna 5J644 to Jackson tower. Come in, Jackson—I've got a fire here. Come in, Jackson."

No answer.

Allen adjusted the frequency on his radio. A gust of wind pushed his plane sharply to the left, and Allen pulled back on the stick to compensate. The acrid smell of an electrical fire filled the cockpit.

Allen changed the frequency on his radio. "Cessna 5J644 to Jackson tower. Come in, Jackson. Cessna 5J644 to Jackson tower. I'VE GOT A FIRE HERE. COME IN, JACKSON."

> The acrid smell of an electrical fire filled the cockpit.

Allen was lost. The smoke inside made it difficult to see his instruments. Worst of all, there was silence. Try as he might to find the correct frequency to reach the tower, there was nothing.

"Talk to me," Allen said out loud, staring at his taciturn radio. "TALK TO ME!" he repeated in a shout. "I'M DYING IN HERE!"

CAN WE TALK?

In this chapter, you and I are going to talk about talking. Before we go any further, though, there are a few things that need to be confessed. First, you and I are probably not very good at talking. In fact, chances are we're downright miserable at it. And second, if your wife is even close to normal, she will sometimes be feeling like Allen Lange at two thousand feet. She's desperate, and she's dying in the silence.

I ran across this simple true-false quiz a while ago.[17] It's for wives to take, but before you give it to her, go ahead and guess how she'll respond to each of these questions:

1. I know more about sea anemones than I do about my husband's feelings. T or F
2. My husband's priorities seem to be work, sports, his car, the yard, church, and then me. T or F
3. My husband would rather floss with razor wire than discuss our marriage. T or F
4. My husband would rather jam his head on the end of a sharpened pencil than go to counseling. T or F
5. Sometimes I feel alone in this marriage. T or F
6. I feel alone most of the time in this marriage. T or F
7. I can't describe to you how alone I feel in this marriage. T or F
8. I really wish my husband would change in a few areas. T or F

9. My husband is a great person and I love him, but I'm frustrated because he and I don't seem to be on the same team. T or F
10. I'm willing to do just about anything to change our relationship for the better. T or F

Look back over the list again. Do you think your wife might circle *True* for at least one of these questions? More than one? How many more than one?

Running Away

Scott and Monica fell in love in college. Scott had come from a long line of thoughtful and contemplative people—measured people, so to speak. "No need for small talk" was spot-welded to his DNA. Monica was beautiful, warm, effervescent, outgoing, and talkative—all of which Scott loved about Monica—and Monica boasted to her friends that Scott was the strong, silent type—a man who knew exactly who he was and where he was going.

> When he arrived home that night from work, he found an empty garage and a note on the kitchen table.

But it didn't take long after their wedding for these two qualities to meet nose to nose. In fact, Monica had a "sinking feeling" on their honeymoon. Scott's emotionless two- or three-word answers to her questions gripped her with a strange sense of loneliness.

Twenty-five years later, I picked up the phone on a Thursday afternoon to check in with Scott. He and I had been neighbors as youngsters in the Illinois town where we had grown up, and our friendship had lasted a lifetime. I loved Scott like a brother, and Bobbie and Monica had become very close friends, so you'll understand why his words broke my heart.

"Monica is leaving me today," Scott said evenly. "Andrew [the youngest of their four children] graduated from high school on Monday. We had a party for him on Tuesday, and I think Monica's leaving me today."

Scott's prediction was perfect. When he arrived home that night from work, he found an empty garage and a note on the kitchen table.

Two years before, at her thirtieth high school reunion, Monica had reconnected with Brent, her first serious boyfriend. They, along with a tableful of old friends, had talked late into the night. Scott had decided not to attend the reunion. He wasn't crazy about traipsing along with his wife and spending the evening with total strangers. Before the night ended, Monica and Brent had exchanged phone numbers and e-mail addresses.

That Thursday afternoon, almost exactly twenty-four months later, Monica packed everything she could fit into her sports car—including her dog—and drove five hundred miles to move in with Brent. Monica was a Christian. A highly decorated grade school teacher, a person who had volunteered to serve countless times in the nursery during worship, someone who had taught Sunday school for years. She had read Bible stories to her two boys and two girls and had prayed with them at bedtime since they were small. She was a nearly flawless mother. A year before packing up her car and her dog, she had celebrated her fiftieth birthday. But now, like a defiant and unbending teenager, Monica was running away.

"My family thinks I'm visiting my hometown for a few days," she e-mailed us a week later. "But I've moved in with Brent. I'm never going back. Never."

And except to return once to gather the things she hadn't been able to pack into her little car the first time, Monica kept her word. She never went back.

From their first year of marriage, Monica was Allen Lange at two thousand feet in a floundering aircraft. Her cockpit was filled with smoke—and for most of their twenty-five years together she had been unable to reach the Jackson tower. Scott hadn't *meant* to be distant or aloof. He truly loved his wife. He just wasn't a natural conversationalist. And, because of the silence, Monica was dying up there.

As far as she was concerned, running away was the only chance she had to survive.

Talking, Not Negotiating

He left a desperate message on my machine. "I've got to talk to you," he said. "Soon!"

Stan and I had had many passing conversations in the halls at church, at wedding receptions, and at funerals. But even though I didn't know why Stan had called, I was certain that, as I drove to the coffee shop for our emergency meeting, this talk would be different.

Although a highly respected lawyer, that day Stan didn't look the part. His eyes were red and swollen, his hair was tousled, and his clothes looked as though they had been dragged from the laundry hamper. He told me that he and Jill had been separated for a month. At first he had assumed they could simply work it out. Up to this point, he had never lost an argument with his wife, and he was sure it would be a matter of time until she "started to think rationally."

> Stan had taken his courtroom skills into his home. And in the end, he had lost his case.

But Stan had been wrong, and he was getting desperate. He explained that, although he still had a key to the house and could come and go during the day, he no longer held a key to Jill's heart. He was certain she had changed the lock. Permanently.

"I think I've lost her," Stan said. At this, his countenance broke. His face turned to a flood of tears. "I've been an idiot," he confessed as he described the marriage that could have been. He described how he had, again and again, beaten her down with his words, always "winning" with condescending words of blame or anger. A crack litigator, Stan had taken his courtroom skills into his home. And in the end, he had lost his case.

As he looked back, Stan replayed all the missed opportunities. He recalled times when Jill had approached him with sincere concern about their "communication problem." Stan had ridiculed her. Then he ignored her. When she suggested they visit with a counselor, Stan punished her with days of the silent treatment. When Jill tried tenderly to ask if they could "just talk," he would sarcastically quip, "Okay, you start."

Jill's countenance would drop, and she'd walk away. She rarely argued. She knew better than to try to negotiate with a man who made hundreds of thousands of dollars a year winning at this game. Incredibly, Stan would chalk up these kinds of encounters as victories.

But now, after only a month of separation, Stan saw himself and his estranged wife with stunning clarity. He knew he was no closer to reconciliation than the day he had moved out. His marriage and his children were slipping away. He had no idea what to do, because his habitual refusal to talk to his wife had burned the very bridge he now needed.

Stan was Allen Lange at two thousand feet, frantically searching for the right frequency—and he was dying up there. What made it worse was that Stan was responsible for his emergency—and he knew it.

OFFERING A SAFE PLACE

Author Leo Buscaglia was once asked to judge a contest that honored children who had done good things. A mother submitted a story of her four-year-old son who, at the time, lived next door to an elderly man. Several days earlier, the man's wife had died, and the little boy had walked over to the neighbor's house to cheer him up. Finding the man sitting on a large chair in the living room, the child climbed up on his lap and laid his head against his chest. The man was crying.

When the boy came home, his mother asked, "What did you say to our neighbor?"

"Nothing," the lad responded. "I just helped him cry."

Sometimes the secret to good conversation with your wife is the part where you don't say anything at all. One of your jobs as a husband is to give your wife a safe place—a place where she can be weak or frightened or lonely. Sometimes you may just need to help her cry.

ENDORSEMENTS

Almost every wife I know of loves to hear her husband talk *about* her with unsolicited endorsements spoken in her presence.

Several years ago our daughter Missy told us about a conversation between her husband, Jon, and Jon's Uncle Tom. Tom's wife had lost a battle to cancer, leaving Tom to raise his two small children alone. A very successful businessman, Tom had decided to hire full-time help in caring for his children.

"I've hired a nanny," Tom told Jon. "And she's terrific. Not only are the kids happy, but when I come home from work, I find the house in order. Dinner is ready, the kitchen is clean, even my underwear and socks have magically left the clothes hamper and are folded neatly back in my closet."

Jon's eyes left Tom. He looked at Missy, then back at his uncle. "I know just what you mean," he said with a smile. "I get that every day myself. My home has the same kind of magic."

Missy told me that she held on to those words for months. They provided encouragement when she found herself consigned to mundane chores like laundry. They inspired her and kept her from feeling use-

> Early in his marriage, Charlie challenged himself to say something kind to Martha every day.

less or unimportant. Even though they hadn't been directed at her, Jon's words of endorsement unlocked Missy's heart and deepened her love for her husband.

The late Charlie Shedd, author of several best-selling books on sex and marriage,[18] was one of the happiest married men I've ever known. His secret was a very simple thing. Early in his marriage, Charlie challenged himself to say something kind—a new something he hadn't said before—to Martha every day. His comment may have been a thank you, a kind word about her heart for people, a statement of appreciation for her love for God, or an expression of delight over something she did or said.

When I first met Charlie and Martha, they were well into their third decade of marriage. Martha told me with a smile that there were "very few days" that Charlie hadn't kept his promise. She looked forward to his daily endorsements. And she loved him for his commitment to keep them coming. Charlie was a happily married man because Martha was a happily married woman.[19]

Endorsements work.

CONVERSATION WITHOUT DESTINATION

Did you know that women don't need a reason for calling each other on the phone? It's true. And not only do they make such calls, they can talk for thirty minutes when both of them know that there was no agenda in the first place. This may be as amazing to you as it is to me—but it's true.

You and I, on the other hand, rarely do such a thing. It can even be difficult to check in with our parents, because we know it'll be one of those conversations without a destination.

> She may need some conversation without a destination.

More often than not, I'm driven in my conversations to a goal. I call my barber to set up an appointment. "Next Tuesday? 4:30? Got it. Thanks." In my business, I call clients or customers with the same agenda: "You and I know we've got work to do. Let's cut the small talk and get to the point. This call isn't the only one we have on our lists today." We don't actually say these words on business calls, but most of the time it's exactly what's going on.

But now you're a married man. You're going to have to learn that the most important person in your life may want to talk without any sort of strategic plan in mind. She may need some conversation without a destination.

Example 1: A Destination Conversation

Your wife: "You've been so busy that it seems like we don't talk like we used to. We never just sit and talk. It seems like you talk to other people, but you don't talk to me."

You: "No problem. Let's talk. Name a subject, and we can talk about it."

Your wife: "AAAHHHH! I shouldn't *have* to ask you to talk. I'm your wife. Before we got married we used to stay up till the wee hours of the morning just talking. Now I barely get a grunt out of you."

You: "Don't you see what's happening? I can't win. When I don't talk to you, I'm in trouble. When I offer to talk to you, I'm in trouble. I can't win."

What you are missing here is that your bride doesn't want to have a talk that will "accomplish something." She doesn't want to reserve a rental car or make a hotel reservation. This talk does not have a finish line. She just wants to talk.

Example 2: A No-Destination Conversation

Imagine a different strategy on your part:

Your wife: "You've been so busy that it seems like we don't talk like we used to. We never just sit and talk. It seems like you talk to other people, but you don't talk to me."

You: "You're right. I've been so preoccupied that I've not paid much attention to you recently. I'm sorry. I've got so many things I'd like to tell you about, but why don't you go first. Tell me all about your day."

Your wife: "AAAHHHH! I shouldn't *have* to ask—Wait a minute. What did you say?"

You: "I said, 'You're right, and I want to hear about your day.'"

Your wife: "Well, okay. Hmmm—well, it all started this morning as I was getting ready to walk out the door to go to work. The garbage disposal went out—I couldn't believe it—wait a minute, are you *sure* you want to hear about this?"

You: "Absolutely!"

After your wife finishes talking, she turns to you and asks about your day. Do you say, "It was fine. Where's the paper?" No, you say, "Well, I met Ralph for coffee this morning. It looks like Jimmy is going to UVA in the fall. He's applying for a music scholarship at Julliard, but they don't think he's got much of a shot, so they're guessing it's going to be UVA. When I got to the office, the coffee machine had gone berserk and there was an inch of standing water in the workroom. Nancy had already called maintenance, but the water was already seeping into the carpet in the reception area. Stephanie announced that she's pregnant and that she's going to stay home once the baby's born . . ."

> It's *the fact that you talk* that makes the real difference.

Get the idea? For your bride, it's not so much *what* you talk about but *the fact that you talk* that makes the real difference.

One of the reasons we chicken out of agendaless conversations is our fear of not having something significant to cover. Something profound (like a change in the weather patterns) or something measurable (like last night's basketball scores). Actually, conversations without destinations can be wonderful. In fact, they're like the guys walking up and down the beach slowly swinging their metal detectors. You just never know what treasure you might find.

The other reason for learning how to meet your wife's needs in good conversation is that she's absolutely desperate for it—just as panicked as Allen Lange was when he couldn't connect with the traffic control tower. For her it's almost a matter of life and death.

Bobbie and I are working on our fourth decade of marriage. And I wish I could tell you that these destinationless conversations are effortless. They aren't. However, they *are* easier than they used to be. If you stay with it long enough, I promise that it will get easier.

WHERE'S ALLEN?

"Cessna, this is Jackson tower, come in! We've got you in our sights. Landing lights are on."

The connection is made. Allen is safe at last.

FRIENDSHIP: THE SECRET INGREDIENT IN EVERY SATISFYING MARRIAGE

Let there be times when the conversation is not supposed to be "deep." This is hardly a waste of time. It is marriage. And without it the marriage starts to starve.

WALTER WANGERIN, *AS FOR ME AND MY HOUSE*

It was late. As I turned into our driveway, my headlights washing across the front of our home like a great wave, I noticed that one of the lamps in the living room was on. *Great,* I naively thought to myself, *Bobbie must still be awake.* I couldn't wait to fill her in on what had just happened.

Pulling the car into our detached garage, I jumped out and ran down the sidewalk, entered the house, and hustled into the living room. Sure enough, Bobbie was sitting on one end of the sofa, next to the end table and lighted lamp. The fact that she was neither watching TV nor had any reading material on her lap should have tipped me off. But we had only been married for a few months, and I wasn't very adept at reading the signs. Plopping down next to her, I eagerly began to tell her about my evening.

At the time, I was employed by a well-known international youth ministry. I had the responsibility of working with students at three local high schools. I coordinated the club meetings held in kids' homes and did lots of one-on-one counseling. On this particular night, I was bursting with the news that one of "my kids" had decided to turn his life around. He had been a heavy drug user, and his parents had threatened to send him away to get help. Then I had come along, befriended the young man, and, by the grace of God, had actually motivated him to clean up his act.

On and on I went, telling Bobbie the story.

Now, remember that I was new at the marriage thing. I didn't notice that Bobbie wasn't celebrating the good news. The cool breeze emanating from her end of the couch should have told me something, but this was about *me* and *my* story, so I rode it all the way to the end.

I waited for Bobbie's response. There was nothing. Only then did I look squarely into her eyes, and it dawned on me that she may have heard the words but really hadn't been listening. Even though it happened a long time ago, I can tell you exactly what she said in the end. These were her first words—uttered with no change in facial expression—following my nonstop success report: "I don't care."

I was stunned.

"You don't care?" I said in my best shame-on-you, guilt-inducing voice. "You don't care?"

"No, I don't," she said, her steely green eyes leaving no doubt. "You're late," she continued. "You told me you'd be home by 9:00, and you didn't even have the courtesy to call me. You're spending all your waking hours with those kids, and this isn't the *first* time you've come home later than you promised. Where do *I* fit in?"

I didn't say anything. It was my turn to be silent.

"You're out there saving the whole world. And I'm home alone, waiting for you—and I'm sick of it!"

There are no words to adequately describe my utter shock at that moment. I had never heard a wife talk to her husband like this. (It wasn't one of my *normals*.) I remember thinking—because my self-centeredness was off the charts—that I had made a terrible mistake in marrying this wild woman.

More than thirty years have passed since that awful night. Bobbie and I have learned how to speak words more clearly and with a little less bite. But I know exactly what she was telling me. It was, in reality, a very simple truth—a truth that had nothing to do with disdain for the young people I was working with (she loved them as much as I did) or her own spiritual condition (she loves God and is a living example of his grace everywhere she goes). Here's what Bobbie was saying to me. It's a powerful thing and one of the reasons why that night was one of the most significant turning points in our marriage: "I'm your wife. But I also want to be your friend. You'd never treat a friend like this."

Of course, it took years (literally) for us to completely unpack what Bobbie was feeling that night. But I am so thankful she had the courage, very early in our marriage, to try to tell me the truth—and to express her expectations—about our relationship. She didn't just want to be married to me. She wanted us to be friends.

> She didn't just want to be married to me. She wanted us to be friends.

Sometimes, "walking down the aisle" changes the bride and groom from good friends into lovers only. This change can only be described as extremely dangerous—and in every case, it's relationship-threatening.

A PROFOUNDLY SIMPLE TRUTH

Over the past decade, Dr. John Gottman, a University of Washington professor, has taken a number of the most widely accepted assumptions about marriage and turned them on their ear. He's one of the only researchers in the field of marriage studies who has brought rigorous scientific methods to bear on predicting what makes marriages work and what makes them fail.

After detailed interviews with a couple, Dr. Gottman actually observes them in what has become known as his "love lab." With precision, Gottman and his colleagues have developed a process of watching married couples and pinpointing hundreds of specific behaviors.

Each couple is allowed to "live normally" in a nicely furnished apartment outfitted with video cameras, one-way glass, and microphones in every room except the bedroom and bathroom. Holter monitors are worn by each of the participants.[20] Then, from 9:00 A.M. until 9:00 P.M., they are carefully observed.

After years of surveillance and analysis of hundreds of couples, Gottman claims to be able to predict the future success or failure of a marriage with an accuracy rate of over 90 percent. And usually his conclusions are drawn within just five minutes of observation.[21]

You're undoubtedly thinking, *How does he do it?* Dr. Gottman has identified specific behaviors that are marriage destroyers and others that are marriage protectors. Far and away, the *most* significant marriage protector boils down to one word (are you ready to be underwhelmed?): *friendship*. Not money, not exotic getaways, not creative romantic rendezvous. No, merely friendship. Gottman makes this observation:

The determining factor in whether wives feel satisfied with sex, romance, and passion in their marriage is, by 70 percent, the quality of the couple's friendship. For men, the determining factor is, by the same 70 percent, the quality of the couple's friendship. So men and women come from the same planet after all.... Friendship fuels the flames of romance because it offers the best protection against feeling adversarial toward your spouse.[22]

There's very good news for you and me in this discovery. Successful marriage may not require us to learn anything new. Building a friendship with your wife early in your marriage is a matter of accessing skills you learned as a youngster. You know the rules. You know what it takes to find a friend and to keep one. All you have to do is to apply this knowledge to the most important relationship you have.

MORE CONTROL THAN WE THINK

Let's pretend that you and your wife are locked in a heated argument. Words are loud and biting. Maybe there are some tears. Then the phone rings. You reach to answer it. "Hello," you say in such a friendly voice that the caller may think you were watching a ball game on TV when the phone rang. It's a close friend. The conversation isn't a long one, and although your wife cannot hear the other person, she hears the tone of your voice. She also realizes how quickly you were able to switch its timbre when you realized who it was that called. You did it instantly with your voice—and your attitude—because you chose to do so.

> Successful marriage may not require us to learn anything new.

Some husbands and wives assume that, when it comes to conflicts with each other, they "just can't help" but speak to each other with disrespect and unkindness. But it's not true. We *can* help it. In fact, we *always* find the resources to speak respectfully and kindly to those whose friendship or business we value enough—and this should, obviously, include our wives.

But there is more to friendship than just avoiding negative dialogue.

JUST NORMAL STUFF

Treating your wife like a friend includes engaging in conversations that may not be dramatic at all. Consider this example:

You walk into the kitchen early on a crisp autumn Saturday morning. Your wife is already up, standing at the window with a cup of coffee in her hand. You find the newspaper on the kitchen counter, sit down, and pour yourself some coffee.

> *Your wife (gazing out the window):* "Look at those leaves. Aren't they incredible?"
>
> *You (looking up from the paper and glancing out the window where she's standing):* "They sure are." (You follow your comment with an affirming "hmmm" sound.)
>
> *Your wife (still looking out):* "This is my favorite time of the year."
>
> *You (looking at the paper):* "Hey, listen to this!"
>
> *Your wife (turning from the window and walking toward the sink):* "Listen to what?"
>
> *You:* "The Johnsons are finally selling that store."
>
> *Your wife (opening a cabinet):* "No kidding? We thought they'd never sell."
>
> *You (still looking at the paper):* "I guess someone made them an offer they couldn't refuse."
>
> *Your wife (walking over toward a lamp but pausing before she reaches out to turn it on):* "Could we run to the hardware store this morning? We need to get some lightbulbs."
>
> *You:* "Uh-huh."

Did you catch the theatrics, the tension, the passion?

You're right. It wasn't there. Nothing dramatic. Nothing heroic. But this is the very kind of interchange that can do wonders to build that marriage-protecting friendship. Gottman calls this process "turning toward each other." And he claims that these simple gestures of attentiveness—these casual exchanges—practiced thousands of times throughout your marriage, can build a comfortable friendship that can protect your marriage against the things that could easily destroy it.

The kind of dialogue shown above can happen among friends without any effort.

> The friendship-building skills that you must apply to your marriage are skills you already have in your repertoire.

For example, if you and your closest friends were out of town for a weekend golf outing and found yourselves at the breakfast table together early one morning, this kind of conversation would have happened with no effort at all. It bears repeating: the friendship-building skills that you must apply to your marriage are skills you already have in your repertoire.

Compare the conversation pattern of "turning toward each other" to that of a husband who continually ignores his wife. They talk *over* each other, *at* each other, *about* each other, *behind* each other's backs— rarely *with* each other.

But solid friendship includes more than conversation. Sometimes it affects your calendar.

TIME

Something that posed a huge threat early in our marriage was carving away time to spend together. The relentless and unpredictable pace of our lives made it difficult to find enough time to be together. And, given the pressures—most of them urgent—of my life, it was much too easy to assume that Bobbie could wait. The phone call couldn't wait; the airplane couldn't wait; the conference in Dallas couldn't wait. But Bobbie—*she* could wait.

Without the courage to confront the problem and without a willingness to say no to a host of good opportunities, Bobbie and I could have drifted dangerously apart. My decision to take a serious look at my calendar came at Bobbie's insistence. Instinctively she knew that distance would devastate our relationship. She saw the potential dangers, and she was determined not to be distracted from her goal of finding time to be together. Sometimes she made a game out of it—packing a picnic basket and bringing it to the office when I had to work late. Who could resist the checkered tablecloth spread out on the office floor? Sandwiches, potato salad, ice tea—and no ants. I'm thankful because I know the friendship we now enjoy is a result of her relentless pursuit of my calendar.

The Slot System

Mark and Susan's story is very similar to ours. But their approach to reserving enough time for each other was more measured. In fact, early in their marriage, Susan and Mark took a long walk that, according to Mark, put them on a course that saved their marriage. Susan was concerned about the negative effect that the unrelenting demands of ministry could have on their marriage. And so, before the walk ended, she had presented a plan—a simple strategy to protect their marriage from the corrosive effects of too much time apart. Mark was introduced to what they now call the *slot system*. The truth at work here is this: without some kind of planning, your marriage will be ruled (and overruled) by your schedule rather than the other way around.

Since that conversation, Mark has seen two measurable results: (1) Because the slot system worked so effectively, their conflicts about time spent together have been rare, and (2) Mark and Susan have taught this system to hundreds of couples—with rave reviews.

When they teach this system, they begin by dividing a typical week into twenty-one separate slots. It looks like this:

Sunday	Monday	Tuesday	Wednesday	Thursday	Friday	Saturday

Each day has three slots—morning, afternoon, and evening. Mark and Susan concluded that they needed a minimum of six slots together in a normal week. Each slot includes a meal and a block of time. The morning slots begin with breakfast and end before lunch. The afternoon slots begin with lunch and end around 5:00 P.M. Dinner is in the evening slot, which ends at bedtime.

The Slot System—Exhibit A

Let's look at how the slot system worked for Todd and Melanie. Mark had conducted their wedding two years earlier, and now they had made an appointment to see him again. These two had entered marriage with their eyes wide open. They had brought a willingness to do "whatever it takes" to make their marriage thrive. In fact, one of the agreements they had made in premarital counseling was that if their relationship ever got below "excellent," they would make an appointment to see Mark—which is why they were now sitting in Mark's office.

Melanie began. "Something's missing," she said. Todd nodded in agreement. "We married each other because we wanted to dance," she continued. "But it feels like we're just trudging along, trying to make our life together work."

"It's like our car isn't running on all cylinders," Todd offered. "Like our wheels are turning without bearings."

When Mark asked Todd and Melanie how they were doing in making time for each other, they both laughed—almost always a good sign in marriage counseling.

"What's so funny?" Mark asked.

"It's just nuts right now," Todd offered. "What with starting a new business, I'm working late most nights. I typically get home around 8:00 at night. I'm exhausted. And that's when we get into our worst fights."

Mark then asked about weekends.

Melanie explained that Todd was working nearly every Saturday. Most Sundays Melanie led the children's choir at church and Todd helped out with the youth group in the afternoon. "We've been good about having our date night on Saturdays," she concluded. "But lately, there's just been a lot of tension, even when we're doing something fun."

Todd and Melanie had forgotten the one nutrient their marriage most needed: *time together*. Scheduled, *quantity* time together does for a marriage what an oil change does for a car; it guarantees that all the parts of the engine function smoothly with a minimum of wear and tear.

Mark pulled out a blank "slot system" sheet and asked Todd and Melanie to take a look at their upcoming week. "Fill in the things that are already scheduled," Mark said. "Then find six slots where you can be together, even if you have to move some things around. And don't just think of these slots as romantic getaways. They could be taken up with running errands together, watching TV, taking a nap, having dinner together with friends, or just hanging around the house."

As Mark explained the process, Todd and Melanie swallowed hard. They knew their schedule would not easily yield to this kind of demand. While they were pondering, Mark made a few suggestions to Todd. "If you have to work late, instead of working until 8:00 on two nights, why don't you work until 10:00 one night, then come home by 5:30 the next night. That gives you a slot with Melanie. Or, instead of working from 10:00 until 4:00 on Saturday, why don't you go early and work until noon. That'll give you two slots with Melanie on Saturday."

Surprisingly, after only ten minutes of negotiating, Todd and Melanie had come up with this plan for their week:

Sunday	Monday	Tuesday	Wednesday	Thursday	Friday	Saturday
1. Breakfast & church together	**W**	**O**	**R**	**K**	**!**	◯
◯	**W**	**O**	**R**	**K**	**!**	5. Home improvement projects
2. Youth Group at our house	◯	3. Dinner at home	◯	◯	4. Dinner with John and Louise	6. Date night

Once they had picked their six slots and numbered them from 1 to 6, Mark drew five circles in their schedule. "Part of the beauty of this system," he explained, "is that it not only gives you an appropriate amount of time *together,* it also provides you with pockets of freedom for each of you to plan your *own* activities—without feeling guilty or pressured to beg for permission from each other."

The circles in this schedule represent times when you and your wife are free to work a few extra hours or plan an independent activity—going to a sporting event with friends, enrolling in an art class, or whatever. With this plan, you'll achieve a good balance between sufficient time together and guilt-free time apart. You'll find yourself protected from feeling smothered by too much time with each other or alienated by not having enough.

Whenever Mark teaches the slot system, someone invariably asks about those times when six slots a week are simply impossible—out-of-town business trips, unforeseen crises at work, and the like. He acknowledges that this happens to him regularly. However, he goes on to make a critical point—one I'd encourage you not to miss. Mark and Susan have determined that by making six slots their norm, their marriage is well prepared to handle those times when six slots just aren't going to happen in a given week. "We have chosen," they explain, "to set the default button on six, so that it's *normal* to have enough time together and *abnormal* to miss each other for a whole week."

Pay attention now. Here's the most important thing Mark says about the slot system: "Give up on the myth of *quality time* with your wife. Trying to squeeze *quality* out of an hour or two a week is going to be an exercise in frustration. But carving out specific blocks of *quantity* time is always the most fertile ground for growing *quality* time in your marriage."

THE ZERO-SECRETS POLICY

> Untold secrets often become a stench that hides in the walls of your marriage.

My grandparents' house smelled. It wasn't an overpowering stench; it was just enough that when we'd visit, it would greet us like an unfriendly host. When my grandparents entered a rest home, the new owners of their house made a complete renovation—and I'm convinced that one of the reasons was to get rid of the smell.

Untold secrets often become a stench that hides in the walls of your marriage. You can't see it, but you both know that something "smells" wrong. We say to engaged couples that if they can't handle revealing secrets when they're in the thick of romance, they surely won't be able to handle it when the protective buffers around their marriage have worn thin.

The seeds that can later sprout and destroy marriages usually hide in secrets:

- the female friend at work in whom you confide
- the job you lost because you got caught stealing
- the secret e-mail address your bride doesn't know about
- the fact that you cheated your way through school
- the quantity of alcohol you consume when she's not around
- the pornography you view on a regular basis

When we suggest that couples adopt a zero-secrets policy, someone (usually the guy) often asks, "Are you saying that I need to tell my wife every time I lust after another woman?"

Our answer is a resounding, "Sort of."

Your wife doesn't need to get a catalog of every lustful thought you have, but telling her that this is something you struggle with will shed light on it and release it from your secret memory bank—and it will also create accountability.

Twenty years ago I worked on the second floor of a new office building. My desk faced the front window overlooking the parking lot. Early one day, I looked up from my desk in time to see a woman walking from her car into the building. She looked like a model. Her face and her body were flawless. Her stride was silky and strong. My heart raced as I watched her until she disappeared into the building directly under my window.

Wow, I thought to myself, *I wonder who THAT is.*

The next morning, quite by accident, something caught my eye again. I looked up and saw the same woman walking from her car. My eyes did not leave her until she was out of sight once more. For the next few mornings, the woman's appearance was no longer a surprise. I watched for her. I waited for her. I stood at the window to get a better look. During the day, my mind would drift back to her. I began to think about how I might meet her—perhaps wait for her and act as though I was leaving the building as she approached. I had allowed my mind to go too far. I had crossed the line, and I knew it.

"I've got to tell you something," I said to Bobbie the next weekend. "There's a woman I see walking into the building every day ..."

For the next few minutes, I explained what had happened and how this mystery woman had captured my imagination. The burden of keeping a secret from Bobbie was more than I wanted to carry. I told her that I was sorry and needed her forgiveness for my foolishness. She thanked me for telling her and willingly forgave me.

> Secrets that hide can become serious infections. They need air in order to heal.

By the way, although I noticed the woman on Monday morning, my eyes left her before she made it to the front door. Because I had told Bobbie, the thrill of watching was gone.

Secrets that hide can fester and become serious infections inside your marriage. They have the power to ruin your friendship. They need air in order to heal.

One Last Thought about Secrets

Your wife may have secrets of her own that need to be shared with you. These are secrets you may not want to know about, but they're secrets she may need to tell you. Telling you about these will relieve the burden she's been carrying—the burden of hiding something from you. When she does tell you, she will need your words of assurance, your forgiveness, your affection—and not your judgment.

8

CONFLICT: ONLY YOU CAN PREVENT FOREST FIRES

*Aravis and Shasta got so used to fighting and making up
again that they decided to get married so as to do it more
conveniently.*

C. S. LEWIS, *THE HORSE AND HIS BOY*

———◆◆◆———

Although the fire station was all the way downtown Wheaton,
Illinois, I could hear the sirens the moment they started wail-
ing. I suppose my ears were particularly attuned that afternoon,
because the fire trucks were coming to see me.

When I was a kid, long before the concept of recycling ever hit the
scene, we separated our trash. The purpose, however, was not to recy-
cle it but to burn it! There were two huge washing machine boxes in
the garage—one was for tin cans and glass, the other for "burnable
scrap." Then every two or three weeks, one of the boys—my three
brothers or I—was charged with wrestling the box onto our Red Flyer
wagon for the short trip to the "way back" to be burned. (Actually,
unlike mowing the grass or cleaning the basement floor, this wasn't a
chore I dodged.)

On this particular day, my brother—I was twelve, and he was
five—came along. It was better to have someone walk along to help
steady the oversized box on top of the undersized wagon.

When we reached the burning area, Danny and I turned the box
over and dumped its contents. We hadn't noticed the wind until the
box was empty and we had to chase a few wayward pieces of paper

that skittered into the tall grass. I asked Danny to stand guard in case any burning papers made it over to the tall grass, and then I lit the fire. So far, so good. But once the stack of stuff was engulfed in flames, I got to thinking, *I wonder what would happen if I took some of this fire and laid it next to the tall grass.*

"Don't do it," Danny warned when he saw what I was doing. *What do little brothers know?* I thought to myself.

"You'll start a big fire," he said, his eyes widening. "I'll tell Mother." (The ultimate little brother warning.)

I was unaffected by my brother's words—and so, given the wind and the dry conditions, we had a for-real prairie fire going in no time at all. At first, the grass fire was very small, not too much for our stamping and stomping. Then I held my little brother back for a brief moment, just to let the fire get bigger. More interesting. At that moment we both realized that we were no longer in control.

> "I wonder what would happen if I took some of this fire and laid it next to the tall grass."

Spotting the flames from the kitchen window, my mother called the fire department—the number was dutifully taped to the wall telephone (remember, there were *four* boys living here). Then she grabbed a bucket from under the sink, filled it as quickly as she could, and ran to the blazing field. In order to help her run more swiftly, she held the bucket in her arms rather than at her side, the water violently sloshing back and forth.

Just as I looked up to see my mother running toward me, she tripped on a stick and fell headlong onto the grass. The bottom of the bucket slammed against the hard ground and the water shot straight up like a geyser, then it returned to earth, soaking her from head to toe.

Although my dad traveled around the world for a living, he wasn't far *enough* away at that moment—I think he was in Greece—because I got what was coming to me when he returned. I might have been able to avoid a spanking, given the dry and windy conditions, had it not been for Danny's truthful report. My attempt to bribe him only made it worse. (By the way, when I told my story to Mark, he laughed and told me about the first time the fire trucks showed up to put out *his* prairie fire—he was ten years old. What is it about boys and matches anyway?)

WHERE THERE'S SMOKE . . .

It probably didn't take long after you and your bride walked down the aisle until you learned something about your marriage. Your arguments didn't go away. You had some when you were engaged, and you hoped that getting married would put an end to them—at least to their frequency and intensity. How wrong could you have been?

You've been able to control some of these conflicts, but like our youthful pyro-experiences, a few have gotten completely out of control. Smoke has been visible for miles. And when it happens, you and your bride may take on the characteristics of one of these five animals. See if you can identify yourself—and her.

An Ostrich

When the conflict escalates beyond a casual disagreement, the ostrich puts his head in the sand. *This isn't happening,* he lies to himself as he walks away from his wife. Picking up the remote, he clicks on the television, hoping to find something that will drown out his wife's voice—especially if she's . . .

A Tiger

This is the classic winner-take-all fighter. At the first sight of an escalating fight, her fangs glisten and her claws extend. The way to get the upper hand in this fight is to injure the opponent, and the longer she's married to him, the easier it is to find just the right words to hurt him. Of course, ignoring a tiger only escalates her fury, like if she's married to . . .

A Turtle

At first glance, this husband looks like an ostrich, but don't be fooled. His head only pulls back into his shell until just the right moment, and then it darts out and snaps vicious and hurtful words. When his wife fights back, his head has disappeared again. Of course, even if his head is tucked back into his shell, there isn't much comfort if he's married to . . .

A Skunk

Agile and cunning, this fighter—with or without intent—stirs up a fight, then sprays its victim with a barrage of awful and often unrelated generalizations. The skunk may run from the argument, slam doors, or even shout from the other room, but there's a hint of sport in this fighter. It's almost as though she enjoys the smell she creates. Of course, the only way the skunk can feel guilty about leaving such horrible odors behind is if she's married to . . .

A Puppy

Anger is almost invisible on this person's menu of emotions. His favorite retorts are "whatever" and "it's no big deal." He often tries to avoid the issue by saying something he thinks is funny. He hates fights and will do anything to keep peace, but sometimes he creates messes that have to be cleaned up by someone else. Even if it means taking all the blame, his goal is to keep a disagreement from escalating into something unfriendly.

TURNING SKIRMISHES INTO STEPPING-STONES

After years of marriage, observation of other couples, and counseling experiences, we've come up with some strategies that have helped to tame these nasty animals—or to use the earlier imagery, some tactics to help keep the fire sirens from going off. These have not prevented small blazes from springing up now and then; but by and large they've kept them from escalating to the point where our home—and the neighbor's homes—became threatened by the carnage.

In fact, for some men, these strategies have successfully turned skirmishes into stepping-stones, helping their marriages go from ordinary to great.

Fire Safety Strategy #1: Embrace Imperfection

The foundation for this strategy begins with a false expectation. You had it when you got married, and your wife had it, too. Don't worry, it's a hope shared by nearly every bride and groom, and it goes something like this: "I love this person very much, but there are a *few* things that need to be adjusted in her personality and habits. I'll get to those just as soon as we're married."

Oh, and here's another dream shatterer: "Our relationship is meant to be. God brought us together—so when we get married, we won't fight."

If you had been fortunate enough to marry a perfect, sinless woman, these hopes may have been possible. Or if she had been that lucky in marrying a perfect you, these dreams may have also come true. But neither of these things happened. You and your bride came from the ranks of the imperfect, and you both married out of the same flawed inventory.

I've spent most of my career in the publishing business, which means that I have read—or scanned—thousands of manuscripts over the course of the past thirty years. One of the things I've noticed is that my immediate focus is on the mistakes in the work, not on the good that's there. Being a skillful editor is a good thing for me professionally. But in my marriage, focusing on my wife's problems and making note of them—especially with a red pen—spells big trouble.

Ironically, after twenty years in the business, I stepped out to write my first book. And when I received my manuscript back from my editor, I discovered red marks everywhere. At that moment I realized *my own* need to be edited and the pain my editing had inflicted on others.

Since you also recognize imperfection in yourself (at least I hope you do), this strategy is best implemented with a nonverbal acknowledgement to yourself that being married to you must be hard work. Since we all struggle with self-centeredness, this can be a pretty tough admission. But once you've silently made peace with your own flaws, it will be easier to admit them to your wife, even during an argument.

> The ship that can maneuver the easiest should yield to the less nimble craft.

"You're right," you could say when she accuses you of messing up. "You're right, and I shouldn't have done—or said—that." You cannot imagine how effective this can be in helping extinguish the early flames.

Dr. Henry Brandt, one of the pioneers in the field of Christian counseling, discovered a secret weapon in helping married couples come to terms with their inevitable differences. Dr. Brandt would begin his initial session by asking a single question, first to the husband and then to the wife: "Before we start on your list of grievances with each other, I would like to know—what do you need to confess?"

The recognition of your own imperfections opens the door to understanding your wife's flaws. Believe it or not, when you take this as a challenge, you may be better at it than she is, so it's appropriate for you to go first.

I'm not much of a sailor, but I've come to know one of the basic laws of avoiding tragedy on the sea: The ship that can maneuver the easiest should yield to the less nimble craft. As you begin to disclose your own imperfections, your wife will feel safe in unveiling her own.

Fire Safety Strategy #2: You Can Disagree without Fighting

Just because it's natural—and healthy—for you and your wife to have conflicts and disagreements, it doesn't mean that these *have* to turn into fights. Dr. John Gray, of Mars and Venus fame, says that heated arguments are not a helpful way of dealing with disagreement. The problem is that fighting turns the focus toward "defending and winning" and away from solving the issue at hand.

During our first year of marriage, Bobbie and I discovered that there were things we said during our disagreements that could immediately infuriate each other, escalating the discussion into a blazing prairie fire. So we took a bold step. During a calm discussion following one of these battles, we sat down to discuss our own private "rules of engagement."

The Geneva Convention

On June 24, 1859, Henri Dunant[23] witnessed the Battle of Solferino in northern Italy. Seeing the bloodshed, Dunant immediately began enlisting local peasants to carry the wounded from the battlefield and take them to local churches, where doctors tried to relieve their suffering.

Deeply troubled by the inhumane treatment of wounded soldiers, Dunant and four other men organized an international conference of thirteen nations in Geneva, Switzerland, to discuss ways to make warfare more "humane." At the end of the conference on August 22, 1864, the representatives had signed the Geneva Convention. This agreement provided for the neutrality of ambulances and military hospitals, the protection of people who helped the wounded, and the return of prisoners to their country. It also adopted the use of a white flag with a red cross on hospitals, ambulances, and evacuation centers—whose neutrality would be recognized by this symbol.

> Fighting turns the focus toward "defending and winning" and away from solving the issue at hand.

Even though the Geneva Convention has gone through several revisions in the past 150 years—including the denunciation of chemical weapons in battle—it has stood like a sentry over hundreds of battles. And tens of thousands of soldiers have been saved because of its protection.

During our first year of marriage, Bobbie and I agreed that the inevitable clashes in our marriage should be under the protection of our own "Geneva Convention." And so we decided on the following nonnegotiables—situations where we'd *never* mistreat the wounded or use mustard gas:

1. *We will not criticize each other in public (including—some day—in the presence of our kids).* When one of us has been hurt by the other, the victim will come directly to the spouse as soon as possible in private, explaining his or her perspective.

   Do say (while driving home from a party): "What you said to your friends about my eating habits really hurt my feelings. It's unfair, and it embarrassed me."

   Do not say to your wife (while standing with your friends at the party): "Isn't that your third trip to the buffet? Haven't you had enough?"

2. *We will not address areas of disagreement when we're at our worst.* Bobbie and I learned that serious discussions are rarely well served when we're exhausted from a busy day or when we're not feeling well—emotionally or physically. Our condition usually made a pointed conversation more frustrating, and we rarely reached a solution.

   Do say: "I'm eager to talk about this as soon as we can, but I know we're both very tired. I don't think it's a good time to try to deal with this issue. Let's talk about it over coffee in the morning. Please don't forget that I love you—but right now we both need to get some rest."

   Do not say: "I don't care how you feel. The Bible says, 'Don't let the sun go down on your wrath.' Well the sun is down, and I'm ticked. And would you *please* quit crying."

3. *We will not resort to name-calling.* This includes referring to each other by our parents' first names. (Maybe you've discovered that your wife and her mother share some of the characteristics that most frustrate you.)

   Do say: "It really bugs me when you do that."

   Do not say: "Nice going, 'Geraldine.'"

4. *We will not, in the heat of the battle, bring up information shared in moments of sincere vulnerability.* From the time you and your wife decided that marriage was where you wanted to end up, you engaged in intimate conversations about your deepest fears, regrets, or failures. Arguments are out-of-bounds for the retrieval and regurgitation of this information.

   Do say: "I know how angry this kind of thing makes you. I'm sorry you feel this way."

   Do not say: "What else would I expect from the granddaughter of an alcoholic?"

5. *We will not use each other's physical characteristics as ammunition when we're arguing.* As with references to intimate secrets or making unfair comparisons to each other's parents, unkind comments about our bodies are forbidden.

   Do say . . . absolutely nothing about this.

   Do not say: "Keep your big, fat, knobby German nose out of my business."

These are the articles of our Geneva Convention. And whether you borrow some from us or start from scratch, having your own list is going to keep your battles inbounds. Because, as a man, you're wired to compete and win at war, it's going to be tough to refrain from using your "trump cards." But don't succumb to the temptation. They're chemical weapons. Please don't use them.

Here's the way we monitor our Geneva Convention: if any of the rules are broken,

> Because, as a man, you're wired to compete and win at war, it's going to be tough to refrain from using your "trump cards."

the offending party immediately loses the argument. It's over—on the spot. I'd encourage the same kind of inflexibility in your marriage.

Fire Safety Strategy #3: Try the Instruction Manual

The Bible has a few specific and unambiguous directives for you and me. Obeying these will work wonders in keeping your arguments from breaking out into "first year of marriage" bloodshed.

1. **Be considerate, . . . and treat [her] with respect.**[24] Immediately following this directive, aimed specifically at husbands, is the prospect of a terrible thing that will happen to us if we disobey, namely, that our prayers will be hindered. It's incredible, but true. If you stoop to disrespecting your wife, a lid gets put on your prayer life. It will be as though your prayer "radio" will no longer be tuned to God's station for his leading in other areas of your life. Imagine the devastating consequences of missing God's voice when he speaks to you through circumstances, other people, or his Word.

This passage from 1 Peter goes on to refer to your bride as "the weaker partner." What an interesting thing to say. Here's what it means: The word *weaker* has nothing to do with your wife's tenacity or discipline, or her standing before God. It refers to her worth, her delicacy, and her built-in sensitivity. Because of these gifts, which are unique to your wife, the admonition to you is to be careful. Gentle. Thoughtful. This can be illustrated by the way you would recklessly play touch football with your buddies in an open field compared to how you'd play inside a china shop filled with priceless and very fragile antiques. Because you know the damage a simple incomplete pass could cause, you'd play your game very differently.

2. **Do not be harsh with [her].**[25] I was on a business trip, sitting in a breakfast diner enjoying a big bowl of "home-cooked" oatmeal. Glancing through a copy of *USA Today,* I was interrupted by the sound of a shouting man. Looking up from my paper, I caught a young man— a dad, I presumed—screaming for all he was worth directly into his child's face. I was dumbfounded. And I wasn't the only person in the place who saw this, because the whole restaurant became instantly quiet.

Before I tell you what I was thinking, let me tell you what I *wasn't* thinking: *Wow, that kid certainly must have done something egregious to earn this punishment.* Nor did I think, *Poor dad, having to put up with lots of nonsense from his insensitive and thoughtless child. Maybe now the kid will get the message.*

Here's what I *did* think: *What on earth is the matter with that guy? He ought to be locked up for treating a child like that!*

What would it—what *does* it—look like when a husband treats his wife harshly? Even in private, away from public scrutiny, it is a very ugly thing. An indefensible thing. When a man speaks harshly to his wife, he is instantly in the wrong. Every time.

The tone of your voice has everything to do with what happens in an argument. You may have already discovered that *how* you speak to your wife is as important—as fortifying or as destructive—as *what* you say to her. Some husbands may defend themselves by saying, "I'm not being harsh; she's just too sensitive." And your excuses will be as feeble as that dad's excuses would have been in the diner.

> When a man speaks harshly to his wife, he is instantly in the wrong. Every time.

Remember that her tenderness comes as standard equipment. She *is* going to be more aware of the pitch of your voice. It's who she is, and it's one of the reasons God gave her to you. She is your ideal partner.

Fire Safety Strategy #4: When God Whispers in Your Wife's Ear, Don't Miss the Message

This strapping, exceptionally good-looking husband strolls into his million-dollar home at 8:00 every night. He gets home at this time every night because he has an everyday appointment with Leonard, his bartender. "I'd be home earlier," he says to his wife, "but my job is so stressful that, without a little liquid attitude adjustment, well, I'd be impossible to live with."

When he strides through the door, he expects—and receives—a brilliantly prepared gourmet meal. The kids, who finished dinner an hour ago, had better be quiet and well behaved. If one of them is watching *his* big-screen TV, Dad sends him scampering to a set in another room so he can download another sporting event via his satellite dish.

He has nothing but disdain for his wife's parenting methods, claiming that the children's misbehavior *must* be her fault—since he's never home. He second-guesses her every move. She lives in constant fear. And he lives with mortal unhappiness.

"Early in our marriage," she confesses, "I wanted to tell him the truth about how he made me feel. In fact, I know this is *exactly* how his father treated his mother and him, too. It's just doing what he learned when *he* was a boy."

Although this woman has been married for almost twenty years, she tries to communicate in tender ways with her husband. Tough talk isn't an option; she's far too frightened for that. Her closest friends have heard her loving suggestions and her gentle pleas to her husband. And the man's inability—unwillingness, really—to listen to the whispers of his wife only adds to his losses. Not listening to his wife when they were first married will eventually lead to his ruin—and hers—one way or another.

> Early in your marriage, there's no one in the history of your life who wants to see you succeed more than your wife does.

When you read the biographies of great men, you'll discover—almost without exception—the strength and wisdom of their wives. These women provided far more than lifelong companionship and progeny for these men. They became wise counselors, advisers, and advocates. Some received credit for the efforts from the public, but most weren't recognized for their enormous contribution until they and their prominent husbands were gone.

Early in your marriage, there's no one in the history of your life who wants to see you succeed more than your wife does. As you build this relationship into a great marriage, you're going to face disagreements and even an occasional fight. These are inevitable. But know this: The same fire that sends danger across the tall, dry grass in an open field can be used to purify precious metals. As you learn to fight fairly and to never stop listening, these brushfires with your wife just may be the very things God uses to shape your 51 percent of a terrific marriage.

MONEY: CROUCHING TIGER, HIDDEN CRISIS

If a husband and wife are not communicating about finances, I'll guarantee you that they're not communicating about anything.

LARRY BURKETT, FINANCIAL COUNSELOR

———◆◆◆———

Sometimes the Discovery Channel is the only thing worth watching on television. Having drawn that conclusion, Bobbie and I tuned in recently to a feature called *Big Cats at Home*. It seems that there are folks scattered across the country who have a great affection for big cats—especially lions and tigers. And these people have brought these huge felines into their homes, treating them like normal house pets. The footage of these youthful animals was delightful. Cute, playful, and harmless-looking "kittens" romped on living room floors with their owners.

Eventually, however, these babies grew up. "Cute, playful, and harmless-looking" no longer served to describe them. Gliding back and forth behind backyard fences may be a beautiful sight on television, but the size of their claws, the glistening of their teeth, and the mystery of their disposition would change your perspective if you happened to live next door. Fearful neighbors have tried to force owners to get rid of their cats, but, amazingly, there's no federal law that prohibits people from raising a lion or tiger at home. (On the show, we saw some of these "house cats" that weighed over five hundred pounds! Nice kitty.)

Of course, the feature also included some pretty gruesome tales about these cats—especially the tigers—who, without provocation or warning, had attacked their neighbors or even turned on their keepers. The Discovery Channel treated us to some awful before-and-after photographs of people who had been victimized. Several had been killed.

The show's producers drew the following uncompromising conclusion: If you choose to own a tiger—or any other big cat—treat it with the utmost respect. And keep it caged at all times. Remember that a tiger can, without notice, attack—and when it does, you *will* get hurt.

CAUTION: MONEY—PROCEED AT YOUR OWN RISK

Tigers and money have a lot in common. They are both very beautiful. People stop and gawk at what they can do—jumping through fiery hoops at the circus or picking up the tab for the newest German sports sedan. They are both extremely alluring, but they can both be very dangerous if not caged properly.

And one of the reasons a book about the first year of your marriage must discuss the wonder and danger of money is that there is a good chance that you and your bride have quite different views about it:[26]

- "I'll bet that cat could run down a deer and smoke it in a split second."
- "He's so cute. Here kitty, kitty."

You may think you'll be able to tame this tiger. Trust me: it'll never happen. Your job in this first year is not to domesticate this big cat called *Money* but to cage it. And a tiger's always easier to cage before it gets big enough to do some serious damage.

Once the tiger's caged, you and your bride can spend the rest of your marriage safely enjoying its beauty and its power.

MONEY'S FALSE PROMISE

The attraction of money, of course, is what we believe it can do for us. It's why people board tour buses to view the estates of the rich and famous. Audible oohs and aahs can be heard at every turn. "Will you look at the *size* of that place!" someone will exclaim.

> A tiger's always easier to cage before it gets big enough to do some serious damage.

"Did you see all the cars in his driveway?" another will say.

I wonder what these people say about their humble little bungalows after driving back home in their twelve-year-old cars. "If only we could drive a new car and live in a house like some of those we saw on the tour," they're bound to say. "If we could have *those* things, then we'd be happy."

These same "tourists" stand in grocery store checkout lines every week. While they wait they scan the covers of their favorite weekly magazines. Every time they do, they see photographs of these same "rich and famous" people looking quite sad and pitiful. The headlines tell of "separations" and "settlements," "rehabs" and "bouts of depression." They shout about "abuse" and "estrangement." He gets the airplane; she gets the Montana ranch. He gets the cars; she gets the jewels. We're not sure who gets the children.

Maybe happy, maybe not.

Early in our marriage, our pastor, Richard Freeman, was preaching one Sunday morning about money. He was leading up to the fall "stewardship campaign," when the congregation would be asked to "subscribe to the annual budget." Everyone had their seat belts fastened.

> "I know where to go to find a list of the most important things in your life. You've already written it down."

But Rev. Freeman surprised us that morning with a truth now seared into my brain forever. "I know where to go to find a list of the most important things in your life," he announced confidently. "You've already written it down."

I was fascinated with this thought. *Prove it,* I'm sure I said to myself.

Then Rev. Freeman pulled something out of his pocket. It was his personal checkbook. Turning to the check register, he opened it and held it up. "I know where your priorities are," he said, "because here's a list of Lois Marie's and mine."

I had never thought of it like that, and I knew he was right. The way we spend our money *does* show where our priorities lie.

NORMAL . . . AGAIN

In chapter 4 we talked about family systems—about what you and your bride grew up believing was normal. Any discussion about money needs to deal with this, too. If your parents argued about money, that was normal for you. If your dad paid the household bills because he didn't trust your mother with the checkbook, that was normal. If your dad "surprised" your mother with new cars; if your mother went shopping like it was a daily sport, even when she didn't

> Through their courtship, their engagement, their wedding ceremony, and their honeymoon, the tiger sleeps.

need anything; if your parents lived with heavy credit card debt; if your parents tried to hide their expenditures from each other; if your parents always waited until they could pay cash before they bought something—all of these things were normal for you. You're bringing them into your marriage as standard equipment.

CROUCHING TIGER

The other reason we're talking about money is that if you ask couples before they're married if they think money will be a big problem, most will say no. They might as well be saying, "We're not worried about money. We'll be livin' on love." And because this tiger has, so far, never done much damage to the couple, the typical bride and groom do very little about him. Through their courtship, their engagement, their wedding ceremony, and their honeymoon, the tiger sleeps. No cage necessary.

But a few months into the marriage the kitty wakes up, and things begin to change. Dramatically.

- "The sofa that Grandma gave us is heinous. We *need* a new one."
- "A golf membership would make it so much easier to take my clients out. We *need* one."
- "I've let my wardrobe deteriorate. I *need* new clothes for my job."
- "I'm tired of cooking. Let's go out again."
- "Hey, would you look at that? No money down—zero percent interest!"

In order for you to cage your tiger before it gets too unruly during this first year, here are a few "Caging Habits" that have helped many couples who want to do the right thing with their money but aren't quite sure how.

Caging Truth #1: Make a Budget and Live within Your Means

I'll never forget the first personal financial seminar I attended as a young man. The leader was a man named Ron Blue. His clients included some of my favorite professional athletes, as well as several prominent Christian leaders.

Ron walked to the microphone, thanked his host, and greeted us. "Do you want to know the secret of financial success?" he asked. Then he answered his own question.

"You'll find financial success if you make more money than you spend and do it for a long period of time."

A couple of the students chuckled, but Ron didn't smile. Instead, he went on to explain that financial *trouble* begins when people spend more money than they have.

"It happens all the time," he said. "It happens to good people— good people like you and me, people who are unwilling to live within their means."

A few hundred years ago, spending *more* than you had would have been impossible. Can you imagine a pioneer slapping his MasterCard down to buy a horse on credit? But every time you receive your credit card bill, it tells you what your "credit limit" is. "Come on," it seems to be begging you. "Think about the good things you could buy with this *unspent* money. Go ahead. Why wait?"

Spending the money you don't have breaks Ron Blue's simple rule. Its consequence is the prevention of financial success.

The easiest way for you to stay within your means is to put a budget together—*together*. I wish Bobbie and I had done this in our early years. Once we started creating a budget together, our frustrations and arguments about money were exponentially reduced. What's more, creating a budget together gave us mutual accountability. Over the years, I have observed that a man who refuses to be accountable to his wife on financial matters is often a man who avoids accountability—of any kind—to anyone

> Financial trouble happens to people who are unwilling to live within their means.

else. The beauty of accountability *to a budget* is that, at least in some sense, when you allow your budget to determine your spending decisions, you avoid being pitted against each other. In effect, you let the budget be your referee.

If you need help in creating a budget (or what may be called a spending plan), there are some terrific software programs you can buy to get you and keep you going as you manage it, month by month.[27]

Caging Truth #2: Remember That Your Wife Has Valuable Insights about Money

It was clear from the attitude of this soon-to-be husband that he had already gotten off track. He was about to marry a brilliant, talented, wealthy, recent Ivy-League college graduate, but it was clear as he and his bride sat in the premarital counselor's office that he intended to call the financial shots at home. He spoke to her in a tone dangerously close to that of an unhappy father scolding his child. As he explained his financial plans, he punctuated his points with words that made the counselor cringe.

- "She just needs to understand a few things when it comes to money."
- "I'll give her an allowance each month. When it's gone, it's gone."
- "After we get married, she's not going to be allowed to just blow money like she does now. We've already talked about this—and she understands."

It never occurred to this young man that his bride had a perspective and wisdom about money that needed to be valued. It never occurred to him that his words were thinly veiled attempts at controlling his bride. And it never occurred to him that this thoughtless control would eventually drive her away—maybe to a new mailing address without him.

There are few places where young husbands make more mistakes than when they're dealing with money. Here's a good rule to remember: If you speak to your wife about money as though she were a child, then she will believe that your concern over money is more important to you than your love for her.

Early in our marriage, Bobbie and I found ourselves embroiled in deep conflict over money. I was working on a youth worker's salary, and she had grown up in a home where money was quite freely spent.

"We can't afford that," was something I said all the time.

It wasn't that Bobbie was intentionally fighting against me; it was that she really couldn't understand our financial situation. So we decided that she would take over the checkbook. Instead of putting myself in the position of telling her what we could and couldn't afford, she could see it for herself.

This decision was a great one. Bobbie became so adept that now she was watching *my* expenses like a hawk. Our biggest first-year fight—by a long shot—was when I bought a James Taylor cassette without asking her permission. Talk about taking the ball and running with it!

Caging Truth #3: Be Careful about Taking Money from Your Parents

The chances are good that both sets of your parents have more money than you do. And it's probable that they really love you and want the best for you. So it stands to reason that there will be times when your parents are willing—whether or not you ask them—to loan you money.

Be careful.

Here's what I mean. Let's imagine that you have a circle of very close friends. And we'll imagine that one of these friends—let's call him Harold—is a loan officer at the bank. You and Harold always have a great time together. You're always relaxed when he's around, and he seems to feel the same way about you.

One day you decide to buy a new car, and because you don't have enough cash, you call your good friend, Harold. A few hours later you drive to the bank to pick up the check. Harold's waiting for you in his office and hands you the check as you walk in. You know that Harold is more than happy to loan you the money, and you have every intention of making good on the loan. However, the moment after you sign the papers

> "The rich rule over the poor, and the borrower is servant to the lender."

and the check passes from his hand to yours, you feel something strange. It takes you a few weeks to figure out the feeling, but the next time you're with him it hits you: *Harold used to be my good friend. There was nothing between us except the fun of being in each other's presence. But now I'm a debtor to Harold. He holds a note with my name on it, and I'm obligated to him.*

Whether you like it or not, your relationship with Harold has changed—maybe until the loan is paid off. Maybe forever. You used to be friends, pure and simple. Now you're his debtor. King Solomon of ancient Israel said it well: "The rich rule over the poor, and the borrower is servant to the lender."[28]

Building a strong, unencumbered relationship with your bride's parents is an important—and sometimes challenging—goal to set. And your bride wants the same with your parents. Now it's *possible* to borrow money from them and not have it affect your relationship. It's *possible* that changing your status from son-in-law to debtor won't change anything at all. But it probably will.

If you choose to borrow from them—as a last resort—put together a payment plan in writing and stay on top of it. Pay it off early if you can. Talk about it openly when you're together. If you don't, this indebtedness can spoil (literally) your relationship.

There's one more thing about your parents' money. If they offer to *give* you money, caution is also a good idea. I have a very close friend who received a check from his wife's mother for Christmas. "Your dad and I want you to put this toward a new color television," the note inside the envelope read.

This was back in the early 1970s when color sets went for about five hundred dollars. But the check was for only a hundred dollars. That meant that this Christmas present was going to *cost* my friend four hundred dollars! And if you think he was going to be comfortable *not* having a color television the next time they visited, you'd be wrong. Some gift, huh?

Ron Blue has a wise perspective about the issue of parents giving gifts to their married children. The gift, he notes, should not obligate the couple to something they cannot afford. "Don't give them *lifestyle* money," he says. In other words, don't let your parents give you money that forces you into a lifestyle you can't afford or sustain. A hundred-dollar check toward a five-hundred-dollar color television is a perfect example; another is the down payment on an expensive home you'd have trouble maintaining.

Ron and his wife, Judy, have given their married children things like appliances. (Who *doesn't* need a good washer and dryer?) He advises parents to help their married children by sending money to pay down the principal on their mortgage or to start a savings account for their children's education. All of these are good ideas.

Caging Truth #4: Treat Your Bride Like Your Business Partner

Whether or not your wife assumes the check-writing duties, this fact is certain: Not only will you be honoring her by including her in your financial strategy, you'll also be doing yourself a great favor. Her insight will be extremely valuable.

When Mike Hyatt and I started our publishing company in 1986, we mortgaged and leveraged everything we owned. It was a scary proposition to think that no longer would we be able to refer to the funds as "my money" and "Mike's money." The money was "ours."

We made all of our financial decisions together. If I had decided to step out and hire a marketing expert or invest in a new computer system without Mike's permission, I would have sent him a disturbing message: "Even though I say that you're my partner, I'm going to make these important decisions without you."

Treat your wife like your business partner. Think strategically about expenditures and investments together. Do your best not to talk about "my" money and "your" money.[29] Someday, if children come along and your wife decides to be an at-home mom, you may be *forced* to treat your money as "ours." I can't think of any good reason to wait for that day. Establish your "partnership" right away.

Caging Habit #5: Put Giving into Your Regular Budget

How I use money is a snapshot of what's truly important to me. At a single glance I can see what I value most. I may think that giving to my church or other worthy charities can wait until I have more money, but I know from experience that if Bobbie and I hadn't gotten into the habit of being generous early, it would have been impossible to do it later.

Practicing charity came to me as a gift from my parents. It was one of my *normals*. My parents were tithers—they gave away at least 10 percent of their income every year. So one of the early financial decisions Bobbie and I made was to be sure that, at the end of the year, our donations totaled at least 10 percent of our income. We didn't do this so that God would be obligated to bless us in some special way; we did it because we had learned that this was the right thing to do. And we discovered that stewardship was its *own* reward, which is exactly why the Bible says that "you're far happier giving than receiving."[30]

The donation we could barely afford in our first year became a pattern of generosity that we're both thankful for. In the end, it's easier to make strategic decisions about giving money away when you're first married and living on less than when you find yourself with more someday. It may be easier to give ten cents out of every dollar than a hundred-thousand dollars out of every million!

If you stop making mortgage payments on your house, the lender will eventually foreclose on you. If you neglect to keep up with your car payments, the bank will send a flatbed truck and winch your car away. But if you stop giving to your church or to the support of missionaries, they'll suffer quietly.

Holding your money with an open hand will be a reminder to you that it's a gift in the first place. It's why your church typically labels its fund drive as *stewardship*. A steward never "owns" anything. Instead, he is charged with taking care of someone else's property. Your open hand will remind you that money is a blessing to be shared rather than an asset to be hoarded.

Besides, closing your hand will spill lots of it.

Caging Truth #6: Set a "Fun Money" Spending Limit

I was on the phone with a businessman I really respect. He runs a large division of a 150-year-old multinational corporation, and he runs it very successfully. My friend loves his work, and he reminds me of this every time we talk.

> Holding your money with an open hand will be a reminder to you that it's a gift in the first place.

Somewhere in our conversation he mentioned his spending limit. We had been talking about an investment that I thought would be a good idea for his division. "I'll have to talk to the CEO," he said. "A hundred-thousand dollars is above my spending limit."

My friend is happy in his work, because within this "spending limit" he has the freedom to make choices. His entrepreneurial instincts—exercised inside these boundaries—make his work inspiring and motivating.

Early in your marriage, you and your bride should set a no-permission-necessary spending limit. It may be ten dollars, a hundred dollars, or more. Also, you may want to set a "frequency limit"—once a week, twice a month, or whatever is agreeable to both of you. This money will give you both a sense of freedom without jeopardizing your budget. When you're out and you see something that falls within your agreed-on limits, you can go for it.

Mark and Susan advise newlyweds to adopt a similar approach. They call it the *Marriage Insurance Premium* (MIP)—a certain amount of money set aside each month for you to spend without your spouse's permission. Having a MIP creates an expanse of freedom for each of you, a space in which you can make small financial decisions in ways that fit your style and personality. Without it, you and your wife could easily feel constricted and trapped.

Caging Truth #7: Pursue Contentment

Early in our marriage, if someone had told me that making a lot more money would not make me happy, I would have laughed out loud. Of course, I was familiar with the cliché about money and happiness, but I *knew* it was foolish and doubtful.

Down through the years of our life together, however, Bobbie and I have watched some of our friends gather wealth. In some cases, fabulous wealth. And we've made many acquaintances with "people of means." In some cases, fabulous means. And we've made the following observation—one that has, so far, yielded no exceptions: If these people were happy before they got wealthy, they still seemed to be happy. And if these people were not happy before their ships came in, money didn't change this situation either.

> Spending your way to happiness will never happen. You'll never reach the top of this mountain.

When I was twenty years old, I—along with thirty-nine friends—crossed the United States on a bicycle. There were, however, three ten-thousand-foot passes lurking between the Pacific and the Atlantic Oceans. One thing I remember about climbing the western slopes of these behemoths was that, as we rounded bends in the road—thinking we were at the top—there were still *more* hills to climb. Getting to the very top felt like an endless assignment.

Spending your way to happiness will never happen. When you *finally* buy that thing "you've always wanted," your little bicycle will round the bend in the road, and voilà, there's another "if only I could have that" waiting for you. You'll never reach the top of this mountain.

So what should you do? Take a deep breath, and realize that your climb for acquiring things looks more like a hamster's wheel than a goal you can achieve. You're far more likely to spin than win. Understanding this fact—and believing its truth—will begin to help you on your journey toward contentment.

Caging Truth #8: Money Is a Neutral Substance

You can go into a bookstore and find books about money that claim to be written from a Christian perspective. Some of these books will tell you that money—especially having a lot of it—is a very bad thing; on the other hand, you'll be able to find titles telling you that having lots of money is God's way of rewarding you for your obedience. Can you imagine such opposite positions—both of which purport to represent a Christian perspective?

Here's where we're coming from. We think it cuts to the heart of the issue: "The love of money is a root of all kinds of evil. Some people, eager for money, have wandered from the faith and pierced themselves with many griefs."[31]

Water is a neutral substance. It can be a thirst-quenching lifesaver after a basketball game or a jog through the neighborhood. But a person can also drown in water. A baseball bat is also a neutral substance. A slugger can use it to park a line drive over the centerfield fence and win the game for his team, or a thug can use it to kill an innocent victim.

Money is a neutral substance. It can be used for good things, or it can lead to a person's demise. The variable isn't the money itself but the way in which it's treated. The nonnegotiables about money are these:

- Don't fall in love with it; use it—but use it wisely.
- Don't spend more than you have—except for a reasonable mortgage, stay out of debt.
- Share financial decisions with your wife.
- Give away as much of it as you can.

Out of respect for what it can do—both good and bad—hold your money, however much you have, with an open hand. This *restrained* tiger is a beautiful thing.

10

SEX: BATTER UP

There are three things that are too amazing for me,
four that I do not understand.
the way of an eagle in the sky,
the way of a snake on a rock,
the way of a ship on the high seas,
and the way of a man with a maiden.

PROVERBS 30:18–19

———◆•◦◆•◦◆———

I want both of you to close your eyes and think of as many sexual fantasies about each other that you can."

Though Mark and Susan have done premarital counseling with more couples than they can remember, they'll never forget being asked this question in their own premarital preparation. The question was not a complete surprise, since the minister who asked the question trafficked in the unexpected. This was a man who had an uncanny ability to bring Jesus into the most unlikely places in the most unexpected ways.

"I'll give you sixty seconds," the minister said.

Mark, happy to obey his pastor, closed his eyes and started thinking. What Susan was going to do with the question wasn't his immediate concern.

"Time's up!" the minister announced with a flourish. Mark looked straight at him, feeling a little squeamish about what he had just done while sitting in church—in the pastor's office!

"Now let me tell you what just happened," the minister began, releasing Mark from having to describe what had just galloped through this mind.

Pointing to Mark, the minister continued, "This young man just thought of twenty or thirty different possibilities. But his bride-to-be is still trying to think of the first one." Mark glanced in Susan's direction. Her blush and shy giggle communicated the pastor's accuracy.

At that moment, Mark realized what you and I already now know. The anatomical differences between husbands and wives don't compare to the immense differences in the places we'll never see—our brains and our hearts.

MEET MR. CLUELESS

Years later, Mark found himself seated across from a young couple just three months into their marriage. Because of scheduling snafus, the couple was only able to complete four of the five premarital sessions before the wedding. So the fifth and final meeting was now taking place a few months *after* the wedding.

In this session, Mark typically discusses the process (and power) of building a mutually satisfying sex life. "Men have a tendency to misunderstand their wives' needs when it comes to sex," Mark said. "They often assume that, because they are satisfied, their wives must be satisfied as well."

> The anatomical differences between husbands and wives don't compare to the immense differences in the places we'll never see—our brains and our hearts.

As he talked, the bride nodded in agreement. She knew exactly what Mark was saying. The groom, on the other hand, was becoming less and less attentive, his eyes scanning the family photographs on Mark's desk and the Bible commentaries in the bookcase.

The wife had had enough. "Are you getting this?" she asked, just enough edge in her voice to let her husband know that she wasn't pleased with his attitude.

"Come on, honey," the young man replied, a distinct dash of bravado in his voice. "Do you *really* think we need help in this area?" His eyes moved from his bride to Mark, and the swagger in his countenance intensified. His next words confirmed that here was a man in the process of being made utterly stupid by his own virility. "I'd say we've pretty much got this part down."

The young bride sat up straight in her chair and looked directly into her husband's face. "You've definitely figured out how to make *yourself* happy, big guy," she snapped, "but you've still got a thing or two to learn about me."

The silence that followed was poignant and intentional. Mark wanted to let the wife's words soak deeply into her husband's mind. The flush of his face revealed that her pointed remark had made a direct hit.

TAKE ME OUT TO THE BALL GAME

Let's face it, intercourse is intercourse. Making our body parts fit together is not terribly complicated. "No assembly required" may as well be printed on our marriage licenses. But for your wife, this isn't enough—not even close to enough. Making the emotional and physical connections in ways that are completely satisfying to her is a whole different . . . ball game.

From the time we were youngsters—sixth grade rings a bell—we and our buddies started talking about "running the bases." And I'm not talking about baseball. You remember hearing guys joke about getting to first base with a girl—then second base, and so on? I don't recall anyone ever putting specific definitions to these markers, but I think we assumed that holding hands and kissing were included in running out a single. French kissing may have described the dash from first to second, but above-the-waist petting definitely announced your arrival there. Hitting third base meant full-body petting—anything short of intercourse. And, of course, home plate was the ultimate.

Do you remember what each of these felt like the first time you experienced them? For most men, regardless of their age or lifelong sexual exploits, these "firsts" were unforgettable. I've noticed some interesting things about the way most boys talk about these bases during their adolescence.

Unforgettable First Arrivals

The *first time* is an incredible experience—even first base.

Because my dad was a minister, sitting in church was as common to our family as sitting at the kitchen table. So, of course, my first encounters with nonfamily girls were at church. Anything remotely resembling "social interaction" in grade school is a total blur, but church was different. I remember noticing girls during my adolescent Sunday school

> Making the emotional and physical connections in ways that are completely satisfying to her is a whole different . . . ball game.

years, primarily because they always sat with each other and had terminal cases of the giggles.

I was sitting next to her in church the first time I made contact with a girl's hand. We both had our arms folded across our chests, which allowed our inside hands to reach out and touch. They did. My heart raced. I'm sure my ears turned bright red. My entire body tingled. I felt like Kirk Gibson in the first game of the 1988 World Series. The pastor may have been waxing his most brilliant eloquence, but I was completely missing it.

This was incredible. I was alive.

Base Fatigue

I coached my first Little League team in the fall of 2000. I learned that, even for youngsters, getting to first base may be a thrill but who wants to stay there? Dancing the jig a few feet toward second is an art form. Of course, the purpose is to entice a pickoff attempt from the pitcher in the hope that the throw would be wild so they could scamper down to second.

It's quite a simple thing. Once you get to a base, your interest isn't in staying there but in moving on. Staying on the same base for any length of time at all is—well, it's a little boring.

Baserunning Experience

Once you've spent time at first base, the next time you run the bases you hustle past it on your way to second. Been there, done that.

When our daughters turned sixteen, they had our permission to "single-date"—out for the evening with one boy. Young men were aware of our "dating rule at age sixteen," so as we approached the girls' birthdays, Bobbie and I couldn't help but notice the boys circling the field.

We had another rule in addition to the minimum age limit. Boys who were interested in taking our girls out had to be interviewed by me.[32] Our second daughter's first date was going to be with an older boy. He was eighteen. During the interview I asked Steven if he had had a long-term dating relationship before.

"Yes, sir," he said.

"How long did you date her?" I asked.

"Oh, about a year," was his reply.

Because this was Julie's very first dating experience and because Steven was something of a veteran, I gently warned him about his baserunning speed. "Don't assume," I said—beads of perspiration were forming along his temples as I spoke—"that you can quickly move to where you've been with another girl. This is Julie's first experience,"

"Yes, sir," he said again, his lips turning purple from oxygen deprivation.

LEARNING TO TALK ABOUT SEX

Several years ago, an older couple walked into Mark's office. What the husband said in the first few minutes would have been laughable if it hadn't been so tragic. "It's been years—maybe ten—since my wife and I have had any sort of physical intimacy," he confessed. "It's gotten so bad I've decided we needed some counseling."

Marriage disintegration usually begins in secret places—places no one else can see, places husbands and wives avoid. And sexual intimacy is one of the most frequently circumvented subjects. Many couples learn the magic of open dialogue about every dimension of their lives together—every dimension, that is, except sex. And because of this neglect, sex often becomes an area of simmering frustration and tangible defeat.

Early in your marriage, you need to learn to express your needs clearly, and your wife needs to do the same. And I'm not talking about sarcastic comments during sex. "Can I get you something to *read*?" doesn't qualify as productive sex talk.

"I really want to make love to you tonight," a husband needs to feel free to say kindly to his wife over breakfast.

"When you do that to me, it drives me wild," a wife must be able to say without inhibition.

> "When you do that to me, it drives me wild," a wife must be able to say without inhibition.

When we mention the need for this kind of openness—especially to unmarried, engaged men—we're often met with a verbal (or nonverbal), "I could NEVER say that!" Then we remind them of the Old Testament's challenge to concentrate our efforts for the *whole first year* on learning to bring pleasure to our wives. And how can a husband possibly learn to please his wife without talking about what pleases her?

To get to the answer, we begin once again with our family of origin—our *normals*. If your parents showed no physical affection in your presence, that was a *normal*. If you never saw them touching each other tenderly, you may have been convinced that your parents found you under a lily pad, because they *never* would have done THAT to bring you into their family!

If your parents talked about how dirty and awful sex was, that was a *normal*. If your parents walked around the house in their underwear (or less); if you saw your parents flirt with other adults in public but not with each other; if you never heard a single word of advice about sex when you were small; and if you were (and are still) certain that your mother is incapable of saying the word *intercourse*—all of these things were normal for you.

> Perhaps we'd be in a much better place if we had used the playground as our sexual image instead.

Your challenge is to recognize your sexual *normal,* and either celebrate it because it was so healthy or learn from it because it wasn't. Then you can begin to feel free to talk about it with your wife. Chances are better than 50/50 that she's eager to talk with you.

OUT OF THE BASE PATH AND ONTO THE PLAYGROUND

Learning about sex in baseball terms probably got us off track back there in sixth grade. In baseball you "slam, slide, dive, hit, smash, drive, blast—and win." So you've concluded now that sex is something you *do.* You step up to the plate, or you wind up and deliver. You do something *to* someone.

Perhaps we'd be in a much better place if we had used the playground as our sexual image instead. Here's what a playground provides that baseball misses completely.

Variety

I'm sure you've never seen a playground that has only one kind of structure to play on. Can you imagine how silly it would be to drive past a school and see a dozen seesaws and nothing else—or only swing sets or only jungle gyms?

Baseball has rules—hundred of rules. Just because a player decides it'd be more fun to run on a fly ball than tag up, it doesn't change the rule. Three strikes is an "out" every time. There is no room for flexibility at all. In fact, some free spirits wonder why they call it a "game."

The fun of the playground is the pleasure of variety. When it comes to sex with your wife, treat the experience as though you're on the playground, not between a couple of chalk lines. Changing settings, times of the day, positions, and locations are all perfectly legal. You will not be charged with an error on account of your creativity. Of course, because it's play, be sure that your playmate is having fun, too. This is profoundly important to keep in mind.

Spontaneity

I really don't know why they do this, but baseball games almost always start at fixed times—strange times like 1:05 P.M. or 7:20 P.M. And at the beginning of each season, the players know exactly who they'll be playing and where for the next six months.

Even among individual players, strict workout regimens rule each day. A player, just because he feels like it, cannot decide to take batting practice before breakfast or lift weights during the sixth inning. There's simply no room for impulsiveness or spontaneity.

But your intimacy with your wife is very different from baseball. It is not something that has to be regularly scheduled. It's neither your right to make unyielding demands with regard to frequency nor her privilege to go on strike.

Laughter

There's almost nothing funny about a baseball game. You hear cheers, boos, shouts, insults, and calls for the umpires' heads. There's very little laughter, unless the humor is directed at a player's unplanned blooper. But if you roll your windows down near a busy neighborhood playground, you're going to hear squeals of delight and laughter.

One of the most visible indicators of a healthy marriage is the ability to laugh. Watching silly movies and sharing jokes between you and your wife are just as important as spine-tingling sex. Some women would say, in fact, that one leads to the other.

Mark and I have a mutual Christian friend who is a sex therapist. She says, "There are 150 positions for intercourse, and only two of them can be successfully accomplished without laughing."

Everybody Wins

Can you imagine a child complaining to his mother that he "lost at the swing set" or that he "was defeated at the merry-go-round"? The beauty of the playground is that *play* is the goal. In order for there to be success, one group doesn't need to grind another group's nose in nasty defeat. Because play is the only goal, both sides win.

> The beauty of the playground is that *play* is the goal.

"Tonight I'm at your complete service," a husband may say to his wife before bed. "Your wish is my command—anything you want will be my pleasure." Call this guy a "loser" in baseball, but in lovemaking he captures the Cy Young award, the batting crown, and the Most Valuable Player award in a single night.

Of course, his award ceremony is celebrated a few nights later when his wife makes the same unconditional offer to him. I think we've just defined a win-win.[33]

MISSION POSSIBLE: LEARNING YOUR WIFE'S SECRETS TO GREAT SEX

There are different kinds of thrilling moments in baseball. Certainly the clutch home run is a biggie—like Kirk Gibson's in 1988. The no-hitter and the triple play are amazing and extremely rare. But one of my favorite baseball delights is the inside-the-park home run. In fact, with the reduced size of many of the new ballparks, these are becoming more and more infrequent.

Even if you're not a big baseball fan, you probably already know that when a player hits a ball into one of the outfield gaps and legs out a home run, he *must* touch all the bases. If he doesn't, the opposing team can contest it—and he can be called "out."

Okay, so you knew this. But did you know that even if a batter clears the fence with a dinger, he *still* has to touch all the bases or his home run doesn't count as a home run? Robin Ventura was reminded of this rule in the 1999 National League Championship Series against Atlanta, when he hit a towering extra-inning home run into the right-centerfield bleachers with the bases loaded. His teammates ran from the dugout and mobbed him as he rounded first. The game was over, and the Mets had won. But because Robin never made it around the bases, he was credited with a "grand-slam single."

Now that you're married and "getting to home plate" is normal fare, you may be tempted to take an immediate left turn out of the batter's box, simply dashing to third base and back. In fact, you may even be tempted to stay right there at home plate. Hey, every at bat is a winner. Right?

> For a man, the thrill of sex is the destination. But for his wife, it's all about the journey.

Well, actually, no. And this is exactly what the young bride was trying to tell her groom in Mark's office that day. If her husband doesn't remember his baserunning skills and practice them regularly, she'll lose interest in no time at all.

For a man, the thrill of sex is the destination. But for his wife, it's all about the journey. As far as she's concerned—even though she's married and "scoring" is a given—if he doesn't touch all her bases, his home run doesn't count.

So what are some of your wife's secrets to great sex? What does it mean to "touch all the bases"? We're glad you asked. (Take a minute right now and turn to pages 113–14 on the flip side of your book. Read what a woman thinks this "baseball game" should look like.)

Touching

Do you remember the life-size wall chart in biology class that showed the human nervous system? Coming out from the guy's brain were lines that looked like rivers and tributaries, branching out again and again until they covered his whole body.

Try to remember where you saw the greatest collection—the highest concentration—of nerve endings. A chapter on sex may send you to the wrong place, because the answer is—your fingertips.

There are no words to describe the power of touch, especially to a woman. It's almost as though there's a nerve that runs straight from her fingertips to her heart.

Many husbands fall into the pattern of never touching their wives except in a sexual context. And these men wonder why their brides are less than enthusiastic about those touches. The truth is that the places she wants to be touched often don't even show up on our baselines.

Some days she may want you to brush her hair. Another day she may need a neck massage. On a different day the biggest turn-on for her may be having her feet rubbed. If the only sexual game you know is baseball, you will likely strike out.

> So when you're sitting next to her at a concert or riding along in the car, reach over and hold her hand.

So when you're sitting next to her at a concert or riding along in the car, reach over and hold her hand. When you're striding from your parking spot at the mall, take her hand. When you sit across from her in a restaurant and you're waiting for your food, take her hand while you talk together. You probably did these things when you were dating her—and there's no good reason to stop now!

Kissing

I'm no expert on rules that prostitutes follow, but there is one that's universally known. When they're with a client, there's absolutely nothing that's unacceptable—out-of-bounds. Every conceivable position or fantasy the client may have is fair game. It's what he's paying for. However, kissing is strongly discouraged. This act communicates a love and an intimacy that even the most bizarre forms of sex cannot match. Don't you find that amazing?

Too many couples stop kissing once they get married. Even though you've only been married for a short time, perhaps you've noticed this yourself.

I married a woman who loves to kiss. It makes me tired just thinking about it, but when we were engaged, we could literally—I'm not making this up—kiss, *just* kiss, for hours. Sometimes we'd stop (I'd be taking gulps of air) and talk about how much fun it will be when we're married.

"We can kiss all night long," Bobbie would say.

It wasn't exactly what I had in mind, but I let her run with the thought.

The next time you're making love, stop what you're doing and give your wife a deep, long, passionate kiss. Give her an exact replica of the one you gave her when you asked her to marry you. See if I'm right about this kissing thing.

Talking

Here we go again—talking about talking. But here I'm not talking about free and open conversations about the *subject* of sex. I'm not referring to candid "what gives me pleasure" talks or "I need us to make love tonight" comments.

No, this kind of talk is as important to a woman as any kind of foreplay could be. It's tender talk, affirming words, the kind of gentle things you spoke when you were try-

> The tender words I have in mind have no destination but her heart.

ing to win her heart in the first place. These are sounds she needs to hear again in a setting that's quiet and conducive to soft conversation:

- "I love the way you smile."
- "I'm the luckiest guy on the planet because of you."
- "You have the most beautiful eyes I've ever seen."

Ordinarily your lives are filled with "task talk":

- "Could you pick up the dry cleaning?"
- "What time is dinner?"
- "Have you seen my Palm Pilot?"
- "Hey, it's Thursday. Would you mind taking out the trash?"

The tender words I have in mind, however, have no destination but her heart. No goal to achieve, but simply to remind her that if you had it to do all over again, you would.

All these things—touching, kissing, and talking (and maybe a few more you and your wife can discover together)—will guarantee home runs that show up in the record books.

PRESSURE AND REJECTION: TURNING OFF THE SPIN CYCLE

The most common—and destructive—pattern a couple can experience is the unnecessary cycle of pressure and rejection. If it hasn't happened to you yet, it will.

There will be times when one of you is particularly interested in lovemaking at the very time the other seems to be indifferent. As a result, the pursued partner feels pressured, and the pursuing partner feels rejected. This is not an amusing scene at all. Left unaddressed, this situation can degenerate into a seething resentment that can spread poison throughout your whole relationship.

Though this pattern isn't the least bit surprising, what is remarkable is how few couples *ever* discuss it, much less work out possible scenarios to ameliorate the situation. Many couples simply cross their fingers and hope things work out on their own. It's a strategy that can set you up for a lifetime of frustration.

And, in spite of the stereotype of the pursuer and pursued, it's not always the man who is the aggressor. (Does it surprise you that the most popular sexual stimulant in history—Viagra—is a product for *men?*)

Here are a couple ideas that may be helpful. If they sound like kid stuff, it may be because they're nothing more than guidelines—*rules* are for baseball, remember? These may help you and your bride enjoy sexual play without wounding each other's heart. Though none of the following ideas are perfect, they are sure to work better than the common "gee-whiz, I sure hope this works out, knock on wood" approach that many couples fall into.

The "Almost Never Say No" Ideal

Because most couples will agree that sex is almost *always* a good idea, here's your sexual default: "If you're really in the mood, I can get there." And face it, you'll most likely look back on what you've just experienced, and, regardless of who was up for it and who wasn't, you'll both admit that it really *was* a good idea.

Right now, early in your marriage, you may want to adopt this "almost never say no" policy. No, it's not an unbreakable rule. It's just that you'll decide that it will always be your priority to *try* to meet your spouse's needs.

The spirit of this default is not unlike what happens when your wife says to you, "Hey, I'd love to go out for a walk tonight." Even though you may not be in a walking mood, you take a deep breath and lace up your walking shoes. You may give a qualified yes by saying, "I'd love to walk with you, but if it's okay, let's just go around the block once. I'm exhausted." In the same way, the spouse invited into unscheduled lovemaking may say, "Actually, I don't think I'm up for thirty minutes of WWF main event, but if you're up for something quick, sign me up."

When you're the one doing the asking, it may be wise to remember that your bride's response to this encounter may not make her an Academy Award finalist. "Way to put your heart into it, honey" after this rendezvous could put you in a difficult negotiating position later on.

Quid Pro Quo

Regardless of her best "never say no" intentions, there *are* going to be times when your bride is just not going to say yes. Because you're at the playground and not at Yankee Stadium, let it go. Believe it or not, there will be times when the shoe is on the other foot and you'll be needing a healthy dose of understanding from your wife.

Although we discourage lighted scoreboards mounted on your bedroom wall, we *do* encourage keeping informal track of your own noes and yeses. There's nothing wrong with hearing, "Hey, this didn't work into my plan the other night, and even though I'm still not feeling like Cleopatra—sure, let's."

> Because you're at the playground and not at Yankee Stadium, let it go.

What's important in these "not tonight, honey" moments is that the rejection of the act of lovemaking doesn't mean that you or your wife have suddenly contracted terminal leprosy. Your or your wife's no to making love didn't mean anything but simply that. Nothing more.

If you're on the receiving end of the no, don't take it personally. If you're doing the rejecting, a little tenderness accompanying the "no, thanks" will go a long way.

In addition to these two guidelines, you and your wife may come up with some playground principles of your own. We know a couple who does "rock, paper, scissors" when they can't agree. And the losing spouse can always ask for "best two out of three" if he or she is *really* serious. The secret is to discuss these playground principles *before* the situation presents itself, when harmony and rational thinking are at work. When unruffled people are engaged in problem solving, constructive ideas are usually the natural result.

MADE FOR EACH OTHER

One of the things God put into marriage and your sexual union is the mystery of *interdependence*. You begin to literally *need* each other. Let me explain.

Bobbie and I were having dinner with our daughter, Missy, and her husband, Jon. Since Missy was nursing her newborn, she had timed the outing with the baby-sitter so the baby wouldn't need to be fed before she returned. The restaurant service was quite slow, so our dinner experience took longer than we had expected. Although Missy wasn't in pain—that's easy for me to say!—she *was* beginning to get a little uncomfortable. "I'm going to need to nurse pretty soon," she said. (Did you notice she said that *she* needed to nurse?)

Just then, a baby began crying from a quiet corner of the restaurant.

"Oh, dear," Missy said, quickly lifting her dinner napkin up to cover herself. Because Missy's body was primed to nurse, the sound of a crying baby triggered her breast milk on cue, soaking the front of her dress. Jon quickly gave her his sport coat.

Isn't it amazing how God connects a mother and her baby in this way? When the baby is born, there's nothing more satisfying than the taste of his or her mother's milk. And once that process begins, a mother has just as much need to *give* her milk as her child has to *receive* it. There's interdependence at work.

The analogy ought to be obvious. When you and your wife step into marriage and begin to engage in regular lovemaking, your bodies begin to "look forward" to each other—to literally long for each other in a spirit of interdependence.

The Sobering Side of This Truth

In the story of Missy and her baby, let's imagine that her baby woke up and was crying for something to eat. Instead of waiting for the mother, the baby-sitter whipped up some baby formula and fed the child. Like magic, the baby drank a bottle of formula and went back to sleep.

Then suppose Missy walks in. "How's the baby?" she asks the sitter.

"Great. He woke up about an hour ago and started to cry. I fed him a bottle of formula, and now he's sleeping again."

This may have been fine for the baby, but his mother would have been miserable.[34] In this incredible relationship between child and mother, God gave them *both* a drive—a hunger—to be satisfied by each other.

You know where this is going, don't you? "How 'bout it?" between you and your wife is more than just a matter of enjoying a playful romp on a grassy knoll. It's more than just the fulfillment of one of those fantasies that Mark conjured up during his own premarital counseling. Sexual intercourse is literally the satisfying of a craving that God gave you for your wife. And it fulfills a hunger that she has for you, too.

The reality is this: you *need* each other sexually.

SPOILING YOUR APPETITE

It's physiologically possible for you to relieve your pent-up need for your wife *without* her—to spoil your appetite, so to speak.

Of course, infidelity does exactly this. As guilty as you'd be of stealing if you hot-wired your neighbor's new car and drove it off, you're robbing your wife of what belongs to her. Yes, your heart belongs to her. Yes, your future belongs to her. But your *body* and what it provides for her—the hunger it satisfies—also belongs to her. And because great sex includes more than just landing on home plate, any kind of baserunning activity with anyone else but your wife is a truly bad idea for at least two important reasons:

1. It robs your wife of what *belongs to her* exclusively. The damage that's done creates a lifetime scar—and in many cases it spells the beginning of the end.
2. You and your wife have become adept at lovemaking through lots of trial and error, and therefore your new experience will *not* be as good. This may come as a surprise to you, but it is almost always true.

Psychiatrist and family therapist Frank Pittman, after counseling with thousands of couples who had had extramarital affairs, concluded, "Most affairs consist of a little bad sex and lots of hours on the telephone."[35] Another study confirmed Pittman's assessment, citing real numbers: While 67 percent of men and 55 percent of women found marital sex to be very pleasurable, only 47 percent of men and 37 percent of women describe extramarital sex to be very pleasurable.[36]

> Sexual intercourse is literally the satisfying of a craving that God gave you for your wife.

But even in the face of the statistical data, many men still find themselves enmeshed in affairs. And almost 100 percent of these men fall into illicit relationships through talking and touching and kissing. (See how powerful these things are?) Some men we've talked to even reported how much more freely they were able to *pray* with their new love than with their wives. They insisted that in the early stages there was "nothing sexual" about their relationship. However, if this kind of "nonsexual" affair is not terminated, it *will* eventually lead to intercourse—remember the Little Leaguers dancing the jig away from those boring bases?

> "It's only my body; I *still* love my wife"—a common excuse that has a predictable outcome.

What's more, just because a man is happily married and sexually satisfied, there's no guarantee that he's not a candidate for an affair. In counseling, some men have even said, "It's only my body; I *still* love my wife"—a common excuse that has a predictable outcome. Even couples who recover from infidelity carry deep scars for the rest of their lives. Talk to someone with one of those scars. He'll tell you what I'm telling you: *It's not worth it!*

Temptation to infidelity will be a relentless adversary your whole life. So be on guard. Act like a recovering alcoholic with plenty of money, who lives across the street from a liquor store. He *could* walk across the street—he may even *want* to walk across the street, but he *knows* that "just one drink" will kill him. So he stays right where he is and hangs on to his sobriety. "One day at a time," his bumper sticker reads. Your commitment to sexual faithfulness needs to be the same. Never drop your guard because you think you're bulletproof. You aren't.[37]

Virtual Affairs

Real infidelity isn't the only way your body can be stolen from your wife. You can do it virtually. Every man can remember his first look at a pornographic image. I had mine when I was a sophomore in college. Lucky for me, there was no Internet in 1967.

Today pornography is cramming cyberspace and is as available as my toothbrush. Almost every day, I'm invited to see "hot young babes" or "hungry sluts" right here on my computer. Because my software shows me the first couple lines of a message before I download it, I'm further enticed to check out quickly what's waiting for me. Every time I see these invitations there, waiting for me, my heart jumps. My pulse goes up *every single time*.

I will always be a drunk just across the street from plenty of booze, and I know it. What I also know is that if I cave in, I will be guilty of committing grand theft. My unsuspecting wife will lose something precious because of my foolishness.

I want to. I'd like to. I'm really curious to see what's waiting for me. I take a deep breath and hit the delete key. And you must do the same. Forgive me for sounding as dogmatic as your junior high gym teacher, but there's no leeway here; there's just no middle ground. I've seen firsthand—and in the lives of close friends—what this "drug" does to a man's soul.[38] Please hit the delete key. You *must* hit your delete key. Not for me—but for your wife *and* for you. If you cave in, it'll ruin you.

Just One Look

Because I travel quite a bit, I often walk through airports. The way some of these are designed, a person can get a full aerobic workout merely transferring from one plane to another. As I walk the concourses, I see lots of interesting people. Some of these people are women, and some of them really shouldn't be wearing what they're wearing in public.

I truly have no control over taking the first glance. But I've promised myself—and my wife—that I'll not look again. When my eyes send a signal to my brain that indicates something like "really large breasts at 10 o'clock" or "tight short skirt at 3 o'clock," I *choose* not to look back.[39] It's not that I'm afraid I'll actually *do* something illicit right there in the airport. It's just that I know I'm standing at another threshold of a virtual affair. If I step across it, I will be stealing from—and dishonoring—my wife. So I don't look again.

Is it easy? No, but you'll get used to it.

ALL THE MARBLES

I love watching athletes celebrate great victories. A golfer hugging his caddie or a baseball player being mobbed at home plate after hitting a game-winning home run often brings tears to my eyes. Because my own athletic prowess never reached broadcast proportions, I cannot identify with what it means to win on such a grand scale. Or can I?

Orel Hershiser, baseball's most dominant pitcher in 1988, unanimous winner of the Cy Young award and the Most Valuable Player award for the National League Championship Series and the World Series, was asked about what it felt like—winning in front of the whole world. His response may surprise you: "Of course I was thrilled beyond words. Completely in awe. But this feeling is no different from when you make the honor roll or watch your bride walk down the aisle or hold your own child for the first time or close a big business deal. You *know* that feeling."[40]

It's true that each of these things is a thrill. However, because I know him, I know there's one more thing Orel could add to his list: *the satisfaction of fidelity.* Winning at the challenge of intimacy with your wife and overcoming the relentless temptations of infidelity will bring you an even greater satisfaction than winning the World Series or the Stanley Cup or the Masters.

Your discipline, hard work, and self-denial will have paid off—and you'll have more fun on the playground than you could have ever imagined.

11

IN-LAWS: WHO ARE
THESE PEOPLE AND
WHAT DO THEY WANT
FROM ME?

*When a man walks his daughter down the aisle and turns
her over to another man, it's like handing a priceless Stradi-
varius violin to a gorilla.*

JAY KESLER, PRESIDENT EMERITUS, TAYLOR UNIVERSITY

I'm an in-law.
I got this way by walking our two daughters—Missy in 1994 and
Julie in 1999—down the aisle at First Presbyterian Church in
Nashville, Tennessee. The feeling I had during each of these very long
walks was identical. Let me see if I can describe it for you:

These women came into my life in 1971 and 1974, respectively.
Moments after their birth, I was presented with their pocket-size bodies. I looked into their little faces. I lifted theirs to mine and kissed their
tiny rosebud mouths. Their eyes rolled back and forth, trying to focus;
their miniature arms and legs flailed. The feelings in the deepest corners of my heart were wonder and overwhelming delight. "Daddy," I
whispered to them. "I'm your daddy."

Now these babies were women. Their hands rested on my right
forearm, and we moved along in procession to the glorious organ
music that filled the sanctuary like a thick mist, penetrating every nook
and crevice. I was numb from the top of my head to the bottoms of
my feet.

As I walked slowly down the aisle next to these brides, I wish I
could tell you that the feeling was the same rapture I felt when I gave

them their first kiss in the hospital. But it wasn't. This wasn't a wedding; it was a funeral. And deep in my soul, I knew it

It Was Also Another Birth

Are you shocked that I'd say something like this—comparing our daughters' weddings to a funeral? First, let me assure you—without the slightest hesitation—that the men our daughters chose to marry are incredible. Jon and Christopher are the answers to the prayers we said as Bobbie and I knelt alongside our young daughters' beds:

"Lord, please bless the boys that Missy and Julie will marry. Please protect them today. Help them to be obedient to their parents. And teach them to love you. Amen."

The girls would also pray for these boys—wherever they were:

"Help them not to fall off their bikes and hurt themselves."

Our prayers had been answered. We couldn't have been more thrilled with the young men who stood at the end of that long aisle. Bobbie and I loved them and were overjoyed with Missy and Julie's choices.

So my dark feeling wasn't because I disliked Jon or Christopher in any way. What I knew, however, was that this spelled the death of something—*and* the birth of something else.

Until this moment, I had been the most important man in their lives—the daddy, "the Big Kahuna." As their parents, Bobbie and I had been the go-to folks for decisions, both big and small. Our home was their home. But on this day—in one instant—all of that died.

> This wasn't a wedding; it was a funeral. And deep in my soul, I knew it.

"Who gives this woman to be married to this man?" Mark DeVries asked me. His eyes and mine were swimming in tears.

What was born in that ceremony was a new "most important" man, a new go-to guy, a new home—a brand-new marriage. And on those two wedding days something else was born—roles Bobbie and I had never known before: father-in-law and mother-in-law. Our twenty-three-year and twenty-five-year relationships with our daughters were instantly demoted to second-string. For each of them, there was a new superstar in town.

Not until these weddings did I fully realize what I had done to Bobbie's parents when I married her and moved them down a notch to the status of *in-laws*. I tell you this to help you understand why your in-laws are acting strangely. But as I said, *you're* in charge of this relationship now, even though you're the new kid on the block.

SIDE WITH YOUR WIFE

The first law of in-law relationships is this: Always side with your wife first.

Louis and Joanna had been married for less than a year when Joanna forgot her mother-in-law's birthday. I say "*Joanna* forgot"—because both Louis and Joanna grew up in homes where the unspoken and unquestioned rule was this: the wife takes responsibility for remembering birthdays, anniversaries, and all gifts for both sides of the family.

Even so, the direct attack from her father-in-law caught her completely off guard. He called her at work, but he skipped the normal pleasantries. There was a sharpness and intensity about his anger as he spoke: "How could you forget her birthday? This year, of all years—when she's done so much for you!"

Forget the fact that Joanna's husband, Louis—the woman's own son—had forgotten this birthday as well. Forget the fact that, just three months into the marriage, there were enough adjustments for a new bride to make. This father-in-law was incensed, and he gave full vent to his anger, leveling Joanna with a stout reminder of her failure.

Hours later, when Joanna met up with Louis back at their home, she still wasn't over the trauma. Louis could tell she'd been crying. "What's the matter?" he asked, hoping it wasn't something *he* had inadvertently done to hurt her.

Joanna poured her heart out, telling Louis of the phone call from his angry dad. She began to cry again, apologizing for forgetting his mother's birthday.

Louis stood up and calmly walked across the room to the telephone. Without saying anything to Joanna, he punched out a number on the keypad.

"Hi, Mom, this is Louis," he said. Joanna held her breath.

"Listen, I'm *really* sorry I forgot your birthday. I hope you had a wonderful day yesterday anyway. I'll get you one of those belated cards as soon as I can. Hey, better late than never," Louis quipped, his voice light and warm. He paused.

"Can I speak with Dad?" Louis asked.

After a couple moments, Joanna heard Louis speak again.

"Hello, Dad, this is Louis."

Joanna presumed that the pause signaled his dad's "hello" back.

"Dad," Louis continued with unmistakable precision, "I understand you called Joanna today about missing Mom's birthday. This was not hers to remember, and blaming her was wrong. I love you, Dad, but doing this is unacceptable. She's not your child; she's my wife. I expect you to never talk to her like that again."

Louis stopped talking. Joanna presumed that his dad was defending himself.

"No, sir," Louis broke in, his voice still calm and strong. "This is not up for discussion, Dad. Sorry."

Once again, Louis listened and then he spoke.

"I appreciate you saying that. Thanks for understanding. Goodbye, Dad."

For Louis and Joanna, this single conversation did more to short-circuit future in-law conflicts than years of therapy could have. What Louis did that day was to declare—to both his parents and his bride—where his primary loyalty would rest. And in doing so he created a sense of security for his wife. After that day she virtually never felt any competition with her in-laws. Louis's solidarity with her in their marriage was not in question.

The words of Scripture bear repeating: "A man will leave his father and mother and be united to his wife."[41]

I hope you never have to have this conversation with your dad. This transition from being your dad to the in-law in your marriage may be happening seamlessly. But if you ever face what Louis faced and don't take this kind of decisive action—if you fail to "leave" your primary loyalty to your parents to "be united" with your wife—you will be in serious trouble. Your neglect will put your bride and your parents—especially your mother—on a lifetime collision course. If you don't draw the line, these women will spend the rest of their lives competing for your affection.

"He's *mine*," one of them will say.

"No he's *mine*," the other will respond.

As cruel as it may sound, you have no choice but to choose your marriage over your loyalty to your parents. If you do what Louis did, you'll survive. If you don't—then let the games begin.

ESTABLISH CLEAR BOUNDARIES WITH YOUR OWN PARENTS

Growing up with an abusive alcoholic dad who eventually abandoned his family had an undeniable impact on Doug. And even though Doug's mom was devastated by her husband's behavior, she had sacrificed everything for her son's welfare. At times she was working three jobs in order to pay the bills.

And so when Doug's new wife, Lisa, began to experience some tension with her mother-in-law, Doug immediately sided with the woman who had always been his hero—his mother. Doug's mother often shared her "concerns about Lisa" with Doug. Because he loved and respected his mother so much, he believed that her advice, though not always presented in the most gracious terms, was given "for his own good."

Over the years, Doug tried to make subtle—and sometimes not so subtle—recommendations to Lisa about changes she should make in her habits, her behavior, or her personality. Increasingly, Lisa suspected that her husband was only parroting his mother's concerns. Lisa became more and more defensive, resisting even the slightest suggestions. And the icy intensity between Lisa and her mother-in-law began to bleed over into the marriage.

Doug knew he had to do something, so he stopped by Sam's office on his way home from work. Even though Sam was a few years older, there was a solid friendship between them—and Doug respected Sam's judgment.

In a few minutes, Doug asked a question that caught Sam's attention: "How can I get Lisa to make these reasonable changes my mother wants her to make?"

Sam's chair squeaked as he leaned back, folding his hands behind his head. "It sounds to me like you need to run away from home," Sam said, a gentle smile crossing his face.

Doug was shocked. "Run away from home?"

Then, from memory, Sam quoted, "For this reason a man will *leave* his father and mother and be united to his wife, and they will become one flesh." He continued on: "You've been trying to live in two homes, Doug. When you got married, you may have moved your possessions in with Lisa, but your heart is living somewhere else—it never left your mother. This is *your* deal, my friend—not Lisa's. Until you leave your mother and completely move in with Lisa, you're never going to get this fixed."

The sun had just disappeared on the horizon as Doug pulled into his driveway, but for him it was more like a sunrise. He was going to make a change. From now on, he had determined, whenever Lisa and his mother were on opposite sides of an issue—any issue—Doug was going to side with Lisa.

> "When you got married, you may have moved your possessions in with Lisa, but your heart is living somewhere else."

After a few weeks, Doug realized that his plan was going to be more difficult than he thought. At first, his mother was restrained about Doug's loyalty to Lisa. But when it became a consistent pattern, she became more vocal about it. Doug held his ground, which was even more difficult, because Lisa was still skeptical.

In the first two months, Doug's mother tried anger, tears, guilt—and even a surprise "intervention" and the reading of a twelve-page letter in Doug's office. Doug did his best to understand his mother's pain. Gently and lovingly, but without flinching, Doug explained to his mother that he *had* to leave home and emotionally move in with Lisa. Competing with Lisa was a battle his mom was going to lose.

Almost a hundred days after Doug's meeting with Sam, Lisa's shell began to crack. She overheard Doug on the phone with his mother. Lisa heard him defend her, sternly asking his mother to drop the subject. After months of commuting from his mother's home, Doug had finally run away.

We've seen many "Dougs" who dance between their mothers and their wives, hoping that they'll never have to declare primary loyalty to either one. These men have tried to coach their wives and placate their mothers. It never works.

During your first year of marriage, instead of attempting to negotiate a peaceful settlement between your mother—or your dad—and your wife, you be sure to let it be known that your primary loyalty will never be in question. *You will always side with your wife.* It's the only chance you have to save your wife's relationship with your parents.

EXES AND OTHER STRANGERS

Betsy and William were part of Mark and Susan's weekly marriage group. It was Betsy's second marriage, and because she had two boys from her first marriage, she still had regular contact with her ex. As the group talked about principles of healthy relationships with in-laws, Betsy spoke up, a look of new understanding sweeping across her face. "You know," she said, "it seems that a lot of these same principles work well for a relationship with an ex-spouse." Though some in the group laughed loudly, Mark could tell by her expression that she hadn't intended to be funny. He encouraged her to explain.

"I realized a long time ago," she continued, "that I have to move on and forgive my ex for whatever he's done to me. If I don't, I'm only holding myself hostage to bitterness. It's just like when a person can't forgive his parents or in-laws—they get stuck to the very people they're trying to get a healthy distance from."

Betsy had the group's undivided attention as she finished her comments: "When I keep myself tied to my ex-husband with a cord of resentment, it's almost impossible to keep the resentment from spilling over into my marriage as well."

Betsy was right. We cannot selectively harden our hearts with bitterness. The resentment seeps into our marriages, unintentionally poisoning them in the process.

THE HOLIDAY TUG-OF-WAR

If you haven't yet experienced the holiday tug-of-war, you will. And the entrance of your babies on the scene will intensify it. Here are a couple of things to remember about this game:

You and Your Wife Are In Charge

Thanksgiving and Christmas are the biggies. And in spite of the direct or indirect ways both sets of parents will use to try to influence your decisions, do not be controlled by these influences. With the full cooperation of your wife, decide what *you're* going to do.

> If you haven't yet experienced the holiday tug-of-war, you will.

Many couples alternate years—Thanksgiving with your parents this year and with hers next year. Some even it out by doing the same with Christmas, but making sure that Thanksgiving and Christmas are on alternating schedules—Thanksgiving with your family this year and Christmas with hers; then the other way around next year.

Some couples put the holidays on a three-year rotation, reserving the third year for themselves—something that will be even more important once you have kids of your own.

No Time for Surprises

Whatever you and your bride decide regarding holidays, don't keep your decision a secret from your families. Let them know well in advance. Surprises are a good idea under the Christmas tree, but letting everyone know where you'll be for the holiday celebrations shouldn't be one of them.

You may not want to make plans more than a year at a time, but keeping everyone in the loop when you finalize your plans will reduce the frustration of your parents' unfulfilled expectations.

PLANNED, YET FLEXIBLE; FAIR AND UNEQUAL

There will be times when, because of unusual circumstances such as a birth, serious illness, or death, you'll be tilting the balance of time toward one of your sets of parents. And because many couples live much closer to one set than to the other, it's virtually impossible that you'll be able to give equal time to each. Give up on that illusion, and issue each other a good deal of grace when this sort of inequality happens. So right now—before it happens—resolve that it will be okay. Unplanned events are traumatic enough without you and your wife fighting over "we've been spending a lot more time with your parents than we have with mine."

> Whatever you and your bride decide regarding holidays, don't keep your decision a secret from your families. Let them know well in advance.

Be aware, too, that there may be good reasons to spend more time with one family over the other. We have discovered that women often need to spend more time with their families than men do. Of course, there are exceptions to this rule. Regardless, it's critical that you and your wife openly discuss your need to spend time with your own families, as well as any anxieties you may have about spending time with your spouse's clan.

Let's Make a Deal

In a counseling session with Mark, a frustrated Regina told her husband, Bruce, that she didn't appreciate his attitude when he was with her family. She explained to Mark that when they were with her parents, Bruce usually withdrew, often sticking his nose in a book or keeping his eyes glued to the television.

Once the issue was on the table, Mark challenged Bruce to make a simple commitment. "I promise to be totally present *and* pleasant to Regina's family for seven days a year," Bruce said, playfully raising his right hand. "She can choose the days, and she can count on me to be good."

Setting a boundary on the number of days eliminated the "be nice all the time" carte blanche that felt like a life sentence to Bruce. And it worked. In fact, Bruce's promise changed his attitude when he was with Regina's family. He really *did* have a better time.

Bring on a Baby

The chances are fairly slim that you'll have a baby in your first year of marriage, but it *does* happen. Most couples agree that the adjustments to pregnancy and the birth of their baby were far more significant than the alterations they went through when they got married.

When and if you have children, you're going to be an amateur dad, just like you were an amateur husband. Because the birth of your child changes your parents' status to a new unknown—grandparenting—they're going to go through adjustments, too. In fact, you'll begin hearing your parents say, "Well, when you were a baby, we did it this way." Remember to give them grace. Someday you'll do the same to your kids.

Again, as in all of your dealings with your parents and your in-laws, honor them but be your own man and listen carefully to your wife. Your marriage is your first priority; now so is your family. Your occasional friendly reminder of this to your parents will be a good idea.

"Mom," you might say, "I know you didn't breast-feed your babies, but Cindy's decided to go that route. And I support her."

"Dad, I know your heart was set on us naming our son after you," you might gently say to your father. "But we've decided to name him Amadeus. You know how much I love classical music."

Remember that it's *your* job to leave your parents' home. You've got a family of your own to establish. Gather as much advice as you need, but make your decisions confidently. To do otherwise is to invite chaos.

Oh, by the way, when that baby comes along, don't forget that the strength of your solid relationship with your wife will be the most important thing in your child's emotional health. When you walk in the door, in spite of the temptation to coo and fuss over the baby, greet your wife first. And don't be afraid to regularly invest in baby-sitters, so your bride will know that she's still number one. There may be times when you feel that you've lost your wife, that you can't possibly compete with a newborn baby for your wife's attention. During those times, be intentional about investing *with* her in the parenting process. Please notice I said *invest*. There's a handsome return on this investment!

REMEMBER, IN-LAWS ARE PEOPLE, TOO

Here's the good news about in-laws: They can be an incredibly important stabilizing factor in your marriage. In fact, in some European cultures, a low divorce rate is due, in large measure, to the presence of a supportive extended family that surrounds marriages with love and encouragement. Relationships with in-laws are healthiest when they avoid the extremes of enmeshment (overattachment) and isolation (overdetachment).

I began this chapter by confessing how it felt to become a father-in-law. How painful it was—even under the best of circumstances—to let my daughters go. There's no question I was guilty of insensitivity when I married Bobbie. I was presumptuously pitting a couple years of courtship against more than two decades of her parents' raising and nurturing her. They had sacrificed a lot more than I had, but I was "winning." I knew my marriage was more important than her relationship with her parents—and my relationship with my parents. But this was a huge adjustment for everyone.

I should have been more sympathetic. When I asked her dad for permission to marry her, he said, "Yes." But then—because I was living in Chicago and she was living in Washington D.C.—he added, "I'm sorry you're taking her so far away."

I said I understood, but it was a lie. I couldn't have possibly understood. But now I do, and someday many of you will, too.

Be gentle with your wife's parents. And don't be harsh with your own. These folks have loved you for a long time, and they really *do* want what's best for you. Whatever else they may be guilty of, in-laws are people, too.

12

HELP: WHEN
SOMETHING'S GOT
TO CHANGE

Marriage is a humbling journey.

BILL AND LYNNE HYBELS, *FIT TO BE TIED*

———◆·◆·◆———

Clint was a high-rolling businessman. Becky was his "trophy" wife. When they walked into a room together, everyone noticed. They owned whatever money could buy, but they were missing what it couldn't. She buried herself in civic clubs and raising her kids. He was seldom home, but when he was, his mind and heart were preoccupied with the next big deal. She grew increasingly distant; he grew increasingly angry.

Before long, this father of two young children was entangled in an affair. In order to make his point, Clint didn't bother to hide anything, being seen in popular restaurants with his new flame. Though his mistress wasn't nearly as attractive as Becky, she was available with no strings attached—no demands, no expectations.

If you were to follow this true story through to the end, where do you think it would lead? You'd probably assume that Clint eventually left Becky, who secured a crackerjack lawyer and took Clint to the cleaners. And you may think that there were months of a custody battle—with this messy divorce making for juicy gossip at all the cocktail parties in town for months. But you'd be wrong.

Here's how the story really ended: Today, over ten years after the affair, Clint and Becky are involved in a special ministry they began at their church. Every week they teach and counsel couples whose marriages are in trouble. (I'm not kidding. This is really happening.)

Clint and Becky stumbled into a healing process that many considered miraculous. And this same process—the one they now teach to young couples—if practiced early enough, can save any troubled marriage. In fact, it can save a marriage *before* it gets into serious trouble.

YOU MARRIED AN EXPERT

During the years when he carried a full counseling load, best-selling author Gary Smalley and his staff had the chance to have the following dialogue—or something close to it—with thousands of married couples.

> *Gary to the couple after hearing the details of their marital troubles:* "It sounds as though you've got some work to do."
>
> The couple nods.
>
> *Gary to the husband:* "So, Dave, what do you think you and Shelly need to do to fix these problems?"
>
> Complete silence. [Dr. Smalley and Dave's wife may as well have put their ears up to a conch shell. Except for a blank stare and slightly panicked look, Dave says nothing. After a minute of silence, Dave's stare drops to the floor in embarrassment.]
>
> *Gary to the wife:* "Okay, Shelly, what do *you* think you and Dave could do to fix your marriage?"

Shelly recaps some of the problems she and Dave are having and then offers a sequence of reasonable solutions. Gary nods as Shelly is speaking. He's not surprised by her insight and wisdom. Dave, on the other hand, *is* stunned and amazed.

> Clint and Becky stumbled into a healing process that many considered miraculous.

The chances are better than 50/50 that Shelly and your wife have something in common. (Truth be told, the odds are *much* better than that.) Instinctively, intuitively, your wife is an expert on these matters, including the relationship and the roles you and she should take to ensure a successful marriage. And like a mother bird protecting her nest from the attacks of the neighbor's cat, she's programmed to do whatever she can to safeguard your marriage from all foes—big ones and little ones.

When you come home late for dinner or when you fail to clean out the garage when you told her you would or when you promise to spend more time with her and nothing comes of it, your wife reacts. No, she overreacts. Why? Because she knows that these "little" actions can signify the brewing of big trouble, and she's going to call your attention to them. She's going to do whatever she can to keep them from accumulating or growing. Small decisions of neglect can kill marriages. Your wife knows it, which is why she tends to make big deals out of little things.

Learn to Recognize Early Warning Signs— and Take Them Seriously

My flight was scheduled for 4:35 P.M., the last nonstop flight of the day from Orlando to Los Angeles. At 4:10 there was no effort to begin boarding passengers. I noticed the gate agent spending a lot of time on the phone. At 4:20, still no activity—no boarding.

"We're in trouble," I said just loud enough for the guy standing by me to turn and stare.

At 4:30 we got the announcement from the agent. "Ladies and gentleman," he said in his best be-calm-and-friendly voice, "we've received word from the flight crew that there is an indicator light on the instrument panel that is flashing a warning." There was an audible moan from the passengers in the waiting area. One young traveler tried to make a joke about how many pilots it takes to unscrew a lightbulb, but no one laughed.

> Small decisions of neglect can kill marriages. Your wife knows it, which is why she tends to make big deals out of little things.

"We've contacted a maintenance crew. Several diagnostics have been run. We're continuing to monitor the situation. We don't anticipate that this will result in a serious delay—perhaps twenty or thirty minutes—but we will keep you informed." Then he said my favorite five words of fiction—pure make-believe: "Thank you for your patience."

Some of the passengers began pacing back and forth; others spoke out in angry tones. Mothers fumbled through purses, looking for something new to keep their fidgety children occupied. I pulled out my cell phone and dialed the airline. I'd heard this "twenty or thirty minutes" story before.

A few minutes later I had a backup reservation for a connecting flight through Dallas. I had a critical meeting with a client the next morning in Los Angeles. Not getting there was not an option.

Nearly every time this happens to me, I wonder, *What are the chances that we'd still make it to Los Angeles if the captain really* did *go ahead and unscrew the warning light?* What do *you* think?

With all the redundant systems built into airliners, the chances are actually very good that we'd make it safely. In fact, if the crew members had kept their mouths shut, none of us would have even needed to know about the problem. We could have been obliviously munching on our pretzels and sipping ginger ale at thirty-five thousand feet if they had just overlooked it and let us board the plane. After all, *most* of the systems were working just fine.

> Getting broken things fixed immediately is just as important in your young marriage.

But here's the truth: pilots can lose their privileges to fly if they ignore such things. They know that, even if the chances for serious trouble are minuscule, this indicator light *means* something. Impatient passengers or not, they're not going anywhere until they get it fixed. And getting broken things fixed immediately is just as important in your young marriage.

"What's wrong?" you say to your wife. You can tell something's bothering her.

"Nothing," she responds, her steely glare telling you that she's avoiding the light on the instrument panel.

You've probably already had this conversation.

What Clint learned as he recovered from his near-divorce experience with Becky—and what Dave learned as he listened to Shelly—was that early in their marriages there were plenty of warning lights they should have seen—lights their wives clearly saw. When it comes right down to it, most men admit that they *do* see them. They just choose to ignore them. *No marriage is perfect,* they foolishly rationalize. *We'll get over this in time.*

Call Maintenance

Pilots spend years in training. They prepare for the most horrific emergencies in simulators. Every time the wheels of their airplanes lift from the surface of the runways, pilots know that they alone hold in their hands the very lives of hundreds of trusting passengers. But pilots don't fix indicator lights. *They call maintenance.*

Admitting they need help is the part most men hate—and this loathing is almost universal. This habit shows itself most often in our inability—unwillingness, really—to stop and ask for directions. We're as lost as last year's Easter egg, we've passed the same 7-Eleven four times, our wife is crying (yelling) because we're late for a wedding, and we are *sure* that we're doing just fine.

"I know the church is right up here," we say with complete confidence.

Most marriages take off with no contingency plans on board. No one asks the question, "What will we do when a warning light goes on? How will we fix it, and who will we call if we can't fix it?" So a man takes off with no strategy for encountering trouble and with no understanding of how or whom to ask for help when he does run into problems.

As we've said, in most cases your wife has a better eye for warning lights than you do. Research has proven that women are more likely than men to raise concerns about their marriages.[42] But you and I are strangely comfortable with unscrewing the bulb (or smashing it with a hammer) and taking off for Los Angeles as though nothing is wrong. And the most tragic thing that can happen is that our flight lands without a hitch. Why? Because the experience of success simply proves to us that there must have been something wrong with the bulb instead of with the airplane. When our wives' warning lights go off, we've now got all the ammunition we need to convince ourselves that the only problem we've got is our wives and their overly sensitive warning systems.

> So a man takes off with no strategy for encountering trouble and with no understanding of how or whom to ask for help when he does run into problems.

One afternoon a minister's wife almost literally dragged her husband into the counselor's office. The first words out of the minister's mouth were, "I have no idea why we're here. We have a fine marriage." This man, professionally trained to counsel others, was completely blind to his own wife's desperate concerns.

During this first year of your marriage, you *must* keep your eye on the instrument panel. If you think you see something, ask your wife to confirm it. If the warning light is on, discuss the situation with her. Don't try to be funny. It's no place for a comedy routine. If you can't talk it through to the satisfaction of *both* of you, be sure to call maintenance.

"Maintenance" may be a trusted older friend, a minister, or a trained counselor. It's someone who will treat your warning light seriously.

Put Up a Safety Net

In January 1933, the construction of the Golden Gate Bridge in California began. Four-and-a-half years later, President Franklin Delano Roosevelt pressed a telegraph key in the White House, announcing to the world that the bridge was open.

During the construction of the bridge that cost thirty-five million dollars, only eleven workmen died. I say *only*, because the norm for construction like this was one man dead for every million dollars spent. The reason for the stellar safety record was very simple. The contractors invested a hundred thirty-five thousand dollars on a safety net that stretched under the bridge all the way from San Francisco to Marin County. As the bridge was being built, thirty men fell, but nineteen were caught in the net and saved. Local newspaper reporters dubbed the survivors "The Halfway to Hell Club."

A safety net under your marriage starts with an agreement to protect your marriage in the face of the dangers you're bound to encounter. And like the Geneva Convention in chapter 8, you and your wife must decide—right now, before you get into the heat of battle—that you will invest in this net.

Having this safety net also implies that you will lay down your weapons. You start building this safety net by agreeing never to employ armaments designed only to destroy and not to heal. Weapons like—

- defensiveness—"Oh, so it's all *my* fault now?"
- contempt—name-calling, cutting humor, or eye-rolling that accompanies such comments as, "So what're you going to do about it, sue me?"
- withholding attention—the impassive, nonresponsive stone wall that moves you to a position of power by shutting down and not responding to your spouse at all.
- personal attacks—instead of asking your spouse to clean up her mess in the kitchen, you say, "You don't care about anyone but yourself, do you?"[43]

Using these weapons only escalates disagreements into arguments, arguments into fights, fights into a war, and a war into casualties— wounded or dead.

A safety net includes not only your promise that you'll not use these kinds of weapons but also a nonaggression treaty stipulating that the unarmed spouse always has the right to demand the laying down of one of these weapons the moment it appears.

"Hey, we promised not to do that," a spouse on the business side of the crosshairs may say. The weapon-toting offender must lay it down. They made a deal. He has no choice in the matter.

Another safety net may be a couple or a group of close friends who are on call in emergencies. One couple we know refers to these people as their "9-1-1 Group." They made a pact with each other that, day or night, they're available and willing to stand with each other and side with the marriage.

Randy and Tiffany created an explicit safety net early in their marriage. After they had been married for a few months and had faced the pain of nearly falling into "the San Francisco Bay" a few times, they sat at the kitchen table one evening after dinner. Randy pulled out his laptop, and together they made a list of things to include in their safety net. Because they were quite discerning, in addition to putting down some of the same kinds of safety-net emergency procedures described above, Randy and Tiffany added preventive measures of their own— things that would keep them from falling into the net at all.

Randy clicked away at his keyboard as Tiffany made her suggestions for him:

- A candlelight dinner once a month. Randy is responsible to execute it, even if he has to buy Chinese and transfer it from the cardboard containers to the good dinnerware.
- Conversations over coffee for fifteen minutes every weekday morning. Longer on weekends.
- Dance to "our" song or watch "our" video once a month.

Randy had a few of his own for Tiffany:

- Laugh when I try to be funny.
- Come to my business dinner parties.
- Initiate lovemaking.

> As you read this, please avoid the temptation to roll your eyes and decide that making such lists is pure cheese.

As you read this, please avoid the temptation to roll your eyes and decide that making such lists is pure cheese. *I'm Mr. Spontaneity,* you may be thinking. *I don't need to be so mechanical. I can make this stuff up as I go.*

Go ahead, but you're betting against the odds. The statistics are not on your side, unless you're hoping to join the "All the Way to Hell Club."

CAN WE TALK?

Hall of Famer Fran Tarkington, perhaps the best scrambling quarterback to ever run for cover, was presented with this riddle:

> Question: "What do life and a three-hundred-pound defensive lineman have in common?"
> Answer: "They both punish those who are unwilling to move."

If we amended this question just a little and put the word *married* in front of *life,* the answer would still be true. An unwillingness to adjust in *married life* will be punished.

You and I have this in common: we prefer not to have our faces slammed to the turf. We'll do almost anything to keep this from happening. Because you didn't know that a giant lineman would be turned loose in your marriage, you made no provisions to protect yourself before you walked the aisle. But since the day you and your bride got married, you've seen his massive form bearing down on you more than a few times.

Strangely enough, here's what this Leviathan might look like:

- How could you have known about her annoying little habits? How could she have *not* known about yours?
- You *thought* you saw her temper when you were dating, but it was nothing like this!
- She thought you liked her mother. You thought she liked your dad.
- You hate green paint. She loves green paint.
- He hates plaid fabric on furniture. You love plaid fabric on furniture.
- She tosses and turns at night like she's wrestling an alligator, while you lie perfectly still. Unfortunately, you're the light sleeper.

- She slams the kitchen cabinets when you're taking a nap in the family room.
- Dirt on a car is invisible to you. "Service engine soon" on the dashboard is invisible to her.
- Her morning breath would knock a fly off a manure spreader. You have gas and scratch yourself.[44]

Because you're new to your marriage, such things may be unfamiliar to you. Just wait. As inevitable as the sun's rising tomorrow and the Cubs still not making it to the World Series, these things—or others just like them—*are* going to happen. And when they do, what are you going to do about them? How are you going to deal with the angst that wells up in your gut when they show up?

You may have heard experts say, "A man can never change his wife." Or, "It takes two people to bring about change in a marriage." The experts are only half right. Countless husbands and wives have had a profound influence on each other. In other words, you *can* bring about changes in your wife. And here are three principles for success. The first one, in light of what I've just said, will surprise you:

Principle #1: Right from the Beginning, Give Up the Illusion of Changing Your Wife

This may be the hardest principle to grasp, because it seems to make no sense. "I thought you said I *can* change my wife. Now you're saying I should give it up?"

Exactly.

As ironic as it sounds, the first and most powerful step to take in changing your wife is to be intentional about *not* trying to change her at all. Whether it's her weight, the way she keeps the house, the way she always seems to be late, her reluctance to make love, or her habit of nagging you, the more you focus on changing her, the more frustrated both of you will become.

This woman you married is imperfect. Too many husbands are amazed and crushed by this discovery. So when this imperfection is exposed, some men use it to justify their rough behavior. You've probably heard a man rationalize and say, "But you don't understand the way she always . . ."

Some husbands make their wives into their number one home improvement project. So they become a veritable repository of "helpful" comments:

- "How much tonnage do you plan to put on this year?"
- "You talk too much."
- "When we got married, I never guessed I'd have to work so hard to get a little affection out of you."

If you ask these guys about their comments, they'll tell you that they're only trying to *help* their wives, or maybe even trying to make their marriages better. Their wives see it quite differently, of course.

> When a man gets fixated on his wife's faults, he forfeits his power to truly love her.

In counseling, a husband can make what some call a "detailed confession of his wife's sins." Of course, he may add a surface confession of his own, such as, "Okay, I'll admit it. I'm not perfect either. But it isn't all my fault. And until she admits that she's had a part in this . . ." If this sounds more like a justification than a confession, it's only because you're paying attention.

It's easy to begin to let your love for your wife fade when your focus is on fixing her—not to mention that your attempts to change her will, in the long run, almost always fail. Even though there may be short-term behavior adjustments, your demands on her will just as likely have a "chemo effect." In your effort to remove the things you don't like, you can inadvertently kill some of the very qualities that attracted you to her in the first place.

Your pressure on her to "stop talking so much" can scrape the spontaneity from your "first love." Your constant oversight of her eating habits can create untold insecurity and low self-esteem. Your pressure on her to perform sexually can literally shut her spirit down.

When a man gets fixated on his wife's faults, the tragedy is that he forfeits his power to truly love her, which is the only way to ever bring about any real change in her. A man who is desperately trying to change his wife is actually in a tailspin of powerlessness. Change in your wife will always be a by-product of your love for her, not a result of direct and relentless demands.

Principle #2: Create an Environment in Which Change Will Happen

Your marriage is a living organism. It is at every moment either growing or dying. And growth always means change. Because you're wired to improve the woman you love, few things can be more dis-heartening than to feel that she's unaffected—no matter what you say or do.

Peter walked into Mark's office and slumped down in the chair in the corner. His body language spoke of a man who had just been whipped, but the happy look on his face spoke of something different. It was as though Peter had used all his physical energy to make the most important decision he had ever made about his new wife. His face reflected how pleased he was with the decision.

"I'm never going to criticize Katie again," he said to Mark.

Mark looked up from his desk, expect-ing an explanation. He knew of Peter and Katie's marriage—of the bitterness that swirled around it, of Katie's utter frustration with her judgmental hus-band. But in one sentence Peter had said to Mark all that he had come to say.

> A man who is des-perately trying to change his wife is actually in a tailspin of powerlessness.

Six months later, Mark bumped into Katie at a church social. Her countenance was transformed. There was a sparkle in her eyes when Mark asked how she and Peter were doing. You see, when Peter made his promise, two things happened in his marriage: Katie began to trust him and feel safe around him, and, once she was convinced she wasn't being watched by a hall monitor and wouldn't be criticized, *she began to take the risk of making changes in her own behavior.*

A culture of change can never grow within a culture of criticism.

Try an experiment to see what I'm talking about. Ask your wife to stand and face you. Hold your hands up, palms facing her, and ask her to do the same, putting her palms against yours. Then slowly push against her hands. Without any instructions, her response to your pres-sure is completely predictable: She'll push back against your hands.

The last thing you and your wife want to do in your marriage is spend your years pushing against each other. Change is only possible when the pressure to perform is removed and then replaced with ten-derness and grace.

Like a gardener who cannot force a seed to germinate, you can't force the little green shoot to sprout up but you *can* provide an envi-ronment that welcomes growth—one that encourages and then patiently waits.

Principle #3: Make the One Decision Most Likely to Bring About Change

Only two words: *Change yourself.* The most powerful thing you have in your toolbox for affecting change in your wife is to focus on the areas where *you* need to change.

When you do, you will begin to appreciate how hard it is to change ingrained patterns—and this will help you in the patience department. Next, bringing about even the smallest changes in yourself will keep you from feeling like a victim in your marriage—like you're powerless unless your wife changes. Finally, nothing will motivate your wife to change like being loved unconditionally by a man who is willing to change himself.

> A culture of change can never grow within a culture of criticism.

Here's an example of how this principle is broken: Suppose your wife has asked you to slow down when you're driving. She's asked you again and again. And suppose you choose to ignore her. In fact, when you're feeling particularly spunky, you defy her by punching the gas pedal the moment she says something. The result is that you're successfully establishing a no-change environment for your wife. And each time this—or something like it—happens, the ecosystem of your marriage grows increasingly rigid and inflexible.

Now here's an example of how this principle should work: Suppose your wife has asked you to slow down when you're driving. She's asked you again and again. And suppose that you slow down—extra credit for you, because you issue a sincere apology as you ease up on the gas pedal. You win. Your wife is no longer angry when you drive, and you've communicated your love for her in a very practical way. (By the way, have you seen the cost of speeding tickets these days?)

And here's something to celebrate: your wife wins too! She feels as though she *can* make a difference in your behavior. And, most important, your marriage wins, because the source of ongoing tension is removed. Because of what you've done, you begin to establish a pattern in which willing change is simply a demonstration of "the way we do things around here."

You go first, because your honest desire is to please your bride, *not* to manipulate her into doing the same. It's the *only* way your wife will make changes of her own.

WE INTERRUPT THESE DIVORCE PROCEEDINGS . . .

You may have heard the story of the man so filled with bitterness toward his wife that he decided a simple divorce proceeding would never do. So he went to his lawyer for advice on how to give his wife the most miserable divorce experience in the history of litigation. The man's lawyer came up with a brilliant plan.

"For the next thirty days," he said, "treat your wife with such unusual kindness that she'll begin to believe you *really* care about her. Then, when we issue the divorce papers, she'll be totally crushed."

The husband agreed that the suggestion was ingenious, and he set out to put the plan into action. For each of the next thirty days—

- he brought her a surprise gift
- he wrote her tender love notes
- he took her on dates to special places
- he listened to her advice respectfully and made appropriate adjustments in his own behavior
- he spoke with such kind words that he could have earned an Oscar for his performance—best supporting actor

Just before the thirty-day period expired, the man received a call from his lawyer. "The papers are ready for you to serve your wife," he said.

"Are you kidding?" the husband responded. "Forget the papers. My wife and I are having the time of our lives!"[45]

MEET IN
the Middle

Welcome to the middle. As you've already realized, the whole point of this book is to get you and your bride talking—both to help her become an expert on the ways of expressing love that mean the most to you and to help you learn the secrets of bringing happiness to her. We've designed the questions here explicitly to help you take the ideas you're reading about and let them impact you and your marriage.

But even before you dive into questions, you'll likely want to take a minute or two after each chapter to ask your bride about something you've read. Starting out with questions like "Are you really like this?" or "If I tried something like the book suggests here, would you like it?" will only help you become more of an expert in loving the bride you have been given.

After each chapter, we encourage you to discuss together the questions called "Touchpoint" and "Crossing Over." "Touchpoint" questions are meant to talk over with your bride, while "Crossing Over" questions will draw out her response to something she just read or give you opportunity to share something you learned in your chapter.

We've designed the "Meet in the Middle" questions in a way that provides maximum flexibility for you and your bride. You may choose to answer the questions on your own, in a regular meeting time you schedule for you and your wife, or with a group of close friends. It's your call. You may even choose different approaches to different chapters—with some chapters, you may answer all the questions, with others, you may pick a few or just one. However you approach this process, we invite you to invest the kind of focused attention in your marriage that will make this year the most important year in your life.

INTRODUCTION

1. How did you get this book? What prompted you to read it?
2. What do you hope to learn or understand better about marriage? About yourself? About your wife?
3. Is there anything about the topic of this book that makes you a little nervous about reading these pages? Why or why not?

TOUCHPOINT

Think about couples you know. What qualities do you most admire and appreciate about other people's marriages?

CHAPTER 1: THE MOST IMPORTANT YEAR: BRINGING HAPPINESS TO YOUR WIFE

1. To what degree do you relate to either "The Conquest Phenomenon" (page 18) or "Choosing Not to Choose" (page 18)? What wake-up call do you hear in this similarity?
2. Consider again the time-tested principles for a solid first-year investment strategy. Will you accept the challenge not to "go to war" or take on extra responsibilities for this whole first year, in order to make learning to love your wife your first priority? If so, what specific behaviors will your "yes" translate into? Who will—or could—hold you accountable?
3. What distractions could contribute to marital A.D.D.? What will you do to minimize, if not totally remove, those distractions? Again, who will hold you accountable to pay attention to your marriage?
4. What random acts of kindness and deliberate efforts to be thoughtful made your wife happy when you were romancing her? Which ones will you do again this week—and which ones next week?

TOUCHPOINT

Pick one of the following statements (or make up one of your own) to be your motto for the first year of your marriage:

- "Failed marriages are not the result of the lack of investment but the lateness of that investment."
- "Making careless investments comes easily; it takes hard work to invest wisely."
- "My job in the first year of my marriage is to become an expert on my wife."
- "Building a relationship with my wife is my most important assignment."
- "When I make my wife's happiness my priority, my wife will find herself compelled to make me happy."

CROSSING Over

Ask your wife about the statistics regarding depression in the first year of marriage. Find out what has caused her the most sadness as she moved from being a bride to being a wife, and ask what kind of support from you might mean the most to her.

CHAPTER 2: NEEDS: THE YES SPIRAL

1. Martin Luther wisely said, "Let the wife make the husband glad to come home, and let him make her sorry to see him leave." What are you doing—or what could you be doing—to make your wife sorry to see you leave?

2. Learn from the example of the behind-the-scenes husband of the Proverbs 31 woman (pages 22–24).

    - *"Her husband has full confidence in her"*: Instead of treating your wife like a child or your mother, what are you doing to nurture her specific gifts? In what ways do you communicate, subtly or directly, that you do not have full confidence in her?

    - *"Her husband is respected at the city gate"*: What do you do to show your wife that you believe in her? What do you say to honor her and celebrate her success?

3. The *Yes Spiral* leads to outdoing each other in showing love. Review the two conversations, one of which reflects the *Yes Spiral* and the other the *No Spiral*. Make it your own experiment this week to say yes to your wife. Note the results as well as how much energy it takes to climb the *Yes Spiral* compared to descending the *No Spiral*. And keep in mind that laying down your life is going to be demonstrated in smaller and less visible or applaudable ways than facing a firing squad.

TOUCHPOINT

In order of importance, jot down five or six things you think your wife most wants from you. Be as general or as specific as you like. Then tell your wife what you're working on and ask her to make her own list—without seeing yours. Then schedule an appointment to compare the lists. You may want to begin the conversation by telling her about the boys looking for the lost pocketknife in the wrong place (pages 27–28).

CROSSING *Over*

Your wife has read about the five things a husband needs most from his wife (pages 30–31). Take a look at the list and let your wife know whether this list is an accurate reflection of what you need from her. And while you're at it, find out from your bride what one thing she would ask from you if she knew you would not turn her down.

CHAPTER 3: SPIRITUAL UNITY: KEEPING YOUR HEAD IN THE ONLY GAME THAT MATTERS

1. God never designed our marriages to be held together simply by sharing an address or sex or sports or activities or even common beliefs. The often elusive quality of spiritual intimacy is what gives a man and his bride a whole person-to-person union. What makes spiritual intimacy elusive for you and your wife? What can and will you do to protect your efforts toward spiritual unity?

2. Learning that Bobbie was pregnant before we had even been married a year made me realize I couldn't "do" marriage. What, if anything, has helped you realize that you can't "do" marriage on your own power and good intentions?

3. Think about spiritual unity or "soul nakedness."

- With "1" being "I'm a quivering puddle of warm Jell-O" and "10" being "I've learned the value of unveiling the secret places of my heart and disclosing my spiritual doubts and fears, and I'm fairly comfortable doing so," rate your comfort with "soul nakedness." Why do you think you're where you are on a scale from 1 to 10?

- What visible practice(s) reminds you that yours is a Christian marriage? See page 34 for a few suggestions.

- Spiritual intimacy with God means including him in your day—especially in the little things. What hinge points (recurring events in your day-to-day life) and/or prayer hooks (familiar places, things, or situations) prompt you to pray? Or what hinge points and/or prayer hooks can or will you establish for yourself?

4. As the Bridegroom of the church, God can teach you and me a lot about being faithful grooms to our brides. God is attentive, accountable, humble, and full of integrity. Which of these four traits would you like to strengthen? What, besides prayer, can you or will you do to grow in this way? Be specific—and then choose one idea to act on this week.

TOUCHPOINT

Ask your bride what one spiritual practice she would like the two of you to establish in your home. Talk together also about where the two of you will connect with a group of other believers with imperfect marriages.

CROSSING *Over*

Your wife read that some people would say that spiritual unity is sometimes as awkward for a husband as physical intimacy is for a bride. Find out from your bride if she thinks this is true for the two of you.

CHAPTER 4: FAMILY OF ORIGIN: A RIVER RUNS THROUGH IT

1. Marriage is like a white-water run in a river raft, and the things we bring to our marriage from the family in which we grew up are

like the powerful currents beneath. Remember the bowl of ice cream Bobbie dished up and the way my dad was uninvolved with his neighbors? When have you noticed that a *normal* of yours is different from your bride's *normal?* Give an example or two.

TOUCHPOINT

Now tackle the exercise you may have only read about in the chapter: do your own genogram (see pages 44–46). Start by drawing a family tree—writing a brief description of each person you named and identifying any marriages you particularly admire.

Give a brief description of each person you named. Giving particular attention to your parents' and grandparents' marriages,

- describe their marriages, good and bad.
- describe how each seemed to deal with conflict in marriage.
- describe the spiritual life that each couple shared.

Look throughout the system and see if there are any marriages you admire. Why? Then see how you do writing your own "Normal Report." Answer these five questions:

- What would someone growing up in this family system see as a normal husband?
- What would someone growing up in this family system see as a normal wife?
- What would someone growing up in this family system see as a normal marriage?
- What would someone growing up in this family system see as a normal way to deal with conflict?
- What would someone growing up in this family system see as a normal spiritual life for a married couple?

What insight(s) about yourself have you gained from this exercise? What areas of potential conflict and danger have you identified?

CROSSING Over

Your wife was also encouraged to draw a genogram. Compare yours with hers. Ask for her assessment of what patterns she saw that you might have missed.

1. In light of what your genogram has shown you about yourself, make up a pretend list of your "ten commandments" of normal. Review the list that begins on page 46. Some of those items may even make your top ten!

2. The more you're aware of your unspoken rules—your own *normals*—the more you can own them, but those patterns are often invisible before marriage (review the discussion on pages 48–51). This invisibility—not having any symptoms—can be very misleading, but identifying patterns of normal in you and your wife's life can prepare you both for the places where you will face the greatest challenges.

3. Which of your *normals* has appeared when, like Bubba, you were under stress? Be specific about the what as well as the when.

4. What recent discussion could have been less heated had you said something like "You know what? The reason I said that to you was because, when I grew up, this wasn't our normal. What you did wasn't bad; it's only that it was unfamiliar to me"? Be specific.

Chapter 5: Roles: When You're Trying to Decide Who Will Be on Top

1. What was your initial reaction to the statement "Marriage is not a team sport. Your assignment today may be your wife's assignment tomorrow. Her task tomorrow may be yours the next day"?

2. Consider carefully the three roles your wife needs you to play. First, you are a *leader*—and servanthood is at the heart of leadership in your marriage. What would a servant do in the scenarios outlined on page 56? What opportunities to lead your wife by serving her have you had this week?

   Second, you are a *warrior*. Optional: In what ways, if any, are you like Ryan, Will, or Mitch (page 58)? What wrong battles are you fighting? More constructively, what habits and attitudes that, left alone, might one day threaten to destroy your marriage do you need to battle against? What is your battle strategy?

   Third, you are a *lover*. What expressions of love mean the most to your wife? Gifts, trips, shopping sprees? Time, tenderness, undivided attention? Something else? If you're not sure, ask her—and then speak her language to tell her you love her!

TOUCHPOINT

Ask your wife if she agrees that your three most important roles in your marriage are as a leader, a warrior, and a lover. See which of the roles she believes is the most important to her and if there are any other roles that she sees as important for you to play.

CROSSING Over

Ask your wife about the three primary roles for wives suggested in her chapter. Find out if she agrees with these roles or sees others not listed there as more important.

CHAPTER 6: TALK: CONVERSATIONAL FOREPLAY

1. At some point in your marriage, your wife may feel as though she's Allen Lange at two thousand feet. Which of your behaviors and priorities are most likely to make your wife panic as she tries to contact the control tower?

2. What endorsements could you genuinely offer your wife? Practice now—and keep in mind that they will unlock her heart and deepen her love for you.

3. Your wife may need some conversation without destination. In fact, for her, it's not so much *what* you talk about but the fact *that* you talk. What evidence have you seen that your wife loves destinationless conversation—and when is that kind of conversation particularly difficult for you? What will you do to overcome these difficulties?

TOUCHPOINT

Did you guess how your wife would answer the true-false questions? If you haven't, go ahead and guess. Give her a turn, if you didn't. And then be honest about what you're beginning to realize about yourself.

CROSSING *Over*

Find out from your wife about her ideal talk quotient. What would she say is the daily or weekly minimum requirement of talking time she needs with you?

CHAPTER 7: FRIENDSHIP: THE SECRET INGREDIENT IN EVERY SATISFYING MARRIAGE

1. What does it mean to you that your wife doesn't just want to be married to you—that she wants the two of you to be friends? Do you agree with Dr. John Gottman that the most significant marriage protector is friendship? Be specific about what you can do to show your wife that you think of her as your best friend.

2. Friendship means avoiding negative dialogue, "turning toward each other" in conversation, making time to spend together, and living according to a zero-secrets policy. Which of these is toughest for you to live out? Why?

   We suggest that couples adopt a zero-secrets policy.

   - What was your reaction to Robert's account of telling Bobbie about the woman who crossed the parking lot every morning? Be sure to comment on the consequences of sharing his secret.

   - What secret from your wife are you carrying around? When will you tell her?

   - When your wife tells you her secrets, what words of assurance, forgiveness, and affection will you offer instead of judgment? Practice now so they're on the tip of your tongue.

TOUCHPOINT

Without some kind of planning, your marriage will be ruled (and overruled) by your schedule rather than the other way around. The slot system can help. Review the description on pages 79–82. Take a look at your upcoming week and, using the slot system, try to carve out at least six slots (morning, afternoon, or evening) together.

CROSSING*Over*

Find out from your wife what she would have you do if she had an entire day of your time in which you would be with her and do whatever she wanted. Take notes, and give her the gift of investing at least an hour of your time in the ways she has suggested.

CHAPTER 8: CONFLICT: ONLY YOU CAN PREVENT FOREST FIRES

1. Marriage doesn't make arguments go away, but certain tactics can help keep the fire sirens from going off. These have not prevented small blazes from springing up now and then, but they've kept them from becoming uncontrollable wildfires.

Fire Safety Strategy #1: Embrace Imperfection

- Why is it—at times—hard work being married to you?
- When could "You're right, and I shouldn't have done—or said—that" have helped extinguish the early flames of conflict? Practice saying these words out loud so that you're ready the next time sparks fly.

Fire Safety Strategy #3: Try the Instruction Manual

- In the Bible, God directs a husband to treat his wife with consideration and respect, and not to be harsh with her. Which of these commands do you need to work on?
- When did you discover—or when were you recently reminded—that how you speak to your wife is as important as what you say to her? Do you agree with me that speaking harshly to your wife is an indefensible thing and that when a man does so, he is instantly in the wrong— every time? What are some of your favorite excuses for speaking harshly to your wife?

Fire Safety Strategy #4: When God Whispers in Your Wife's Ear, Don't Miss the Message

- Why might you easily dismiss your wife's suggestions or counsel?
- What kind of character refinement might God work in you as a result of brushfires with your wife?

TOUCHPOINT

Fire Safety Strategy #2: You Can Disagree without Fighting

- Draft your own Geneva Convention. Use some or all of the following as starting points:

- We will not criticize each other in public or in front of our kids (if and when they come along).

- We will not address areas of disagreement when we're at our worst.

- We will not resort to name-calling.

- We will not bring up information shared in moments of sincere vulnerability.

- We will not use each other's physical characteristics as ammunition.

- Discuss the possibility of monitoring your Geneva Convention like Bobbie and I do: If any of the rules are broken, the offending party immediately loses the argument. It's over—on the spot.

CROSSING *Over*

Ask your wife to explain to you the five fire extinguishers of conflict from her chapter. Talk together about which of these is the most difficult for each of you to use.

CHAPTER 9: MONEY: CROUCHING TIGER, HIDDEN CRISIS

1. Money and tigers have a lot in common. They are both very beautiful, and they are both extremely alluring—and both can be very dangerous if not caged properly. What indications have you already had that the big cat called Money needs to be caged before it's big enough to do some serious damage?

2. What does your checkbook register reveal about your priorities?

3. What *normal* about money are you bringing into your marriage? Consider the possibilities on pages 99-100.

   In order for you to cage your tiger, consider more closely just a couple of this chapter's "Caging Habits" that can help you do the right thing with your money.

- *Put giving into your regular budget.* Why is giving so important? Is tithing (donating 10 percent) one of the *normals* you or your wife brought into the marriage? If not, what challenge has this fact presented?
- *Set a "fun money" spending limit.* What no-permission-necessary spending limit would work for you and your wife? What frequency limit is appropriate? (Yes, this is definitely another "Touchpoint.")

TOUCHPOINT

Make a budget that will allow you to live within your means. Financial trouble begins—and continues—when people spend more money than they have. The easiest way to stay within your means is to put a budget together—together. If you haven't already, just do it!

CROSSING *Over*

Ask your wife how much she thinks you should set aside for your Marriage Insurance Premium (MIP). Also ask her how you can best communicate love and respect to her regarding money.

CHAPTER 10: SEX: BATTER UP

1. Having acknowledged that a playground is a better metaphor for sex than a baseball game, consider the following aspects of your playground:

   - Variety (be sure that your playmate is having fun too)
   - Spontaneity (it's not your right to make unyielding demands)
   - Laughter (one of the most visible indicators of a healthy marriage is the ability to laugh)
   - Everybody wins (play is the goal)

   Which of these four could use some maintenance work or upgrading?

2. For a man, the thrill of sex is the destination. But for his wife, it's all about the journey, and the journey includes touching, kissing, and talking (tender, affirming words as opposed to "task talk"). Again, which of these do you need to add to the journey?

3. Review the sections "Pressure and Rejection: Turning Off the Spin Cycle" (page 119), "Made for Each Other" (page 121), "Spoiling Your Appetite" (page 123), and "All the Marbles" (page 125). (If you only have time to look back at one section, make it "Spoiling Your Appetite.") What wisdom and warnings seem designed just for you? List these statements someplace for easy reference.

TOUCHPOINT

Early in your marriage you need to learn to talk openly and honestly about sex. But that may not be one of your *normals*. Think about your family of origin. What is your *sexual normal?* (Some possibilities are on page 114.) What about that *normal* can you celebrate because it was so healthy—or what can you learn from it because it wasn't?

CROSSING Over

Ask your bride for one thing she would like you to do differently in order for you to learn to play her version of baseball?

CHAPTER 11: IN-LAWS: WHO ARE THESE PEOPLE AND WHAT DO THEY WANT FROM ME?

1. The most important law of in-law relationships is this: *Always side with your wife first.* When have you—or when could you have—sided with your wife? If you did, what resulted? If you didn't, why didn't you—and what will you do to overcome those obstacles the next time?

2. Bottom line, what evidence from your life (specific actions, decisions, or conversations) reveals whether your primary loyalty is to your wife or to your parents?

3. It's virtually impossible that you will be able to give equal time to both sets of parents. Which of you needs to spend more time with his/her parents? What anxieties, if any, do you have about being with your in-laws? What's your behavior like when you're with them? Remember Bruce (page 135)? Out of love for your bride, can you commit to seven days a year of being present and pleasant with your in-laws?

4. Whatever else they may be guilty of, in-laws are people, too. In what ways can you be gentler with your wife's parents? In what situations could you be less harsh with your own?

TOUCHPOINT

Make a plan to avoid the holiday tug-of-war. What have you decided to do about the two sides of the family and the two biggies—Thanksgiving and Christmas? If you haven't yet decided or told your parents, give yourself a deadline well in advance of the fourth Thursday in November to let everyone know.

CROSSING *Over*

Read to your bride the story of how Louis dealt with his mother's forgotten birthday (pages 129–30). Ask your bride how she would feel if she were in Joanna's shoes. And find out if there have been times in your relationship when she felt as though she wasn't sure if you were on her side or on your parents' side.

CHAPTER 12: HELP: WHEN SOMETHING'S GOT TO CHANGE

1. Small decisions of neglect can kill marriages. Your wife knows it, which is why she tends to make a big deal out of little things. What small decisions of neglect, if any, have you made recently? When has your wife overreacted about a little thing? What are the little things (such as picking up after yourself, not being late, or holding your wife's hand) that matter most to your wife, and what can keep you faithful in doing these little things for her?

2. Getting broken things fixed immediately is important in your marriage. Who would you say is more likely to pay attention to the warning lights in your marriage—you or your wife?

3. Countless husbands and wives have had a profound influence on each other. In other words, you can bring about changes in your wife. But such change in your wife will always be a by-product of your love for her, not a result of direct and relentless demands.

- *Principle #1: Right from the beginning, give up the illusion of changing your wife.* In what ways and with what comments have you made your wife feel as though you are trying to change her?

- *Principle #2: Create an environment in which change will happen.* That environment will never be established in a culture of criticism and pressure. What pressure to change have you been exerting? What is the most important step you can take to establish a culture of acceptance and love— the most likely context for change to take place?

- *Principle #3: Make the one decision most likely to bring about change*—and that decision is to change yourself. What changes that your bride has been hoping for in you could you start making? List a handful, and then choose one to start on today.

TOUCHPOINT

Work together with your wife on building a safety net for your marriage. Put together a maintenance team (a trusted older friend, a minister, a trained counselor, a couple, or a group of close friends) you can call on for assistance when you need it.

What preventive measures would help keep you from falling into the safety net at all? Randy's and Tiffany's ideas (page 143) might help you get started on your list.

CROSSING Over

Read your wife the list of illegal weapons from this chapter (page 142), and see if the two of you can agree on a nonaggression treaty that keeps these weapons of destruction out of range.

Notes

1. "What Happens after the Wedding?" Interview with Pamela Paul, Sheryl Nissinen, and Terry Real (*The Oprah Winfrey Show*, air date: 28 October 2002); Sheryl Nissinen, *The Conscious Bride* (Oakland, Calif.: New Harbinger, 2000), 176.

2. John M. Gottman, *The Seven Principles for Making Marriage Work* (Three Rivers, Michigan: Three Rivers Press, 2000), 5.

3. Linda J. Waite and Maggie Gallagher, *The Case for Marriage: Why Married People Are Happier, Healthier, and Better-Off Financially* (New York: Doubleday, 2000), 67.

4. Waite and Gallagher, *The Case for Marriage*, 67.

5. Waite and Gallagher, *The Case for Marriage*, 67.

6. Cited in Philip Yancey, *Finding God in Unexpected Places* (Nashville: Moorings, 1995), 82.

7. Proverbs 21:9; 25:24.

8. Ephesians 5:25.

9. See the real-life examples in Les and Leslie Parrott, *Becoming Soul Mates* (Grand Rapids: Zondervan, 1995).

10. Deuteronomy 6:5, 7.

11. See 1 Corinthians 12:3–6.

12. Philippians 2:7.

13. The Green River is known around the world as one of the most dangerous on a river raft. Years ago a very popular Pepsi advertisement featured a raft full of adventurers on this very river!

14. Ephesians 5:25.

15. See Gary Chapman, *The Five Love Languages* (Chicago: Northfield, 1992).

16. It's no surprise that some Bible translations describe sexual intercourse by using the word *know*—as in, "And Adam knew Eve his wife; and she conceived, and bare Cain" (Genesis 4:1 KJV).

17. Chris Fabry, *Focus on the Family Magazine* (February 1999), 3.

18. Among Charlie Shedd's best-selling classics were *Letters to Karen* and *Letters to Phillip*.

19. Charlie took the old adage to heart: "If Mama ain't happy, ain't nobody happy."

20. The Holter monitor is a twenty-four-hour continuous recording of a person's electrocardiogram (ECG). It permits recognition of any rhythm changes of the heart that may occur during daily activities.

21. For more information, see Gottman, *The Seven Principles for Making Marriage Work.*

22. Gottman, *The Seven Principles for Making Marriage Work,* 17, 20.

23. For his efforts in beginning the process that resulted in the Geneva Convention, Henri Dunant received the Nobel Peace Prize in 1901. Inspired by the lives of three remarkable women—Harriet Beecher Stowe, Florence Nightingale, and Elizabeth Fry—Henri Dunant wrote, "The influence of women is an essential factor in the welfare of humanity, and it will become more valuable as time proceeds." He was also the founder of the International Committee of the Red Cross.

24. 1 Peter 3:7.

25. Colossians 3:19.

26. Mark DeVries and I do not pretend to be experts regarding your personal finances. There are, however, many helpful books written by Larry Burkett, Ron Blue, and David Ramsey—as well as a number of excellent classes you can take at your church (the ones produced by Crown Ministries, for example).

27. My favorite is QuickBooks.

28. Proverbs 22:7.

29. In most court settlements, a couple's money is treated as "theirs," not "his" or "hers." It's the court's opinion that the money is yours together, and it's a good idea for you to think of it this way, too.

30. Acts 20:35 (THE MESSAGE).

31. 1 Timothy 6:10.

32. I develop this in greater detail on pages 35–38 in *She Calls Me Daddy* (Colorado Springs: Focus on the Family, 1996).

33. If you could use some playground suggestions, here are a few: Bathe together by candlelight, give each other a body massage with scented oil, take a buggy or sleigh ride together, take ballroom dancing lessons, go look at newborn babies in the hospital (this one's huge, trust me!), have a picnic in the country, swing on the swings at a playground, plan a secret rendezvous, have a water-pistol fight, pray on your knees, or watch the stars.

34. I could tell you about breast pumps at this point, but I'll not do it. Some of you may learn about them soon enough.

35. Cited in Dennis Rainey, *Family Reformation* (Little Rock, Ark.: Family Life, 1996), 94.

36. Cited in Peter Blitchington, *Sex Roles and the Christian Family* (Wheaton, Ill.: Tyndale House, 1985), 165.

37. Jerry Jenkins has written a wonderful book about this subject called *Loving Your Marriage Enough to Protect It* (Chicago: Moody Press, 2000).

38. I strongly recommend the book *Every Man's Battle* by Stephen Arterburn and Fred Stoeker, with Mike Yorkey (Colorado Springs: WaterBrook, 2000).

39. The authors of *Every Man's Battle* call this idea "the bounce." Your eyes, like a rubber ball, "hit" the subject and then bounce away. They do not go back for another look—a very good idea!

40. Orel Hershiser, with Robert Wolgemuth, *Between the Lines* (New York: Warner Books, 2001), 144.

41. Genesis 2:24.

42. See Gottman, *The Seven Principles for Making Marriage Work*, 114.

43. John Gottman notes some of these ideas in his book *Why Marriages Succeed or Fail* (New York: Simon & Schuster, 1994).

44. One of the reasons couples choose to live together before they get married is to avoid being surprised by these annoyances after they're married. However, couples who decide to live together before they're married are statistically *more* likely to divorce than those who wait until they're married before living together. Cited in Pamela Paul, *The Starter Marriage* (New York: Villard Books, 2002).

45. Adapted from a story in Neil Clark Warren, *Catching the Rhythm of Love* (Nashville: Nelson, 2000), 28–30.

**The first year of your marriage may not be the
most difficult, but it is the most important.**

You're newlyweds, and this is the best time to do everything you
can to ensure that your marriage can meet the challenges it will face.
Cultivating good habits right away will prepare you for the years
ahead.

With almost ninety years of marriage between them, Robert and
Bobbie Wolgemuth and Mark and Susan DeVries will help guide you
in successfully dealing with the life that happens after "I do."

In this unique flip-over format, the chapter topics are the same,
but one half is written by Robert and Mark for the husband, and the
other half is written by Susan and Bobbie for the wife. As a couple,
you'll each read through your part of the book and "meet in the middle." Together, you'll learn how to have a great marriage that draws
you closer to each other and to God.

Start reading, and make this first year together what it was meant
to be: the most important year in your life.

Robert Wolgemuth has authored or coauthored more than twenty
books, including *She Calls Me Daddy*, *The Most Important Place
on Earth*, *Like the Shepherd*, and the notes to *The Devotional Bible
for Dads*. Robert wrote this book with his wife of more than four
decades, **Bobbie Wolgemuth**, who died of cancer in 2014. She was
a Bible teacher and coauthor of several books, including the award-
winning, bestselling series *Hymns for a Kid's Heart* with Joni Eareckson Tada.

Mark DeVries is the founder of Ministry Architects and the
cofounder of Ministry Incubators and the Center for Youth Ministry
Training. The author of twelve books, he served as a youth pastor
for thirty-four years. **Susan DeVries** has made a career out of being a
wife, mother, and supervising editor for Mark's writing. She has also
partnered with Mark in providing premarital counseling and leading
marriage retreats and classes for couples.

THE MOST
IMPORTANT YEAR IN A
Woman's Life

WHAT EVERY BRIDE
NEEDS TO KNOW

SUSAN DEVRIES & BOBBIE WOLGEMUTH

ZONDERVAN®

ZONDERVAN

The Most Important Year in a Woman's Life
Copyright © 2003 by Susan DeVries and Barbara J. Wolgemuth

The Most Important Year in a Man's Life
Copyright © 2003 by Robert D. Wolgemuth and Mark DeVries

Requests for information should be addressed to:
Zondervan, 3900 *Sparks Dr. SE, Grand Rapids, Michigan* 49546

ISBN 978-0-310-35356-0 (softcover)

ISBN 978-0-310-30484-5 (audio edition)

ISBN 978-0-310-86310-6 (ebook)

Library of Congress Cataloging-in-Publication Data

The most important year in a woman's life : the most important year in a man's life what
every bride needs to know : what every groom needs to know / Robert Wolgemuth ... [et al.].
    p. cm.
Includes bibliographical references.
ISBN-10: 0-310-24006-9
ISBN-13: 978-0-310-24006-8
    1. Marriage—Handbooks, manuals, etc. I. Wolgemuth, Robert, 1948–
HQ734 .M863 2003
306.81—dc21   2002156147

Published in association with the literary agency of Ann Spangler & Company, 1420 Pontiac Road SE, Grand Rapids, MI 49506.

Interior design by Todd Sprague
Cover design by Cindy Davis
Cover photos by Philip Shippert Photography
TRAD decoration from IKEA

First printing February 2018 / Printed in the United States of America

To those who will one day marry our children . . .

*That you would know, enjoy, and protect their hearts
more than we ever could,*

*That you would sniff out the extravagant grace of Jesus
in this wild branch of God's family tree,*

*And that you would dance with them in the kitchen
often enough to make their children as embarrassed
as we made them.*

—*Mark and Susan DeVries*

Contents

Acknowledgments

*T*he most important principles we ever learned about marriage, we learned from real-live people who, over and over again, made marriage look like an arrangement that is, above everything else, incomparably fun. Throughout our lives, these were couples who, without pretending that marriage was easy, never wavered in their common commitment to build exceptional lives together.

First on that list are Robert and Bobbie Wolgemuth, our coauthors, mentors, and friends now for almost twenty-five years. From the time Robert and Mark began meeting regularly when Mark was barely twenty years old, Robert and Bobbie have been examples of integrity and authenticity. They have cleared a path for us, for our marriage, for our parenting, being genuine enough to let us learn as much from their mistakes as from their successes.

It would be impossible for us to calculate the immense influence that these two have had on almost every area of our lives. What a privilege it has been for us to have an excuse to spend countless hours together working on these books.

Without knowing it, three other couples have, for decades, been our "guarantee" that attending to our marriage would be the single, smartest investment we could ever make, even when things were far from easy:

- Dick and Lois Freeman, who taught us to put Jesus and our marriage ahead of our ministry

- Jim and Pat Mathis, who have shown us the power of extraordinary kindness and respect
- Joe and Martha Thompson, who have given us an unforgettable picture of the richness of sharing over five decades with the one person who happens to be your best friend and lover at the same time.

We are thankful for the hundreds of couples who have given us access into their struggles to live out their marriage vows with faithfulness, particularly for the fabulously fallible community of faith that meets at First Presbyterian Church in Nashville.

Over the past two years, dozens of friends have helped keep the principles in these books anchored to reality. Thanks to...

- Chris Carson, Amy Colton, Rusty Douglas, Marc and Jen DeJong, Emily and Jason Huff, Sarah McDavitt Green, Kim Falls Kimberline, Banks and Tracey Link, Mary Price Maddox, Jay Martin, Brian Reames, Drew and Colyer Robison, Eric "Sweet Soul Daddy" Skinner, and Keith and Callie Victory. Your responses to our initial survey shaped this work in ways you will never know.
- the *Partners in Promise* Sunday school class, for letting us test out so many of these principles on you.
- Chuck and Penny Willoughby, Tom and Betty Tyndall, and Dave and Cynthia Lenz, for providing resources, support, and laughter for us at just the right times.

This project is immensely richer because of the input of our wild Wednesday night marriage group: Johnny and Elizabeth, Kemper and Stephanie, Chris and Mary, Patrick and Leah, Billy and Cathryn, Wally and Lee Lee, Steve and Mary Lee, Scott and Elaine, Josh and Keely, Royal and Claudia, LeAnn and Robert, John and Louise, and the periodic guest appearance from Mark Schultz. This group met with us weekly for an entire year. If there is anything that has the ring of "the way things really are," chances are, we have these couples to thank for it.

Our dear friends, Debbie and Kirk Freeman, Sheila and David Hunt, Connie and Blain Norfleet, and Ginger and Chan Sheppard all took time to review the manuscript and give us invaluable feedback.

There are some things that only lifelong friends can say, and the eight of you said it well. Thanks.

Throughout this process, we have been surrounded by a great cloud of witnesses who took on the mission of praying us through these months:

- Mark's men's groups—Jerry, Jim, Luke, Steve, Bud, Ed, Andy, Mike, Jack, Chuck, Roland, Brett, Phil, Chuck, and Steve. (You boys have earned a few dozen Krispy Kreme runs.)
- Susan's women's groups—her 2001–2002 Bible Study Fellowship group, her Old Lady Group (Lee Lee, Louise, Ellie, and Trish), and her RTL group (Elaine, Amy, Leigh, Mary Lee, Donna, Kathleen, Elizabeth, Renee, Shannon, and Cary). These ladies—and their laughter and prayers—have kept Susan sane.

We are, of course, grateful for our own parents, Richard and Louise Whitson, Dorothy DeVries, John and Caroline DeVries, for the examples you set before us.

And finally, to our nearly grown children, Adam, Debbie, and Leigh—thanks for bearing with our chaotic lifestyle (and actually enjoying it), for laughing when we try to be funny, and for never once even hinting that you had the slightest doubt that God had something special to say in these books.

We can't wait to meet those three we have been praying for all your lives.

Finally, our thanks goes to our literary agent, Ann Spangler; our Zondervan editor in chief, Sandy Vander Zicht—who gave allowance to stretch far more deadlines than the legal limit; Dirk "I really like reading edits from four different authors in seven different colors" Buursma; and Lisa Guest, who gave a fresh perspective to the "Meet in the Middle" section of the book.

We are grateful for all of you. Thank you, friends.

Susan and Mark DeVries
Nashville, Tennessee

Introduction

*I*t was almost fifteen years ago when Steve and Mary Lee Bartlett became my husband Mark's first premarital counseling experiment. In spite of the fact that Mark was definitely "making it up as he went along," this young couple seemed to enjoy their meetings with him immensely. They laughed, they dreamed, they talked about all the hot topics.

And now, a decade and a half later, the Bartletts have become such dear friends that, when we began to work on this book, it was only natural that they would be among the first we'd turn to for input. I asked Mary Lee to assess how prepared she felt for her first year of marriage, and I'll never forget her answer: "We had a great time in our premarital counseling, but I just wish someone had told me how hard it was going to be."

And now, after helping nearly two hundred couples prepare for their marriages—sometimes Mark and I together, other times just Mark by himself—we're sure that Mary Lee is not alone. In fact, research is now confirming how very normal it is for a new bride to be surprised by the difficulty of that first year. One researcher noted that as many as 90 percent of brides surveyed reported experiencing some level of depression during their first year of marriage.[1] Another researcher found that *every* woman she interviewed described an often unexpected feeling of disappointment in the first year after the wedding.[2]

Though we've known many brides who haven't had this kind of experience, the let-down feeling is, of course, natural. A wedding is such an

incredible high in a woman's life that just about anything that comes after it is likely to pale in comparison. For some, the post-wedding blues are enough to convince them that they've just made the greatest mistake of their lives. Others feel duped, having believed that Mr. Right would bring automatic satisfaction. And still others enter marriage with a relationship suffering from malnutrition, having poured so much energy into the wedding that the relationship has been left starving for attention.

If you are like most brides, you're longing for a guide to help you navigate the unexpected unsettledness you may be feeling and to help you invest strategically in what we'll be calling the "wet cement year" of your marriage.

Who Are These People and What Are They Trying to Do?

My dear friend Bobbie Wolgemuth and I are excited to share with you some marvelous principles for building an exceptional marriage. But I first want to introduce you to our husbands, Mark DeVries and Robert Wolgemuth—the authors of the other book you're holding.

The Wolgemuth's daughters, Missy and Julie, were in our youth group as they were growing up, and eventually both worked with us in youth ministry. And so it was only natural that they would ask Mark—their youth pastor—to do their premarital counseling and perform their wedding ceremonies. Soon after their weddings the idea of a book came up. Having experienced from a whole different perspective what a powerful influence the right kinds of words can have on a couple starting out, Robert and Bobbie invited us to join them in creating a resource to fortify couples in their first year of marriage.

I want to be clear from the outset that these books are the result of the collaborative effort of the four of us. In one sense, we are four authors of both books. But for the sake of clarity, we have chosen to write each book in only one voice. In the women's book, you will hear my voice throughout, and in the men's book you'll hear Robert's. Our dream has been to create a book that, by its very format, would bring couples together and would help them become experts at understanding each other. And that's why we chose to write two different books— one for women and one for men.

You'll notice that the chapters have similar titles. But they contain very different material. In the women's book, we focus on helping you understand your husband and the power of your responsiveness to him.

The men's book is designed to help a husband gain perspective on how he can learn—during this first year—to "bring happiness to the wife he has married," a fascinating biblical phrase you'll learn more about in chapter 1.

What Am I Supposed to Do with This Book?

As we were writing *The Most Important Year,* Mark and I met with a group of couples weekly to get their input. What we discovered— delightfully—is that these couples just couldn't seem to stick to evaluating the manuscript. From the very first week, even when the drafts of the chapters were in their infancy and even when the group didn't agree with what we had written, the book's format led them naturally into working on their own marriages.

It's important at the outset that you realize this isn't a book to help you understand "the normal man," because the man you married is undoubtedly far from average. It's a book to help you accomplish your mission of becoming an expert on this one man you have been given as your life partner. Here's a process that can help you apply what you are learning—to the end that you and your spouse will know and enjoy each other more than you've dared to dream:

1. **Feel Free to Sneak:** Among the members of our group, we found that wives had a sneaky habit of reading the men's chapters. And every now and then, even the most reading-resistant man would snoop around in the women's chapters, just to see if we were telling the truth.

2. **Ask the Expert:** There will likely be things you read about "men in general" that just aren't true about the man you've married. When you run across those things, ask your husband questions like, "Is this really what you think?" and, "Is this true for you?"

3. **Be the Expert:** Even if you've only been married for a few weeks, your husband may already be confused. You can help him understand and enjoy you more by being warmly responsive to his questions and his attempts to understand your heart.

4. **Meet in the Middle:** In the center of the book, we've provided questions that can jump-start your conversations about these chapters.

Is This Stuff Really True?

The stories you're about to read are true, though many of the details are not. The names and the circumstances have been changed to mask

the identity of those whose stories we are telling. And at times we've combined the experiences of several couples into a seamless story with entirely different names and circumstances.

We also want to acknowledge that the title *The Most Important Year* is true, of course, for those who choose to marry. However, if the first year of marriage were the only "most important year," people of no less stature than Mother Teresa and Jesus would have missed it. But because you and I *have* chosen marriage, and because the first year of marriage *is* so critical in shaping our futures, we are convinced that nothing conveys the heart of our message quite like *The Most Important Year in a Woman's Life* and *The Most Important Year in a Man's Life*.

So whether you are preparing for marriage or have been married for thirty days or for thirty years, we invite you to make this next year *the most important year* in your life.

Susan DeVries   *Bobbie Wolgemuth*
Nashville, Tennessee   *Orlando, Florida*

1

The Most Important Year: Reality Check

The first change the woman must adjust to is no longer being a bride.

SHERYL NISSINEN, *THE CONSCIOUS BRIDE*

———◆•◆————

y now I don't have to tell you. If you're looking for information on how to be a bride, you won't have to look far. There are thousands of books, magazines, bridal shows, and Websites—all offering tips and checklists to help the well-organized bride plan her wedding. And since most of these lists start with "twelve months before the wedding," many of us find ourselves way behind before we even get started—and we haven't caught up yet.

In my research, I found lists that seem to cover everything—from picking out the dress to designing a map to the reception. But I couldn't find a single checklist that included the estimated amount of time a bride could expect to spend on these gargantuan to-do lists.

So I put my own calculator to a few of these tasks and came up with my own estimates. Did you know that the typical bride will spend between 150 and 500 hours preparing for her wedding—the equivalent of one to three months working at a full-time job? After the year you've had, you're not surprised, are you?

If you were like most brides, you probably spent an incredible amount of time and energy creating the wedding that would be "just right" for you and your husband—the kind of day you've been dreaming of and planning for since you were a little girl. And now that the special day is over, there's a good chance you're feeling what a lot of women experience, namely, the postmarital blues. I call it "the princess crisis."

A princess is beautiful, fun to be with, romantic, on a quest to win the affection of a charming prince, and surrounded by others who attend to her wants and needs. But after the wedding day, a bride often ceases to see herself as a princess—feeling more like the duty-bound queen—and when the princess becomes the queen, the real work begins.

You may have noticed one other item notoriously absent from the premarital checklists: time allotted to working on your relationship with your future husband. I took out my calculator again to try to determine how much time a typical couple spends before their wedding working on developing the attitudes and skills they'll need to build a great marriage. The diligent couple will go to premarital counseling—usually five hours or so. And the really committed couples will read a book on marriage—say, another ten hours. At best, the average couple will spend ten times more time preparing for the wedding event than for their marriage.

> At best, the average couple will spend ten times more time preparing for the wedding event than for their marriage.

It's not uncommon for a bride, carried along by the rushing torrent of preparing for the wedding day, to neglect her relationship with her fiancé. And it is not uncommon for couples in their first year of marriage, carried along by the rushing momentum of getting established in a new home—often in a new town with new jobs—to neglect their relationship with each other, only to find themselves wondering at the end of the first year what happened to all the love they once felt on their wedding day.

But *you* have picked up this book because you want something more for your marriage. Welcome!

More Than Commitment

The ever-growing stacks of marriage and relationship books at libraries and bookstores give evidence of how intensely people long to make their marriages work. In fact, in the past thirty years there have been more books written on marriage than there were in the previous two thousand years combined. Yet, despite the deluge of resources, we don't have to look far to realize that *great ideas* on marriage, in and of themselves, do not make great marriages.

Some say that marriages fail because of a lack of commitment. Some say the problem is that couples today lack a proper spiritual foundation. Others say the root of the problem is that couples are simply not willing to sacrifice in ways that their parents and grandparents did. But Bobbie and I are convinced that, regardless of the reason, the demise or the success of a marriage can almost always be traced to the first year together.

Here's how it went with Sheila. All her life she had dreamed of being married—of having someone to share life with, someone to walk on the beach with, to dance with, simply to share the stories of the day with. When she met Ted, she knew she had found the man she had been hoping for. He was strong and stable, quietly eager to please her, and he was ambitious. He knew what he wanted out of life, and she liked that.

But shortly after their wedding, Sheila realized that this man of her dreams had the strange habit of leaving her feeling hurt and lonely. She longed for the closeness they had known when they were dating, but so often it seemed as though he was far away—almost unreachable.

Sheila committed herself to working even harder at being a better wife. She tried to be sensitive to Ted's moods and needs, serving him as unselfishly as she knew how. But she found that Ted simply came to expect these things and seldom expressed appreciation for them.

This went on for years, through the birth and growth of their two children. By the time the kids got busy with lives of their own, Sheila's ache returned in full bloom. She tried to talk to Ted about her long-standing disenchantment with their marriage. Ted was preoccupied with his work and chided her for her "lousy sense of timing."

It wasn't long after their twentieth anniversary that Sheila made the decision to do what she had told herself she would never do. When the divorce papers were delivered to Ted, she finally had his undivided attention. Ted tried to talk her out of it, but Sheila was on a mission. Under pressure from close friends, Sheila and Ted went to see a counselor. But the negativity was so strong by this point that, try as they might, Sheila and Ted could never find a solid foothold on which to start over. They said the line—repeated so often by so many—"We tried so hard; we tried *everything,* and nothing worked."

It's not that Ted and Sheila didn't invest in their marriage. The truth is that they invested sacrificially as they tried desperately to make their marriage work. Their investment was enormous. It simply came *too late.*

The early investment in building an exceptional marriage costs a fraction of what it will take to keep a lousy one on life support.

But the seeds of failure were planted in the first year of the marriage—seeds that over time grew strong enough to corrode their commitment. During that first year, changes could have been made—with minimal effort. But after twenty years of ingrained patterns, even Ted and Sheila's heroic efforts were consumed in a tidal wave of negativity that they felt helpless to stop.

Here's the principle: The early investment in building an exceptional marriage costs a fraction of what it will take to keep a lousy one on life support. The early investment takes less time. It takes less emotional anxiety. Consider the dividends:

- People with satisfying marriages live longer, enjoy better health, and report a much higher level of satisfaction about life in general. In fact, people who stay married, live an average of four years longer than people who don't.[3]
- Forty percent of married couples say they are very happy, compared to 18 percent of those divorced and 22 percent of those never married or of unmarried couples living together.[4]
- Recent statistics show that the average married couple in their fifties has a net worth nearly five times that of the average divorced or single person.[5]
- Divorce dramatically increases the likelihood of early death from strokes, hypertension, respiratory cancer, and intestinal cancer. Astonishingly, being a divorced non-smoker is only slightly less dangerous than smoking a pack (or more) of cigarettes a day and staying married! (I wonder if divorce summons papers come with the surgeon general's warning).[6]

The Most Important Year

As we began our treasure hunt to find the secrets of building a great marriage, we came across this passage from the Old Testament, buried in the middle of the often ignored book of Deuteronomy. Here, hidden just before the instructions concerning the proper use of millstones

when making loan agreements (no kidding), is a single verse that just may make all the difference in the world in your marriage:

> If a man has recently married, he must not be sent to war or have any other duty laid on him. For one year he is to be free to stay at home and bring happiness to the wife he has married.
>
> DEUTERONOMY 24:5

Although the prospects of such a thing may sound hilarious or outrageous to you, take a look at the principles embedded in this verse—principles that just may make your first year of marriage the most important year in your life.

The "Wet Cement Year" Principle—"has recently married"

Have you ever walked down a sidewalk and seen a handprint or someone's name etched into its surface? Think about how much work it took to make those marks and how difficult it would be to change them. Indelible marks are made on your marriage early. They're not very difficult to make, but they're extremely difficult to change.

Scripture is clear that there is—and should be—something undeniably different about the first year of marriage. The implication is that, particularly for a husband, there is a receptivity to change during this year, perhaps as at no other time in his life. We call this "the wet cement year." Once the patterns of the marriage are set, change can and does occur, but it may take something like a jackhammer to bring it about.

> Indelible marks are made on your marriage early. They're not very difficult to make, but they're extremely difficult to change.

Too many women spend the first year of marriage working hard not to make waves, hoping that the little irritants and insensitivities of their husbands will simply go away. But in almost every marriage we've observed, problems not dealt with in the first year simply become larger and more paralyzing as the years go by.

The Slow Learner Principle—"For one year"

Have you ever heard one of these comments come out of a woman's mouth?

- "If he really loved me, he would figure it out."
- "How can he say that he loves me and keep doing the same insensitive things again and again?"
- "If I have to *tell* him what I want, then it doesn't count!"

Consider the contrast between the attitude that lies beneath these comments and the suggestion from the Bible that it will take a man *an entire year of focused effort* to learn how to please his wife. An entire year!

The changes that a couple needs to make (particularly the changes the husband needs to make) *can* be less painful if dealt with in the first year, but they may not come quickly. Our friend Lois was particularly startled at how challenging the first year of her marriage was. Things just fell into place so naturally when she and Andy were dating. But now, it felt as though they were swimming through molasses. Her frustration came primarily because she wasn't prepared. She simply hadn't anticipated how slowly her husband would be able to "figure things out."

Awareness that lasting change will take time can free a wife from having to resort to negative nagging to motivate her husband into change. Being prepared in this way can help her to celebrate the small steps of growth her husband does make as he is learning to "bring happiness" to her.

Let's face facts: Most husbands are clueless when it comes to understanding women. They love their wives and want to see them happy. But they are easily confused about expressing love in a way that truly brings pleasure to their wives. Husbands wonder—

- Is it talking together as you go for a long walk? Or is it taking a short walk together in silence?
- Is it a romantic night together in the bedroom with candles and soft music? Or is it helping with the dishes so she doesn't have to fuss over them in the morning?
- Is it getting flowers once a week? Or is it weeding the garden on Saturday mornings?
- Is it sending a romantic card? Or is it simply putting dirty clothes in the hamper?
- Is it cooking out on the grill at home? Or is it calling ahead to make dinner reservations?
- Is it letting her plan an entire vacation? Or is it planning a surprise getaway without her having to do a thing?

Look closely at the Old Testament passage again. The good news hinted at in this ancient Scripture is that your husband *can,* in fact, learn to understand what brings you pleasure. Your husband is not expected to become a genius when it comes to *women.* He is, though, charged to become the world's greatest expert at understanding what pleases *you!* And to accomplish this, he will need your help.

The Responsive Feedback Principle—"bring happiness to the wife he has married"

Bobbie has a friend who was a first-grade teacher. She told me the story of Zachary, the boy with the unkempt hair. Day after day Zachary came to school with a terminal case of "bed head." *What is this boy's mother thinking?* that teacher wondered.

One day she announced, "Tomorrow is picture day," and then she wrote a note to the children's mothers and sent it home in the kids' backpacks. To her amazement, the next day Zachary walked into the classroom with his hair perfectly combed. *This* was her big chance. Before class began, Zachary made his way toward her desk, and she spoke to him quietly enough that none of the other students could hear. "Wow, Zachary, you'd better get your running shoes on," she said with a twinkle in her eye. "Your hair looks so good that all the girls will be chasing you today!"

She never had to say anything else the rest of the year about Zachary's hair. She didn't need to.

Men are wired a good bit like little Zachary—wired to respond to the positive feedback that comes from the decisions they make. There are few things more powerful a wife can do to motivate her husband than to let him know that his actions and his words are making a difference.

I love the way psychologist Neil Clark Warren makes sense of this process: "My love for another person is strongly related to my love for myself when we are together. If the most potent motivation in my life is to feel good about myself—and I believe it is—then I will love an individual most when she helps me to feel best about myself."[7]

When a wife says, "I like that!" or "That counts for me," her husband feels empowered and motivated and is much more likely to repeat what he did to please her. But a man who believes that he can never satisfy his wife will soon give up trying and invest his energy in places—like his

job—where the results are much more clearly seen. Am I suggesting that you fake happiness so your husband can feel good about himself? Not at all. I'm merely saying that one of the greatest gifts you'll ever give him is to *respond* well to the things he *does* do that make you happy. He needs to know that you noticed.

Investing in the *Real* Journey

In 1845, Sir John Franklin and 138 men set off from England to find a northwest passage to the Pacific Ocean. Their course would take them over the Canadian Arctic.

The ship was well stocked for comfort—a 1,200-volume library, a hand organ programmed to play fifty different melodies, fine china and monogrammed silver place settings, and hand-carved backgammon boards.

But not a single one of the sailors would live to tell his story. For years, no one knew what had happened until an expedition stumbled upon their frozen remains. The ship was found first—frozen solid in the arctic waters of the Canadian north. Apparently, the engines weren't equipped to run in such ominously cold temperatures. And though the ship was outfitted with an auxiliary coal-powered engine, according to the ship's logs, they had no more than twelve days' supply of coal on board. Eventually, the crew was forced to travel by foot.

> Building a satisfying marriage isn't simply about commitment and passion. It's about being prepared for the winters that are sure to come.

Years later explorers came upon the remains of the sailors, frozen in tents or beneath the shelter of the single lifeboat they dragged across the ice for over a hundred miles. But it wasn't the gruesome remains that most surprised these explorers. As they looked more closely at the lost sailors, they were amazed to discover brass buttons and silk scarves. These men appeared to have entered their journey more equipped for elegance than for survival.

Sir John Franklin and his crew entered their adventure with enthusiasm. They had the highest levels of commitment. They had a plan and plenty of passion. They even supplied themselves with an abundance of luxuries to make their journey more comfortable. *But they weren't prepared.*

Building a satisfying marriage isn't simply about commitment and passion. It's about being prepared for the winters that are sure to come. Will you enter marriage with enough coal for the reserve engines, or will your attention be fixed on all kinds of wedding-shower trinkets and gadgets—luxuries that promise to make life more comfortable? The most elegant and memorable weddings in the world become useless ornaments unless couples prepare well.

Before you turn the page, make the decision to do the preparations that will cause this to be the most important year in your life.

2

Needs: Dare to Dream the Impossible

Being helpful to each other will do far more for the strength and passion of your marriage than a two-week Bahamas getaway.

JOHN GOTTMAN, *THE SEVEN PRINCIPLES FOR MAKING MARRIAGE WORK*

---

*I*magine this scene:

It's a Saturday, and you had to work all day. Your husband had the day off. It's 7:00 P.M. when you finally drag yourself through the doorway. But when you come in, you instantly notice something different about your home. No stray papers. The kitchen is immaculate.

In the dining room, you see the flicker of candles. And something smells tantalizing. Over the mellow sounds of your favorite music playing in the background, you call out, "Honey? What's going on? Is someone coming over tonight?"

Your tuxedoed husband appears from around the corner and says playfully, "Welcome, madam. We *are* expecting a very important guest—and she has just arrived. As we put the finishing touches on your dinner, I hope you'll come and make yourself comfortable in our lounge."

As you raise a skeptical eyebrow, this man of yours leads you to a comfortable chair, next to which he has strategically placed your favorite drink and that magazine or catalog you never have time to read.

You pinch yourself to make sure you're not dreaming ...

Mark and I have shared this imaginary scenario with enough groups of married couples to know what to expect: the rolling eyes, the snickers of laughter, comments like, "Yeah right!" or "Come on, be realistic!" or "The closest I'll ever get to that story IS in my dreams."

But before you move this book to the fantasy section of your home library, I want to ask you to consider the possibility that having a husband who cherishes you with this kind—or more appropriately, "your kind"—of extravagance and creativity is not only possible, it's actually crucial if you are to have the marriage you always dreamed of.

> Having a husband who cherishes you with your kind of extravagance and creativity is not only possible, it's crucial if you are to have the marriage you always dreamed of.

And I've got news for you: There really *are* wives who experience this dream on a regular basis—not every night of course, maybe not even every month, but frequently enough to make them shake their heads and wonder how God could be so good as to give them the husbands they have. There is more involved here than just dumb luck. This kind of treatment never happens accidentally but only to couples who have intentionally chosen to find joy in meeting each other's needs in extravagant and surprising ways.

Helping Your Husband Succeed

So what would make your husband treat you this way? Remember that in a healthy marriage a husband finds great joy in bringing pleasure to his wife. One of the most important things you can do during the first year of your marriage is help your husband succeed in doing just that. And to help him succeed, you'll need to develop three specific skills:

1. Know your own needs well enough to understand what your husband can do to bring you pleasure.
2. Express those needs to your husband clearly, specifically, and winsomely.
3. Cherish your husband with as much creativity as you hope he will use cherishing you.

Know Your Own Needs: Why Most Wives Miss the Party

Mark and I recently worked through our standard premarital preparation process with an exceptional young couple. They had convictions about their plans for Bible study and prayer times together after the wedding. They were committed to reading marriage books together. They even agreed to have weekly financial meetings to head off any potential conflicts over money. This was a couple with an uncanny commitment to having an incredible marriage.

In the final session, though, we recognized a pattern that had the potential to severely limit the joy these two would experience in their marriage. We were on the topic of "great sex in marriage." Within thirty seconds, the young bride-to-be, obviously a bit uncomfortable with my candor, interrupted me, "I've just decided that I'm going to leave everything in this area up to John [her fiancé]. That's really his department."

I answered her slowly, "No, Marcia, I'm afraid that's *your* department."

The bride-to-be was confused. As her brows furrowed, she asked, "What do you mean?"

I explained that very few wives I had talked to were truly satisfied with the sexual side of their marriages. I explained that very few men ever actually "figure out" what truly pleases their wives sexually, *unless* their wives teach them. I explained how brides who see sex as "their husbands' department" eventually wind up approaching sex as a chore—an obligation she fulfills for his sake rather than a playful, deeply satisfying experience that she enjoys as much—if not more—than her husband.

Finally, I explained that wives who leave sex as their husbands' department usually become experts at "avoidance strategies." Sometimes it's evening headaches; other nights it's late meetings at church; and still other times, it's "unselfishly" tidying up the house at night until the husband is asleep.

I knew we had this bride-to-be's attention. She said, "That is *not* what I want! But what do you mean when you say it's *my* department?"

Mark explained, "It's not just your sexual needs that are your department. Sex is just an example of a place where it's common for a wife to be completely out of touch with her own needs. It's just that if

you don't know your needs, it's pretty unlikely that your husband will somehow stumble into figuring out how to meet them. For a woman to expect her husband to know her needs better than she does herself— whether it relates to sex or to sandwiches—simply sets both of them up for frustration."

Circling back to the original topic, I affirmed, "It *is* your responsibility to discover enough about yourself over this next year that you become an expert on what your husband can do to satisfy you sexually. As awkward as it may seem right now, that *is* your department."

Let's face it: Knowing our own needs may not feel natural. Many of us grew up with the subtle message that we are not supposed to have needs of our own. We have heard the message loud and clear: "Work harder. Serve more. Stop focusing so much on yourself." Though ignoring our own needs may feel natural or seem unselfish, the truth is that living this way can actually *prevent* our husbands from doing the very thing we long for them to do, namely, to cherish us.

Ask for What You Need: Why Most Husbands Stay Clueless

Some time ago, my friend Cathryn told her husband, Billy, about a surprise birthday party one of his friends had thrown for his wife. Cathryn told Billy how excited her friend was and how fun the whole idea sounded. She talked with great enthusiasm about how special her friend felt that her husband had gone to all that trouble.

> For a woman to expect her husband to know her needs better than she does herself— whether it relates to sex or to sandwiches—simply sets both of them up for frustration.

In a few months, Cathryn's thirtieth birthday came. Billy took her out for an expensive dinner and gave her a very nice gift, and then the two of them came home for a quiet evening together. But by bedtime, Billy could tell that there was something wrong.

He asked, "Are you okay? You look a little down."

Eventually, she admitted, "I thought you were going to throw a surprise party for me this year!"

Billy asked (with typical male sensitivity), "If you wanted a surprise party, why didn't you ask for one?"

Cathryn shot back, "I did!"

What was Billy's mistake? He assumed that when his bride was talking about *her friend's* surprise party that she was really talking about *her friend's* surprise party. What you and I both know is that she was talking about what she wanted from her husband. Cathryn made the common mistake of forgetting what gender her husband was.

I love my husband. He is a marvelous man. He presents seminars, counsels couples, and writes books about marriage. But there are times when he just doesn't get it. And if I hadn't learned over the years to ask clearly for what I need from him, he would still be scratching his head and trying to figure me out.

When we ask couples in trouble what they would love to see happen in their marriages, we often receive detailed lists of what they don't like about their spouse's behavior. But seldom does this kind of negative response help couples get what they deeply long for from each other. Moving from vague criticisms to expressions of specific needs can actually transform a marriage.

For example, a wife might say to her husband, "I want you to be less selfish." The husband might naturally respond with a list of all the unselfish things he's already doing—"I mow the lawn. I'm nice to your mother. I pay all the bills." But her concern about selfishness is much more specific. Her husband has a habit of making plans in the evening without letting her know, so she winds up cooking a nice dinner he ends up not eating or appreciating.

When you find yourself nagging your husband, it's almost always because there is something you want from him that you're not getting. And often it's a sign that you haven't clearly asked for what you need.

Remember Aladdin and his magic lamp? Imagine the genie asking you to make your first wish.

You respond, "I'd like more money."

He tells you to reach into your pocket. You find a quarter, just as the genie says, "How about your next wish?"

You would be thinking, "That's *not* what I meant!"

Your husband is not a genie, but like this genie, he may at times give you exactly what you have "asked for," only to learn later that what he gave you was *not* what you meant. Consider the difference between these two very different requests for the same need:

- "You never touch me anymore."
- "Would you rub my back tonight for about five minutes?"

Your husband will likely see the first request as a criticism and assume you must be talking about sex. With regard to the second request, you are much more likely to get your back massage, and your husband is much more likely to feel as though he's succeeded in loving you.

When we talk to husbands, we hear an almost unanimous chorus: "If I could just figure out what she wanted, I would do it. But it seems like no matter what I do, it's not the right thing." Am I suggesting that *every time* you ask directly for what you need from your husband he will say yes? Of course not. What I am saying is that wives who ask directly for what they need are *always* more likely to have these needs met by their husbands than if they hadn't asked at all. Hockey star Wayne Gretzky is right: "We miss 100 percent of the shots we never take."

One final tip about asking: In addition to being specific and clear about what you need from your husband, he'll be much more receptive if your requests are given winsomely. Clear and specific requests can easily be negated by a spirit of bitterness or anger on the part of the one doing the asking.

Learn to Cherish Your Husband: He's Not Asking for Much

If you hope to create a marriage in which you and your husband cherish each other extravagantly and creatively, the third skill you'll need to learn is the skill of knowing and meeting your husband's needs with the same playful intentionality you hope he uses in trying to meet yours. Without this step, the first two skills can easily be viewed by your husband as demanding and unrealistic neediness on your part.

How do you discover what your husband desires most from you? You might assume that the easiest way to find the answer is simply to ask him. It can't hurt. But if you get less than a clear, specific response, don't be surprised. Willard Harley's book *His Needs, Her Needs* was a real eye-opener for me. Dr. Harley says that the most effective currency a husband and wife have for communicating love to each other is that of *meeting each other's needs*. His theory, after counseling hundreds of couples, is that men and women each have a set of five very different primary needs. Here are the ones he suggests your husband needs from you:[8]

1. sexual fulfillment
2. recreational companionship
3. an attractive spouse

4. domestic support
5. admiration

I'm not saying that these are the needs that all men have or ought to have. I simply offer this list as a starting point for you on your journey toward discovering the needs of this man you have married. So take this list to him, and see if he agrees. If he doesn't, be sure to find out what needs he *does* have.

Another possibility is to ask a few playful discovery questions such as—

- What one thing could I do for you today that would let you know how much I love you?
- If you knew I would say yes, what one thing would you ask me to do with you or for you?
- What would be your perfect night at home? Be as detailed as possible.

Now this is where the fun comes in. Whatever your husband asks, surprise him by doing it sometime in the next week. And add a little extra to it. If he asks for meat loaf and mashed potatoes for dinner, prepare his favorite dessert as well. If he asks you to be more available sexually, initiate an intimate encounter once a week.

It's funny. If asked, most Christian wives would say they'd be willing to die for their husbands. But some of these same wives view it as a grand imposition to demonstrate love in the little ways that meet their husbands' needs, such as being happy with them, enthusiastically greeting them at the door, or flirting back with them.

If husbands of these women ever dare to say that they don't feel much love coming from their wives, these wives are quick to point to all the things they're doing to show love:

> Most Christian wives would say they'd be willing to die for their husbands. But some of these same wives view it as a grand imposition to demonstrate love in the little ways that meet their husbands' needs.

- "Haven't I taken care of the house, done your laundry, and fed the dog?"
- "Didn't I buy you that cool golf shirt?"
- "Don't I pray for you every day?"

Clearly, it's not wrong for a wife to do these things for her husband. The problem comes when she assumes that, because she does the things *she* thinks ought to meet his needs, his needs are truly being met. A wife who "unselfishly" focuses her time on the things she wants to do for her husband, while ignoring the things that matter most to him, should not confuse what she is doing with love. Your charge is to outdo one another in showing love (see Romans 12:10).

The **Yes** *Spiral*

In premarital counseling, we describe this process of meeting each other's needs as the *Yes Spiral*. The more that couples tap into this widening upward spiral, the more likely they are to experience the kind of marriages they've dreamed of. We call it the *Yes Spiral* because it all begins with a willingness to say yes to the request—spoken or unspoken—to meet the needs of your spouse.

Let's take a look at the widening spiral that comes when a husband and wife learn to live with a resounding, mutual *Yes!* toward each other. Here's how the spiral can begin on an ordinary day when you arrive home from work:

> *You:* "Hi, sweetie, I'm home." No response from your husband. "How 'bout a little welcome parade for the princess of the castle?"
>
> *Your Husband:* "I'm sorry. I was caught up in getting my report done." He hugs you and looks into your eyes. "I have a huge favor to ask. I hate to ask you to go out after you just got in, but I was printing out this report that has to be turned in tonight, and I realized I need a few things from Officeland. Could you run over there and get them for me?"
>
> *You:* "Sure. What do I need to get?"
>
> *Your Husband:* "You're the best, honey. Here's the list."
>
> *You:* "Hey, if you get the chance while I'm out, could you call your folks to see when we need to pick up that package? I couldn't get ahold of them earlier today."
>
> *Your Husband:* "No problem." You turn to go, and he stops you. "Hey, you're pretty incredible, you know that?"
>
> *You:* "Come here, you!"

You wrap him in your arms.

Your Husband: "Hey, princess, if you hurry back, I may just have to take you out to dinner tonight." As you leave, he's shaking his head, smiling and saying quietly to himself, "You amaze me!"

A simple—almost silly—conversation, but did you observe how many times you and your husband said yes to each other in this quick exchange?

1. He said yes to your request for a warm greeting, even though he was consumed with his project.
2. You said yes to his request to make an unplanned trip to the store, even though getting back in the car was the last thing you wanted to do.
3. He said yes to your request to call his parents about the package.
4. You both said yes to each other's need for appreciation and affirmation.

> With each yes—in words, actions, or attitudes—the spiral widens, and the two of you feel freer together, more willing to serve each other, more willing to creatively meet each other's needs.

With each yes—in words, actions, or attitudes—the spiral widens, and the two of you feel freer together, more willing to serve each other, more willing to creatively meet each other's needs.

But when the positive responses are replaced by negative ones, the spiral becomes tighter and tighter. You both feel more trapped, less willing to serve, more like you're locked in a room with a porcupine. Here's how the conversation, carried out differently, creates a constricting spiral:

Wife: "Hi, sweetie, I'm home." No response from your husband. "How 'bout a little welcome parade for the princess of the castle?"

Husband (shouting from his office): "I'm sorry. I was just trying to finish this report for tonight. Hey, I hate to ask you to go out after you've just got in, but I really need some stuff from Officeland so I can get this report done and turned in. Could you run to the store and get it for me?"

Wife: "You've had all day. You've been out three times. Why didn't you pick up what you needed when you were out?"

Husband: "I didn't realize I needed it until I got to this point in the report. I've had a few other things on my mind, you know. Here's the list."

Wife (handing the list back): "You'll just have to take care of it yourself. I am *not* going out again. Not after the day I've had! Where's the mail? Do I have any messages? Did you call your parents about when we need to pick up that package?"

Husband: "I distinctly remember you telling me you were going to do it. You know, I can't do everything! I have a job, too, you know."

Wife: "Fine! I don't care if we get the package or not."

Husband (through clenched teeth): "So did you learn this little attitude in your marriage class at church?"

Wife: "Now that was a cheap shot, and you know it."

Husband (getting up): "Excuse me, but I need to go to the store. Don't worry about me joining you for dinner tonight. Now that I've got to make this extra trip out, I'll have to work straight through dinner to get this report turned in on time." He stalks away, fuming. "You amaze me!"

Did you notice how easily each of them became less and less willing to say yes. Once the downward spiral begins, it takes increasing amounts of energy to move against the negative inertia.

Consider for just a minute the investment of energy in these two conversations. The first feels like a walk down lovers' lane compared to the second, doesn't it? But notice that the first conversation required an up-front, against-the-grain willingness to meet each other's needs, even when it wasn't convenient.

I am sometimes asked, "What if I don't really *feel* like doing what my husband needs me to do? You're not suggesting I do it anyway, even though my heart isn't in it, are you?" Well, yes, that's exactly what I'm suggesting!

You find an example of this very behavior in the first dialogue. In the second, the couple simply did and said what they felt like saying and

doing. Love doesn't mean we'll always feel like demonstrating love; it means choosing to demonstrate love—even when we don't feel like it.

Suppose a mother waited to "feel like it" before she changed her baby's diaper. Her child could wallow in his own mess for a long time before she ever "felt like it." Even though her heart may not be in it, she changes the diaper anyway. Why? Because she loves the child, even though she may not *feel* particularly loving at the time.

The decision to meet each other's needs is not primarily about saying the right things. It's not about learning how to perfectly imitate dialogue number one. Rather, it is about possessing an eagerness to say yes to your husband's needs. Since you are, in reality, "one flesh" with your husband, when you meet *his* needs, in some mysterious way you are meeting *your own* needs as well.

But even though you know how important it is to meet each other's needs, there will be times when you're simply not capable. That's okay. In the next chapter, I have some good news for you.

3

Spiritual Unity: More Than Meets the Eye

> As man was incomplete in the Genesis story, so man and woman are incomplete from an ultimate, divine perspective. We believe every human couple needs a critical third partner, and that third factor is God.
>
> DEAN BORGMAN, *WHEN KUMBAYA IS NOT ENOUGH*

We knew Brad and Francine quite well by the time they finished their premarital meetings with us. Both had fiery personalities and shared a common heart for God. As we spent time together, Mark cautioned them that their intense approach to life could make for some challenging and uncomfortable conflict, though I'm not sure they believed him.

By the end of their first year of marriage, they had learned each other's hot buttons and punched them with pugnacious regularity. On most days, their anger simmered below the surface, but at times it boiled over with a destructive harshness that frightened both of them.

Not long ago, we had dinner with Francine and Brad. Shaking her head and laughing, Francine said to us, "We would have easily divorced a hundred times in that first year."

Surprised and curious, I asked, "Why did you stay together?"

They answered in playful unison, "God!"

They would tell you that it wasn't that God stepped in, snapped his fingers, and suddenly made them get along. Rather, it was their common loyalty to the God whom they both deeply loved that gave them the heart to stay together, even when they didn't much care for each other and staying together was the last thing they *felt* like doing.

The Third Partner

Because of the commitment Brad and Francine had made to honor God, they did not simply resign themselves to tolerating a lifetime of mutual annoyance. They were motivated to change the ingrained patterns of resistance toward each other that could have pulled them apart. The good news is that you and your husband cannot both move closer to God without moving closer to each other. I picture it like this:

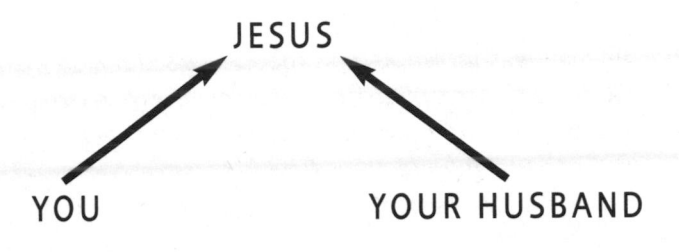

You may recall that men tend to build intimacy best when they are focused on a third object—whether it's football, food, or a military mission. And the greater the third object, the deeper and stronger their bond. Some theologians refer to this phenomenon as the "transcendent third"—something outside two people that draws them together. A husband and wife who have Titans football as their "transcendent third" are brought together by their common football allegiance. But we'd hardly expect this shared fan loyalty alone to enable a couple to overcome even minimal obstacles in their relationship. They need something bigger.

> When a husband and wife are each actively seeking God, they pursue One who is so engaging, so captivating, so transforming, so supremely good, that loyalty to him stabilizes and engulfs all other loyalties.

For some couples, children become the "transcendent third" that gives them leverage to work through annoying behaviors in each other. But focusing on children as the highest "transcendent third" can mask the absence of a true spiritual connection in the marriage. Again, they need something bigger.

But when a husband and wife are each actively seeking God—moving toward *the* "Transcendent Third"—they pursue One who is so engaging, so captivating, so transforming, so supremely good, that loyalty to him stabilizes and engulfs all other loyalties. God is big enough.

Encouraging Your Husband to Grow

With a voice as deep as the Grand Canyon, Doug was a man's man. He had spent the early years of his marriage working in and around the coal mines of western Canada. And though he had traveled as a young boy with his minister-father, Doug considered God irrelevant.

Doug didn't resist when his wife offered to take their young children to church. He was happy to let her. What harm could it do? *After all*, he thought, *kids need good moral input.*

This arrangement worked fine for Doug and Jan until the children became too much for her to handle at the church service. One day she came home and said, "You have to start coming to church with me. I just can't handle these kids all by myself."

To Doug's credit, he agreed and began attending church as the bouncer for his elementary-age kids—and that's when his world turned upside down.

Doug never expected to find "real men" at church; he expected only "pansies." What he found were rock-solid men, just like he thought he was. And so, when one of the men from church asked Doug if he wanted to join their group for a little road trip, an event sponsored by a group he'd never heard of—a group called Promise Keepers—Doug said, "Sure."

In Jan's words, when Doug came back from that event, "everything changed." An encounter with God did something for Doug that Jan could never do. Her husband came home with a commitment to provide spiritual leadership in their home and with a renewed love for her and the children.

It might be easy to assume that Jan had little to do with the transformation in her husband's life, but I don't buy it for a second. What Jan did was to create a climate of such receptivity in her husband that, once he encountered God himself, he became an entirely different man.

It is not unusual for a wife to be further along spiritually than her husband. But there is a certain style, a particular attitude, common to wives who effectively encourage their husbands to move from spiritual apathy to spiritual passion. We've joyfully observed many husbands who have been wooed and won by the irresistible spiritual influence of their wives. These women don't try to argue their husbands into spiritual depth. They don't berate them for not being spiritual enough. They don't claim to know the answers to all the questions. They don't try to

trick their husbands into "witnessing ambushes" cleverly disguised as dinner parties at the homes of Christian friends.

No, there is something refreshing about the wild honesty of these women's faith. Their husbands are attracted to the vitality of a woman whose love for God infects every part of her with a deeper passion, so that she wants to be more patient, more understanding, more winsome, and able to laugh at herself more readily.

What spiritually resistant men usually fear is not that their wives will become too bright and too alive by knowing Jesus but that they will become too boring, one-dimensional, and adventureless. So if your husband is put off by God or by the church, find out what will turn him on spiritually—and wait for your wooing witness to have its effect.

Honor and Respect Your Husband's Pursuit of God

Even if you grew up going to church every time the doors were open, you may be able to remember a time when talking about spiritual things felt uncomfortable. Whether it was being put on the spot when someone asked you to pray or responding to a "simple" Sunday school question in broad daylight, you felt embarrassed. Your husband may feel this "public spiritual insecurity" more acutely than you ever felt it.

Catching your husband doing something well and telling him that you noticed will go a long way toward affirming his spiritual growth.

Remember that spiritual unity does not mean spiritual uniformity. And one of the first ways to encourage your husband to grow in his own relationship with Jesus is to honor his style of living out his faith. It's refreshing to see a man emboldened to take the next step spiritually as the result of a simple, encouraging comment from his wife, such as, "It's great the way you help people—seeing things that need to be done and just doing them," or, "I love the way you cut through all the clutter and get to the real issue when we talk about spiritual things." Catching your husband doing something well and telling him that you noticed will go a long way toward affirming his spiritual growth.

If it feels as though you're on different spiritual wavelengths, don't be surprised. Be patient. Spiritual intimacy, like sexual intimacy, takes

time, as the two of you grow comfortable revealing to each other the parts of your hearts that no one else sees.

Start Out Like You Can Hold Out

When we were first married, we had such ambitious plans for our spiritual life as a couple. We planned to pray together at least daily—none of those perfunctory, placid dinner-table blessings we had grown up with, mind you, but heart-focused, soul-mated prayers that would unite us around eternal things.

We planned to read to each other—devotional books, biographies of great Christians, and, of course, the Bible. And because so much of our early romance centered around music, we were sure that we would spend a lot of time singing "psalms and hymns and spiritual songs" together—Mark on the guitar, me at the piano. Our grand plans, however, failed miserably.

In the span of six months, the busyness of life and ministry kept us from even having dinner together most nights, much less having heart-to-heart prayer times. Before we went to sleep, I'd start reading to Mark, only to be interrupted by the sound of his snoring before I finished the first page. We occasionally prayed together, but our prayers were not the rich, well-prepared five-course meals we had dreamed of—more like peanut butter and jelly sandwiches grabbed on the run. And, after almost twenty-five years, I'm sure one of those leisurely times of singing together is just around the corner!

More than two decades of marriage have given me a little perspective. As newlyweds, we felt guilty for not doing enough. And at times that unnecessary guilt blocked our spiritual unity just as much as our failure did.

In our work with couples before their marriages, we encourage them with this motto with regard to spiritual things: "Start out like you can hold out." We encourage them to do so in two ways:

Pick One Just for You

Choose one spiritual practice that you will agree to do regularly *as a couple*. It doesn't matter whether it's praying together, reading a devotional book, reading the Bible at meals—we emphasize that the key is to do *something* and make it *doable*.

I was fascinated recently to read of a collection of articles by fifty-two Christian leaders on the topic of spiritual intimacy in marriage.[9] Each was asked to write a page of reflections about what they do in their own marriages to cultivate spiritual oneness. The biggest surprise was that *not one of the fifty-two couples did exactly the same thing*.

Do something and make it doable.

You may agree to pray at meals and to keep attending your church together. As a couple, you may decide to read a chapter out of a Christian book each week and talk about it over a Wednesday morning breakfast. Or you may choose to read a chapter from the book of Proverbs together, and invest your time in a young couples Sunday school class. The options are nearly endless.

Connect to an Imperfect Community of Faith

You will also need to have an intentional plan for connecting to a specific *imperfect* church body. We emphasize the word *imperfect*, because we've watched couples spend the early years of their marriages looking for just the "right" church. Some couples hop from church to church—a year or so at one, then on for a short time at another—unable to make a commitment to any of them.

This kind of perpetual searching sets couples up for a lifetime of dissatisfaction with their faith community and can cut them off from the transforming benefits that come only with the accountability of "doing life" with people over the long haul. Like a seed that won't embed itself in the ground in order to avoid getting dirty, couples who "just can't find" a church home miss the vital growth that happens only when we are embedded deeply into the dirty soil of God's people.

Doing these two things—marriage focused and church focused—and formulating a plan will allow you to approach the spiritual dimension of your marriage with joy and eagerness instead of guilt over somehow not doing enough. And during the dry seasons of marriage that are sure to come, your shared love for God may just hold you together when nothing else can.

Family of Origin: White-Water Wedding Guide

Let me be painfully direct here. That special person you are thinking about marrying—the one whose hand you hold under the restaurant table and who looks so irresistible in candlelight—grew up in a fallible family with imperfect parents and depraved siblings.

BILL HYBELS, *MAKING LIFE WORK*

———◆◆◆———

Ah, the Ocoee River—a daring combination of class four and five rapids, the site of the kayaking venue for the 2000 Summer Olympics, and for years a favorite destination of the teenagers in our church. There's just something about the sheer unpredictability of these waters that draws visitors by the thousands to face the challenge.

Several years ago, a family from our church took their own trip down the Ocoee. The boys were in a raft with their dad and several other men, traveling in a convoy of five or six other rafts. With explosive splashes and frantic paddling, these rubber rafts negotiated the first few rapids—with no "swimmers" reported. But after their raft had made it through the third patch of white water, they turned to wait for the rest of the boats in their group. After a few minutes of waiting, they saw a crisis unfold.

Some people were clinging to the side of an upturned raft, and there were swimmers floating downstream. Guides were shouting frantic

commands to each other, and several people were jumping into the rapids with rescue equipment. With the emergency effort under way, word began to ripple upstream and downstream: A man had fallen in and was now underwater, and the teams were scrambling to pull him out before his seconds of breath ran out.

As seconds turned to minutes, and five minutes turned to fifteen, the rescue became a recovery effort, an arduous battle against the water to recover the body of the man who had drowned. As our friends waited and watched, the story became clear. The passenger had been thrown from the boat, and in an effort to get his balance, he simply did what came naturally: he put his feet down, instantly trapping them beneath a huge rock. The force of the rushing water pinned his feet so tightly that he simply couldn't dislodge himself.

Crashing currents can kill. The same currents that bring joy and pleasure bring devastation as well. It's true in white water, and it's true in marriage. What killed this man was not just the currents; it was, surprisingly, *doing what felt normal*. Over the years, he had learned that, when he felt out of control in the water, he should try to stand up. He simply did what came naturally.

> Crashing currents can kill. The same currents that bring joy and pleasure bring devastation as well.

How Did You Get to Be So Normal?

Over the years, we've seen couples in conflict over money or sex or in-laws, but what they're really fighting about aren't these things at all. They're really fighting about *normal*.

Every one of us enters into marriage with his or her own set of "commandments" about what is normal. But when you find yourself in explosive white water that puts you in over your head in your marriage, doing what feels normal can kill your relationship.

When Robert and Bobbie were first married, car trips for Bobbie were seen as opportunities to experience local flavor. Along the way she thought nothing of stopping at "Historical Markers" or quaint-looking shops, while Robert scratched his head in frustration as he watched his finely orchestrated, "point A to point B" itinerary disintegrate into one meandering interruption after another. It was her *normal* going head-to-head with Robert's *normal*. Bobbie's dad happily inter-

rupted family car trips with spontaneous visits along the way. Robert's dad only stopped when the gas tank was *below* empty.

In some marriages, avoiding conflict at all costs may feel normal to the husband, while talking everything out feels normal to the wife. Then, when it comes to disagreements, they get stuck. It's not because the topic is so thorny but because they have such different ideas about the right way—the normal way—to deal with conflict.

The Unspoken Rules of *Normal*

Maybe it's a rule about silence at the breakfast table while the husband reads the paper. Maybe it's a rule that says "the wife always takes care of family birthdays" or "the husband always takes out the trash" or "the wife always buys the groceries." Keep your eyes open in this first year, and you'll come up with plenty of examples of your own *normals*.

Identifying your own sense of *normal* is not as easy as it may look. Most of us assume that our rules of *normal* are universal—that of course every "normal person" sees life this way. Anything else is just plain *wrong*.

When couples come to us for premarital counseling, we spend three of the five sessions focused on this critical issue of discovering each one's *normals*. For many couples, it's the first time they've ever taken a look at the assumptions hiding in the back of their minds.

There is, thankfully, a marvelous tool that can help you and your husband begin to recognize your rules of *normal* in a nonthreatening way. Couples we've worked with have consistently pointed to this tool as the single most powerful part of the premarital preparation. Here's how it works: We start with something called a genogram, which looks like a simple family tree. *Why a family tree?* you may be thinking.

Our rules of *normal* almost always come from our families of origin. Bobbie didn't just arbitrarily assume that a car trip meant stops and adventures; she learned over the course of time that this was normal for her household. On the other hand, Robert couldn't imagine it.

In all our years of premarital counseling, we've never made it a point to ask about a couple's best friends, about their favorite TV shows, or even about their most influential mentors. But we *always* ask about their families. It's not that media and friends have no impact on our values; it's just that when it comes to the imprinting of our unspoken sense of *normal*, there is no single force that comes close to the

power of the family. What makes the genogram so effective is that it allows us to identify patterns of normal "in the family," not in the individual. And let's face it, most of us have a much easier time seeing the weirdness in our family than we do the weirdness in ourselves, right?

Making Your Own Genogram

To do your own genogram, you begin by each drawing a family tree that looks something like this:

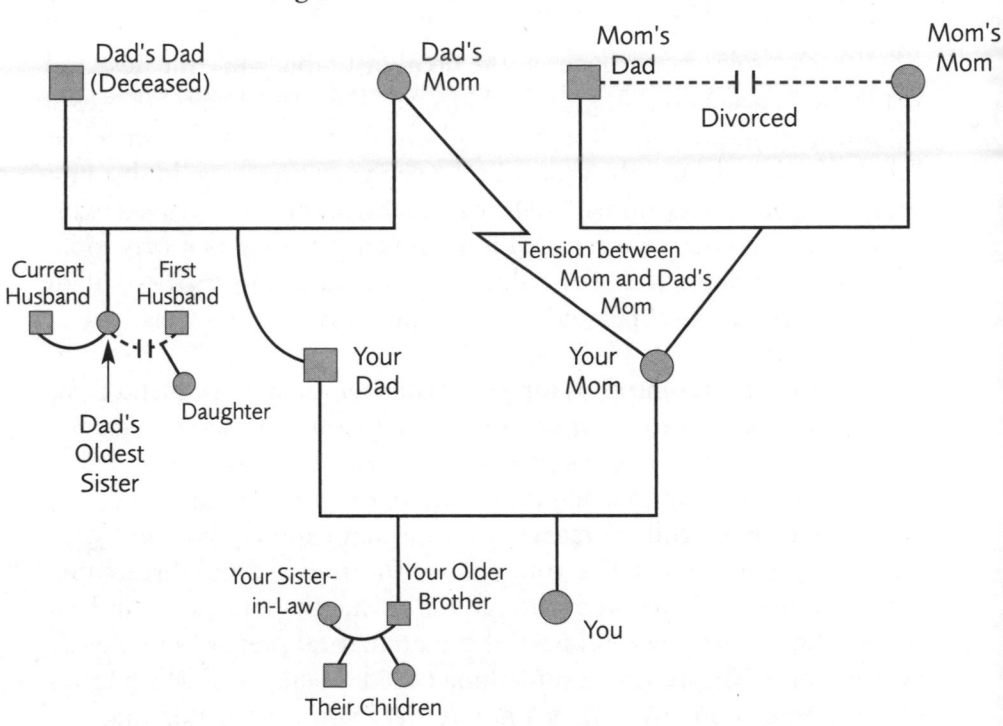

Once the drawing is done, we ask the bride or groom to give us a brief description of each person in his or her genogram. Those descriptions can vary widely from very specific comments—"president of IBM," "lifetime homemaker," or "serving time"—to more general words such as "nurturer," "strict," or "a jerk." As couples give this information, Mark urges them to say the first things that come to their minds, not to think too long about their answers. Their honest and immediate responses always provide the best clues to each one's sense of *normal*.

Once these initial descriptive notes are obtained, Mark asks for more information about parents and grandparents—always asking three questions:

- What can you tell us about their marriage?
- What can you tell us about how they dealt with conflict?
- What can you tell us about their spiritual life?

We also ask the bride and groom to identify any models of great marriages in their family systems or spots of tension between people within each of their families. From this information Mark writes a "Normal Report," which gives the bride and groom a picture of what an average person growing up in his or her family would see as normal. This report answers five questions:

1. What would someone growing up in this family system see as a normal husband?
2. What would someone growing up in this family system see as a normal wife?
3. What would someone growing up in this family system see as a normal marriage?
4. What would someone growing up in this family system see as a normal way to deal with conflict?
5. What would someone growing up in this family system see as a normal spiritual life for a married couple?

As we talk couples through the answers to these questions, the response is amazing. The vast majority of couples really get it. They leave this session with their eyes wide open, seeing their need to enter marriage prepared to do more than "what comes naturally."

Note this, too: Though there's much to be gained by working through a genogram with a trained counselor, you can experience some great success identifying *your normals* using the same process on your own.

Greg's and Carrie's Genograms

By the time Greg and Carrie finished their first premarital session, we liked them immensely. Greg seemed to be a guy who knew what he wanted out of life and marriage. He was a strong Christian with exceptionally high expectations of himself and his marriage. But during our conversation, we noticed a hint of anger just below the surface.

Carrie was a warm, responsive young woman who seemed to hang on every word that was said. By the time they arrived for the second session, they had already finished their assignments and asked if we could meet together for more than the agreed–upon five sessions!

There was nothing unusual about their genograms—showing mostly calm waters with five or six anticipated rough spots. As we talked through these, all four of us realized that there were currents beneath the surface that could present real challenges for this model young couple.

When they learned that we'd be talking about their families, Greg and Carrie laughed, describing his family as "The Cleavers" and her family as "The Simpsons." They both entered the process assuming, without question, that Greg's family was the stable one and that Carrie's was the dysfunctional one. Happily, Greg and Carrie were willing, even eager, to discover their potential danger zones.

Carrie's Family System

Carrie's parents divorced when she was a young teenager. Her father remarried soon after the divorce. Carrie lived with her mother, whom she described as "warm, busy, insecure, and pretty lonely." Her father was "strictly business, stern, cold, and a little on the quick-tempered side," and she described her stepmother as "bossy, selfish, and manipulative."

With a hint of resentment, Carrie also explained that she had never seen her father express physical affection to either of his wives or to her. When we asked why her parents divorced, she said, "I have no idea."

"Have you ever asked either of them?" Mark inquired.

"That's just not a question you bring up with my parents," Carrie answered matter-of-factly.

Looking at Carrie's extended family, we found:

- an aunt—"nice but a little on edge all the time"—who is married to a "very successful" man who works in Europe three weeks out of every month
- another aunt—"the loving one"—is married and divorced. Her ex-husband is a "deadbeat" who's had multiple affairs.
- a "powerhouse" uncle who is married to a "submissive" wife who has "some emotional problems."

Carrie's grandmothers are both still living; their "hardworking" and "stern" husbands both died before Carrie was born. One is a "normal grandmother" who sends cookies and birthday money. The other is described as a "witch" who "always has to have things her way."

As we completed Carrie's genogram, I asked, "Is there anything else you want to tell us about your family?"

"I'm really *so* different from them," she eagerly answered. "I've already promised myself that I will never let the way *they* are affect my marriage."

Carrie's genogram looked something like this:

Greg's Family System

Almost every man in Greg's family is described in "larger than life" terms. Looking into his genogram, we found several interesting things:

- his father is the "undisputed boss" who "is never ever questioned."

- one of his uncles is "explosive."
- his grandfather was humorously described as "the grand pooh-bah."
- one of his uncles is "large and in charge."

He portrayed several men in his family with simple superlatives such as "amazing" or "incredible man." Many of the husbands are very spiritual men, and several are pastors.

The women in Greg's family, on the other hand, are a different story:

- a fair share of "quiet and godly" wives—but these wonderful women are described in miniature in comparison to their husbands
- an aunt with an eating disorder
- a quietly alcoholic grandmother
- Greg's mother, whose chronic back pain has kept her out of commission for the last two years
- Greg's older sister—the "black sheep" of the family
- two female cousins, each of whom have had extramarital affairs

What Lies beneath the Surface?

Did you notice that normal women in both families tended to have more than their fair share of problems? Whether it was Carrie's insecure and lonely mother or her manipulative stepmother or any of the women in Greg's family who had experienced significant emotional or physical problems, the clear rule in both systems was this: "Wives tend to have problems." Even the way the two of them introduced their families with *his* "Cleavers" versus *her* "Simpsons" stereotype gave further evidence that they were already buying into the rule—normal wives have problems.

In both families, women seemed to have a difficult time getting their needs met in healthy ways. From affairs and addictions to vague emotional problems, it wouldn't be considered normal for a wife in this system to ask clearly for what she needs. Husbands in both systems had a pattern of being distant, out of reach, sometimes almost unapproachable. Whether they *appeared* to have it all together (like the men in Greg's system) or simply left the family (like Carrie's dad or her uncle commuting to Europe), the normal husband exhibited a pattern of not being available and of avoiding a wife's everyday struggles.

You may be wondering how this kind of pattern could be a dangerous undercurrent. Let's take an imaginary fast-forward journey five years into this marriage:

When they first got married, Greg was always the strong one, the one who had it together. Carrie loved this about Greg, and she relied on his strength. She liked him "being in charge" and taking care of her.

But now, after five years of marriage, she stares out the window, despair covering her like the blanket pulled up around her. She has her theories: Maybe it was her migraines that started a few years back, maybe it was the fact that she hasn't been able to get pregnant, maybe it was the fact that she hadn't prayed enough. But one thing seems clear to her: she no longer feels anything for this man she lives with.

He's a good man, a spiritual man. She respects him. She feels guilty that she hasn't worked hard enough to keep their marriage alive. But she's tired—tired of him never admitting he is wrong, tired of him ignoring her needs, tired of his arrogant, condescending attitude toward her whenever she brings up a problem.

How did Greg and Carrie get to this place? *They did what came naturally.* Because the men in Carrie's family are consistently distant, to keep Greg at a distance felt normal to her. Or, to overcompensate, she'd become clingy, craving Greg's attention and closeness. In Greg's case, in light of the pattern of troubled women in both families, he would blame Carrie for any unsettledness in their marriage. And Carrie might easily blame herself as well, not knowing how to ask her husband for what she really needs from him.

Carrie and Greg walked away from this genogram session with their eyes opened to the ways that the converging currents of their family systems could pose a very real threat to them. Their commitment now had a clearer focus on what it would take to keep their marriage alive and healthy. Carrie left the session with a fresh willingness to risk being attentive to *her own* needs and becoming courageous enough to share them honestly with Greg. Greg left, no longer infatuated with his own strength and convictions, but now committed to not perpetuating the pattern of placing his wife in the role of "the problem."

The Most Dangerous Enemy: The One You Don't See

It's dangerous to assume that only deeply dysfunctional people bring "issues" into their marriages. There are only two kinds of couples

preparing for marriage: those who seek to be honest about the issues they bring to marriage, and those who pretend they have none. The second group is headed for the rapids unprepared.

Someone once said, "I don't know who discovered water, but I'm real sure it wasn't a fish." When we are surrounded by *normal,* it's hard for us to see that it even exists. The marriages headed for serious trouble are the ones in which one of the partners is blind to the impact of his or her patterns of *normal.* He or she says such things as—

- "My family doesn't have any effect on who I am."
- "I've known this girl for years. It won't be a problem."
- "I'm so glad we don't have any weird stuff in our families."

Five years into our marriage, Mark and I entered some white water without being ready. Mark was sent for three days of psychological testing by a future employer. Looking back now, almost twenty years later, we laugh about this—the kind of nervous laughter that happens after you've just barely avoided an accident. But when we first heard the assessment, we weren't laughing.

> There are only two kinds of couples preparing for marriage: those who seek to be honest about the issues they bring to marriage, and those who pretend they have none.

After Mark completed his three days of testing, we sat in the vocational therapist's office waiting to hear the results. Anticipating a predictable outcome, we were actually looking forward to this report. Mark always performed well on tests, and we expected to hear such words as *highly motivated, exceptional,* and *wise beyond his years.* What we heard, however, was very different.

Turning toward me, the counselor said, "I want you to know that your husband is a very angry man." I stared in disbelief. Mark laughed. He really did. In fact, Mark was sure that the counselor had mixed up his report with someone else's. I'll never forget the way my husband looked at me—the woman he had lived with for five years. He said, "Tell him, honey. Am I an angry man? I'm the funny guy, remember? There may be other angry men in my family, but I'm not one of them."

But to Mark's amazement, I could not disagree with the counselor. In fact, I corroborated his report with supplemental evidence of my own. If you had asked Mark at that time, "How does your family affect

your marriage?" he would have been resolute: "Not very much. Our marriage is nothing like my parents' marriage." What Mark couldn't see was that his family *had* deeply influenced him. He was blind to the obvious. He was about to step into the same profession as the majority of men in his family and had already begun to live with some of the same unacknowledged patterns of anger. It was just *normal*.

During the subsequent months and years, Mark began the process of openly acknowledging his anger, eventually learning that if he didn't own it, it would own him and hold our family hostage. Once he recognized the dangerous undercurrent of anger, Mark was free to be playful about it.

When we lead marriage retreats, Mark loves to tell a story about how my playfulness has, at times, helped to free him from his anger. For reasons that will be obvious, I'll let Mark tell the story in his own words:

> Ten years into our marriage, I came home to a house that looked like three wild children lived there (they did, of course). Toys were strewn all over the playroom. Dishes were unwashed. There was a half-made sandwich on the counter that had obviously been there for hours.
>
> I'd had a particularly difficult day at work. I felt the anger rising in me. I quickly forgot the niceties. There was no "How was your day?" or "How can I help with dinner?" I simply came into the house, set my jaw, and began cleaning—"immaculating," as my children now call it. And before long, I had convinced myself of the absolute injustice of having to come home and clean a messy house after working long hours all day long.
>
> But my bride, who knows my genogram way too well, has learned how to interrupt my petty patterns of anger. I'll never forget that intense moment in the kitchen. After observing me huffing around for a few minutes, she resisted the urge to hook into my anger. She could have easily reacted by explaining that this just happened to be the maid's decade off, or she might have shot back with "I'm sorry you didn't marry June Cleaver."
>
> Instead, she said, "Here's what I want you to do: I want you to take off your tie, lie down on our bed for a few minutes, open that book you've been wanting to read, and then call me in a few minutes. When I get there, I want you to tell me how much you love me. Then maybe we can start all over again."

What Are We Arguing about Anyway?

In the heat of conflict, it's easy to become confused about what the real issues are. Our experience has been this: the more a couple focuses on the content of the conflict—issues like money, sex, in-laws, a messy kitchen—the more likely it is that they'll remain stuck in the conflict. On the other hand, the more a couple focuses on their genogram issues—patterns of anger and reaction, dominance and subservience, or power and helplessness—the more likely they'll move through those issues with love and respect intact.

The mistake most couples make when working through conflict is to focus on the wrong issue. For example, the domineering husband and the submissive wife may have a conflict about sex, but sex isn't the real issue. Or there may be a nagging wife and an unresponsive husband who think their conflict is about the children, but the real issue is the nagging/unresponsiveness pattern.

> The more a couple focuses on the content of the conflict, the more likely it is that they'll remain stuck in the conflict.

Jim and Irene weren't so fortunate. As we met with them week after week, they couldn't get beyond the assumption that their only real problem was money. One night, within earshot of their children, they were arguing about money yet again. The conflict escalated out of control, and Jim slapped Irene so hard that he broke her nose. They stood in startled amazement over what he had done. Blood began to run down Irene's face as their eight-year-old son ran into the room with his piggy bank, shouting, "You can have all of my money!"

Like the child who thinks the piggy bank will help, we can miss seeing the most dangerous currents of *normal* beneath our disagreements. It's these currents, not the subject matter of these disagreements, that will pose the greatest threat to your marriage.

5

Roles: Welcome to My World

A major source of love for a man is the loving reaction that a woman has to his behavior. He has a love tank, too, but his is not necessarily filled by what she does for him. Instead, it is mainly filled by how she reacts to him or how she feels about him. A man's heart opens as he succeeds in fulfilling a woman.

JOHN GRAY, *MEN ARE FROM MARS, WOMEN ARE FROM VENUS*

❧

ack in 1955, in a magazine called *Housekeeping Monthly,* an article for women appeared in the May 13 edition. It was titled "The Good Wife's Guide,"[10] and it outlined, in detail, the unique role a wife should play in a healthy marriage. In that very different world, expectations for wives were so clearly prescribed that they appear laughable to us today.

Here are a few of those tips for being a "good wife"—at least in the 1950s:

- Have dinner ready. Plan ahead, even the night before, to have a delicious meal ready, on time for his return. This is a way of letting him know that you have been thinking about him and are concerned about his needs.
- Prepare yourself. Take fifteen minutes to rest so you'll be refreshed when he arrives. Touch up your makeup, put a ribbon in your hair, and be fresh looking.
- Be a little gay and a little more interesting for him. His boring day may need a lift and one of your duties is to provide it.

- Clear away the clutter. Take one last trip through the main part of the house just before your husband arrives. Gather up schoolbooks, toys, paper, etc., and then run a dust cloth over the tables.
- During the cooler months of the year you should prepare and light a fire for him to unwind by. Your husband will feel he has reached a haven of rest and order, and it will give you a lift, too. After all, catering for his comfort will provide you with immense personal satisfaction.
- Prepare the children. Take a few minutes to wash the children's hands and faces (if they are small), comb their hair, and, if necessary, change their clothes. They are little treasures, and he would like to see them playing the part. Minimize all noise. At the time of his arrival, eliminate all noise of the washer, dryer, or vacuum cleaner. Try to encourage the children to be quiet.
- Greet him with a warm smile and show sincerity in your desire to please him.
- Listen to him. You may have a dozen important things to tell him, but the moment of his arrival is not the time. Let him talk first—remember, his topics of conversation are more important than yours.
- Make the evening his. Never complain if he comes home late or goes out to dinner or to other places of entertainment without you. Instead, try to understand his world of strain and pressure and his very real need to be at home and relax.
- Don't complain if he's home late for dinner or even if he stays out all night. Count this as minor compared to what he might have gone through that day.
- Make him comfortable. Have him lean back in a comfortable chair or have him lie down in the bedroom. Have a cool or warm drink ready for him. Arrange his pillow and offer to take off his shoes. Speak in a low, soothing, and pleasant voice.
- Don't ask him questions about his actions or question his judgment or integrity. Remember, he is the master of the house and as such will always exercise his will with fairness and truthfulness. You have no right to question him.

I'm sure you can imagine the responses we get when we read this prescription to couples. With each line of advice, the laughter only gets louder.

Back in the 1950s, the wife's role was prescribed with rigid clarity. And though this well-defined role was not exactly a recipe for exceptional marriages, there is little doubt that such clarity served at times to make marriages more stable, if less passionate. A man knew his role; a woman knew hers. And though a transformation of these expectations, particularly for wives, was undeniably necessary, the move toward more "egalitarian" marriages has frequently resulted in *less* equality and more rancorous confusion, not unlike a baseball team that plays with the vague idea that everyone should play every position. Balls get dropped, bases are left uncovered, accusations fly, and, more often than not, the team loses.

I was fascinated recently to read about the surprising results of a study of college students at three universities (Brandeis, UCLA, and Whittier College). Here's what the study revealed: "College-age couples who hold traditional views about gender roles are much more likely to make enduring marriages than couples who subscribe to egalitarian precepts."[11] There seems to be something about knowing our positions on the playing field of marriage that brings a protective stability to relationships between husbands and wives.

Whenever I teach about the Bible's perspective on the role of the wife in a marriage, I can feel the level of defensiveness rising before I even begin to speak. Actually, the defensiveness comes quite naturally. Many women have become appropriately angered by the self-serving spirituality of men who assume that their biblical role as husbands gives them the right to dominate and control their wives. But the Bible's message about our roles in marriage is quite different.

At first glance, when we look to the Bible for teaching about specific roles for husbands and wives, what we find seems disappointingly vague. Who pays the bills, who plans the vacation, who cleans the house, who shops for groceries, who has a career, who changes the diapers—none of these are answered in Scripture with regard to gender. But the Bible does something much more profound than prescribing specific tasks for husbands and other tasks for wives. When understood clearly, the roles the Bible describes for wives in marriage can free us from the tired oppositional approach to gender roles that easily results from assuming that men and women are from different planets.

So if a vague egalitarian approach does not work and the traditional model of the 1950s is distasteful at best (oppressive at worst), it may be time to consider a radically different option. The Bible, while not prescribing specific tasks, does give at least three clear directives for women about their role in marriage—describing attitudes that Christian wives are called to take toward their husbands. As you consider what the Bible has to say about roles in marriage, remember that *you* are in the driver's seat. Your husband cannot force you to adopt these attitudes. And, in fact, these attitudes *only* work when they're freely chosen by you.

Image Conscious

> So God created man in his own image,
> in the image of God he created him;
> male and female he created them.
>
> GENESIS 1:27

Even a quick reading of the creation story in Genesis 1 and 2 shows a God who fashions with order and purpose. Each stage of the creation builds, each is more complex, each is better than the one before—until the creation climaxes to its peak. And what, exactly, was this pinnacle?

I've heard Bible teachers explain that creation reached its highest point when God breathed life into Adam. But as I've read the story more closely, this interpretation seems implausible to me. After each stage of creation, we hear the rhythmic refrain, "And God saw that it was good." But after the creation of Adam, after Adam was placed in the garden, instead of hearing the consistent cadence of "it was good," the rhythm of creation is interrupted with four shocking words, "It is *not* good."[12] *What?* you may be thinking. *How can what God has created be somehow* not *good?* "It is not good," God says, "for the man to be alone." Apart from the creation of the woman, the creation story is simply incomplete. The man by himself is not enough.

And like a fireworks display that teases the crowd with a dramatic pause just before the grand finale—waiting long enough that the crowd begins to assume the show is over—God saves his best for last. Scripture does not teach, as some would have us believe, that the woman is an afterthought, a garnish on the real deal of creation, an inferior appendage to the main attraction. If we pay close attention to the story, it's hard to

miss the fact that in this narrative the woman is nothing less than the pinnacle of God's creation, a unique portrait of the image of God.

While Adam was sleeping, God didn't make a secretary, a concierge, a pet, or a maid for him. God made someone who would answer Adam's aching aloneness, one so totally *united* to Adam that they would enjoy an exclusive oneness together.

> While Adam was sleeping, God didn't make a secretary, a concierge, a pet, or a maid for him. God made someone who would answer Adam's aching aloneness.

In revealing the image of God, your husband and you each are part of the dance. God is best revealed not in some sort of neutered, unisex, genderless creation but in a gender-full creation—a creation in which husbands and wives are free to be fully man and fully woman.

Scripture invites us to see God uniquely displayed in our maleness and femaleness—in the passionate partnership between a husband and a wife. In marriage we have a picture of the rock-solid dependability and strength of God, in fluid partnership with the beauty and desirability of God, our unveiled Treasure who is to be worshiped and pursued. Psalm 62 hints at this gender-full nature of God:

> One thing God has spoken,
>   two things have I heard:
> that you, O God, are strong,
>   and that you, O Lord, are loving.
>
> PSALM 62:11–12

We can laugh about and be challenged by the startling differences between men and women. Yet, according to Scripture, these differences are no accident. They are, in fact, the intentional gift of a good God.[13]

Mark officiated at a wedding not long ago in which he made some personal remarks to the bride and the groom. As he spoke to the bride, he said, "Jenny, you are God's gift to Michael." Jenny laughed loudly. Even in the nervousness of the moment, it caught her by surprise that she could be called "God's gift" to anyone.

A woman who doesn't know who she is will settle for much less than God's best in her marriage. She is God's gift to her husband—God's image bearer. Without this knowledge, she will come to believe that she is not worth fighting for. She will come to assume that any unacceptable

treatment she receives from her husband is only what she deserves. She will give up on her grand dreams of loving a man who delights in her.

Help Me!

> But for Adam no suitable helper was found. So the LORD God caused the man to fall into a deep sleep; and while he was sleeping, he took one of the man's ribs and closed up the place with flesh. Then the LORD God made a woman from the rib he had taken out of the man, and he brought her to the man.
>
> GENESIS 2:20b–22

Eve is formed as the suitable *helper* of Adam. I have to admit that, when I first read this word in the creation story, it seemed as though Eve had been given some sort of second-class status, as though the real action remained with Adam. Eve, beautiful though she might have been, appeared somewhere in the background, perhaps cooking for and cleaning up after the real star of the show.

A woman who doesn't know who she is will settle for much less than God's best in her marriage.

But as I've studied this story over the years, a very different picture has come into focus. I was fascinated to discover that, apart from its use in this story to describe Eve, this specific word for *help* is used in Scripture almost always to describe God (not exactly a bit role in the universe, eh?). After the birth of Cain, Eve said, "With the *help* of the LORD I have brought forth a man."[14] Israel's King David later cried out, "Do not hide your face from me, do not turn your servant away in anger; you have been my *helper*."[15]

And in the book of Deuteronomy, we get an even clearer picture of what this help looks like:

> There is no one like the God of Jeshurun,
>   who rides on the heavens to *help* you
>   and on the clouds in his majesty.
> The eternal God is your refuge,
>   and underneath are the everlasting arms.
> He will drive out your enemy before you.
>
> DEUTERONOMY 33:26–27, emphasis added

In the Gospel of John in the New Testament, the Holy Spirit is referred to by the Greek word sometimes translated Helper.[16] The

condescension ("Look, it's Daddy's little helper!") we sometimes associate with the word is completely absent. Instead *helper* paints a picture of one who comes to rescue just in the nick of time.

Back in 1990, Bobbie played that very role in Robert's life. For six years, he and Bobbie had struggled to keep alive the entrepreneurial venture that was a dream come true just a few years earlier. But that February Robert received a devastating phone call from his banker telling him that the note was being called on his business. Suddenly they were faced with the reality of closing their office and sending sixteen employees home with no paycheck and an uncertain future. Because they had pledged their home for the bank loan, their personal equity was gone. Robert's confidence was understandably shaken.

> The wife is the one who is strong enough to believe in her husband when he may be too weak to believe in himself.

The next day, with countless details to manage, Bobbie sprang into action. Like a warrior, she used the only weapons at her disposal—her time, her compassion, and her words. After each employee was told there would be no more work, Bobbie hugged them and cried with them. As the office furniture was loaded into a van, Robert and Bobbie stood together in shocked silence. Then, sitting on the carpeted floor of a once beautiful executive office, with only a phone left in the room, Bobbie began calling clients. As she dialed each number, she prayed for the person who would be receiving the message that their business had been forced to close. After each conversation, she calmly reported to Robert. With confidence and tenderness she continued the recovery operation until every client and merchant had been contacted.

When a husband's back is against the wall, the wife is like the cavalry that charges over the hill. The wife is like Superman or the Lone Ranger, stepping in to save the one who cannot rescue himself. The wife is the one who is strong enough to believe in her husband when he may be too weak to believe in himself. In fact, in those few instances in the Bible when *helper* is not used to refer to God, it always refers to a warrior who rescues others in a battle.

Embracing our role as helpers doesn't prevent us, though, from having a life of our own. Just take a look at how the biblical version of the ideal wife—"the Proverbs 31 woman"—spends her time:

- She runs an import/export business (31:13–14).
- She manages employees (31:15).
- She buys real estate (31:16).
- She receives a financial gain on her investments (31:16).
- She plants a vineyard (31:16).
- She earns a profit from her business (31:18).
- She gives to the poor and needy (31:20).
- She furnishes her house (31:22).
- She dresses well (31:22).
- She is a wholesaler of products to other merchants (31:24).
- She teaches (31:26).
- She runs a household (31:27).
- Her success earns her public praise (31:31).

All of this is accomplished because she takes the initiative. Ironically, behind every Proverbs 31 woman is a Proverbs 31 husband—a man secure enough in his own strength that he isn't threatened by the successes of his bride.

Your husband needs you as a helper. He may not know it; he may not admit it. But he needs you.

Is Submission Really a Dirty Word?

Submit to one another out of reverence for Christ.

Wives, submit to your husbands as to the Lord. . . .

Husbands, love your wives, just as Christ loved the church and gave himself up for her. . . .

However, each one of you also must love his wife as he loves himself, and the wife must respect her husband.

EPHESIANS 5:21–22, 25, 33

When I told Mark that Bobbie and I were going to address submission in this chapter, his eyebrows rose and he got that playful little smirk he gets whenever he thinks I've bitten off more than I can chew. We've both seen how easily this topic can spark controversy. We've seen fire in the eyes of people in our Sunday school classes when we even mention the word. We've watched defenses fly up faster than a force field on the Starship Enterprise.

We are convinced that a biblical understanding of submission holds a key to our experiencing marriage at its best. But in order to use this key, we have to first understand clearly what Scripture means when it urges a wife to submit to her husband. Though there is more than enough room for clouds of confusion on this topic, we can be clear that submission in the Bible means at least two things:

Submission Is Mutual

In Ephesians 5, the primary role of husbands and wives in marriage is defined: "Submit to one another." Here, submission is not related to gender at all. In the apostle Paul's male-dominated culture, the notion of husbands *ever* submitting to their wives undoubtedly sounded scandalous. But Paul was on to something. The truth is that healthy adults all submit to something—whether it is to the truth, to love, to God, to a relationship, or to the board of directors.

No relationship, in fact, can succeed without submission. And in reality, in the healthiest marriages we've ever seen, there is a sort of reverse tug-of-war in which husband and wife make a game of who can give victory to the other partner first.

Submission Is Voluntary

Paul never advises husbands to *make* their wives submit. In fact, the command to husbands is just the opposite. Instead of telling husbands, "Make your wives behave," Paul advises them simply to "love your wives" as radically and sacrificially "as Christ loved the church." Christian husbands who lay the "submission trip" on their wives are missing the point entirely, since the only way that submission can work *for* the marriage is when it is given voluntarily and without compulsion.

The biblical model of submission is this: the willing choice of a wife to submit freely to her husband and his willingness to lovingly submit to her. Watch people who have healthy marriages, and you'll see this kind of willful submission happening all the time:

- the wife who accepts with grace her husband's recommended cuts to the family budget; the husband who accepts the same from his wife
- the husband who moves to a new town because of an unparalleled career opportunity offered to his wife; the

wife who moves for the sake of her husband's career
change
- the wife who occasionally chooses to watch the game
  with her husband, giving up a cozy chair and a gripping
  novel; the husband who attends a concert with his wife
  when she's bought special tickets
- the husband who goes to the romantic comedy instead of
  the action adventure movie; the wife who willingly goes
  to his choice of a show
- the wife who fills the car with gas instead of waiting for
  him to do it; the husband who stops to fill the car's gas
  tank for his wife

Mark and I have an understanding that goes something like this: "If
we ever get stuck and we're unable to agree on what to do, I want you
to win." It is in and through this voluntary kind of yielding that the
marriage always wins.

What Submission Is *Not*

After agreeing together on what submission is, it's important that we
be clear about at least a couple of things that submission is not:

Submission Does Not Turn a Wife into a Passive Pawn

Biblical submission is not about a woman giving up on her passions,
her dreams, her opinions, or her identity in order to please her husband. If your husband wants to move across the country to take on a
new job opportunity and you feel uneasy about it, tell him. Openly
express your reservations. Tell him exactly how you feel and why.
Responding with a "whatever you want, honey" passivity and pretending to be in total agreement are not accurate expressions of submission. They're *dishonest* expressions.

Several years ago, Mark and I were at a stalemate on a decision. We
were behind on several bills. They were "forgiving bills," not like credit
cards that charge interest; they were bills to the doctor, debt payments
to family members—that kind of thing. Normally, I handle the bills in
our house, but one day Mark decided that we needed to go ahead and
pay these bills, even if it meant dipping into our savings. I wasn't convinced of the wisdom of that decision. I pointed out that we were antic-

ipating receiving some additional money in the next couple months. I reminded him of how much we hate to live so close to the edge. I urged him to wait to pay the bills. But after making my case, here was my concluding thought: "But I trust you. And I will support whatever you decide on this one."

We went ahead and paid the bills. Was it the right thing to do? Maybe. Did I yield to Mark's influence because he is "the man of the house"? No. There have, in fact, been many times when he responded in the same way for me—courageously and sacrificially ending a difference of opinion before it became an argument. But in this case, I simply trusted him to make the final call. Either way, we invite each other into maturity and love.

Submission Does Not Require a Wife to Tolerate Abuse

You may be saying, "Okay, a mutual and voluntary kind of submission makes sense, but what about a wife in an abusive marriage? Does the Bible teach that she should submit to her husband if he abuses her, destroying her with caustic words or with violent hands?"

These are the very questions Jean asked me a few years ago as we ate lunch together. She and Frank had been married for less than six months, and she had just moved out of her newlywed apartment. I swallowed hard, bit my tongue, and listened.

Pulling up her sleeve, Jean showed me month-old bruises, and asked if I supported her decision to move out.

My eyes welled up with tears as I looked into Jean's face. "Love," I said, "does not require you to be a willing partner in your husband's destructive behavior. You've done the right thing. Now you must confront him clearly and firmly with a message that says unequivocally, *I love you, but this is not acceptable.*" I said, "Unless he's willing to change immediately, the most loving thing you can do is to separate." I gave her the names of several Christian doctors and organizations in our area that specialized in abuse counseling.[17]

If you or someone you know is dealing with a husband's physical, verbal, or emotional abuse, alcoholism, philandering, or pornography—or any form of violent behavior—please get help. You have no obligation to give in to this. This is *not* submission. In fact, love *requires* your protection of yourself and the vows you made.

Dancing the Roles

In our bathroom we have a picture of dancers in each others' arms. It's a Renoir painting called "A Dance in the Country." A bearded young man is holding his beaming partner in his arms. I get the impression that he has just whispered something into her ear—something she finds exceedingly charming or funny.

Over the years, as Mark and I have talked about the peculiar roles that each of us play in our marriage, we've found no better picture than our "Dance in the Country." We can't dance well together without a willingness to be mutually responsive to each other. We'll never enjoy the music as long as we're rigidly focused on the inflexible "rules" of the dance. The waltz will always work best if our steps are fluid and graceful—sometimes he moves forward and I follow, and sometimes I set the pace.

Great marriages *are* great dances, and those who are willing to move together nimbly will have the most fun of all.

6

Talk: Did Someone Hit the Mute Button?

So you look at us with one of those 250,000 facial expressions you can make as a woman, put your hand on your hip, and say things like, "When are you going to get with the program!" Many men do not have a clue to the program!

GARY SMALLEY, *THE HIDDEN VALUE OF A MAN*

------◆◆◆------

At their first premarital counseling session, Charlie and Meredith couldn't keep their hands off each other. They moved their chairs as close together as they could get them. They talked about how much they loved being together, how conversation flowed so naturally, how comfortable they felt with each other. Mark and I found this kind of open affection refreshing.

We got around to the topic of communication in marriage. As we began to talk about some challenges they were likely to face, they looked at us in disbelief, with expressions you might expect to see on the face of Michael Jordan receiving ball-handling tips from my mother. These lovebirds made it clear that this was information for some other couple, not for them.

"We appreciate your concern for us," they politely interrupted, "but we've got to tell you, this is an area where we just don't need any help."

At this point, I couldn't help thinking of Yoda's promise to Luke. I remembered young Skywalker in his training, saying, "But Master Yoda, I'm not scared." Yoda's head rolled slowly to one side as he responded, with eyes locked on his young apprentice, "You will be. You *will* be."

The vast majority of couples we've counseled have had very little difficulty with conversation—before the wedding, that is. During the

premarital "falling in love" stage, conversation can feel a lot like jumping off a diving board. After the leap, there's plenty of gravity to keep you moving in the right direction, and very little effort is required to get you where you need to go. During this stage, couples typically find themselves talking with comfort and ease. But after the wedding, it can feel a lot more like swimming in the deep end. You only stay afloat with effort.

One woman may enter marriage with an unquestioning "he completes me" attitude. But within the first year, that same woman can find herself in postmarital shock, as simple conversation becomes increasingly difficult with the man who used to be her soul mate. And when Captain Understanding mutates into Dr. Clueless, a bride can naturally feel as though someone changed all the rules without telling her.

There are few areas where the differences between men and women are more obvious than in the area of conversation. And though not every man fits into every stereotypical description, there are certain qualities about many men and their communication styles that, if you learn them in this first year, can save you years of frustration.

Is Deafness Really a Part of His Gender Coding?

We don't have to look far to find complaints and jokes about husbands who just don't seem to listen. C. S. Lewis put these words in the mouth of one of his fictional characters: "Husbands were made to be talked to. It helps them concentrate their minds on what they're reading."[18] More recently, a Christian nonfiction writer wrote these clearly *nonfictional* words: "Husbands, listen to your wives. Wives, speak the truth in love to your deaf husbands."[19] And even Jane Austen, in her book *Sense and Sensibility,* affirms, "Between lovers, no subject, no communication is even made till it has been made at least twenty times over."[20]

I hope you understand. Husbands have a God-given mandate to cherish their wives, to listen to them, to respond to their needs. And most of them enter marriage with the absolute intention of doing just that. So why do these well intentioned husbands often fail when it comes to really communicating with their wives?

Imagine this scene: Your husband is lost. Against his nature as it is, he finally breaks down and decides to ask for directions. (I know this isn't a fiction book, but stay with me.) He sees a man walking a dog in a residential neighborhood, pulls over, rolls down the window, and

asks, "Excuse me, could you tell me how to get downtown?" But instead of answering, the guy keeps walking.

Your husband gives the guy the benefit of the doubt and assumes the pedestrian just didn't hear him. So he pulls forward and speaks again— this time more loudly: "Hey, mister, I'm lost! You want to give me some directions?" This time the man just stares, opens his mouth to say something, then shrugs his shoulders a little, and keeps walking. By this time, your boy is not happy.

Finally, he steps out of the car, approaches to within a few feet from the stranger, and asks for directions a third time. The stranger can see the frustration and anger all over your husband's face, and words immediately begin to fly from the stranger's mouth. But your husband can't understand a thing the guy is saying. Why not? *He's speaking in Chinese.*[21]

Once we realize that the object of our frustration doesn't have a clue what we are saying, anger no longer makes sense, does it? But husbands and wives often find themselves trapped in patterns of anger created by a very similar problem. It's as though we are speaking completely different languages. Call it "Mars and Venus"; call it "his needs and her needs"; call it different "love languages." But there does seem to be general agreement that men and women communicate in very different ways. Because you and your husband both use the same vocabulary and the same grammar, you can easily assume that, when you send a message—which you understand—to your husband, he will understand the message that was sent—exactly as you understood it.

> When you bring a concern to your husband, he'll typically assume one of two things: (1) that you want him to fix the problem (resulting in advice giving), or (2) that he's being attacked (resulting in defensiveness).

Misunderstandings in conversations between husbands and wives do not only occur around situations of intense conflict. They happen all the time, particularly to couples who have never recognized their tendency to speak different languages. Consider this hypothetical conversation:

> *Wife:* "You never hold me anymore. You could tell how sad I was this morning after I heard the news about my mom. I needed you to hug me, but you just avoided me."

> *Husband:* "I thought you needed some space. How was I supposed to know you needed a hug? If you needed a hug, why didn't you just ask me?"
>
> *Wife:* "That's exactly the point. I shouldn't *have* to ask you. You know how much I need affection. Before we got married, you sure didn't have trouble showing me affection. Now it's like I have to turn in a request form just to get you to hold my hand."
>
> *Husband:* "You're doing it again. If I don't hug you, I get in trouble. If I offer to hug you, I still get in trouble. No matter what I do, you're not satisfied."[22]

Something got lost in the translation, didn't it? What this wife is saying is that she loves to be close to her husband and would be thrilled if he'd take the initiative to hold her more often, especially when she's going through tough times. What her husband hears is that he's in trouble for not being able to read his wife's mind. You see, when you bring a concern to your husband, he'll typically assume one of two things: (1) that you want him to fix the problem (resulting in advice giving), or (2) that he's being attacked (resulting in defensiveness). These assumptions are his default settings.

Let's face it. Something in us really does want our husbands to read our minds. I would love it if Mark always knew exactly what to do for me without my having to say a word. But he needs me to tell him!

What the husband in this dialogue is trying to say is that he loves his wife and is willing to hold her or to give her space or to do whatever else she needs, but that he doesn't always know what she wants from him. He is saying that he needs more clarity from her. What she hears, though, is that he doesn't love her the way he used to love her.

Deafness is *not* an inherent part of your husband's genetic coding. He is simply wired to hear things differently from what you intended to communicate. But language differences need not push you apart. If you've ever had a dinner guest whose command of the English language is limited, you know what I mean. We've shared dinners with people whose knowledge of English is equivalent to our knowledge of their language. At first, conversation is difficult, but by the end of the evening,

we are leaning in toward each other, intensely listening in order to understand, often laughing at ourselves as we play impromptu charades.

Differences in the way you communicate with your husband can either launch you into a cold war of misunderstanding or draw you closer, leaving you loving and laughing with each other as you lean in to gain greater levels of understanding.

Relational Amnesia

What happened? Tori wondered, nine months into her marriage. During the three years she dated Wes, they talked effortlessly for hours on end. But now it seemed to be so much work.

Finally she asked her husband, "What happened? I know we know how to do this!"

Wes was more right than he realized when he joked, "Maybe we just forgot."

It happens to most couples. We spend months, even years, in a courtship filled with incredible conversations. But a few months or years into the marriage, it's easy to develop what we call "relational amnesia." Forgetting the ways we used to talk, we settle into patterns of conversation that are unsatisfactory to both of us. When it happens to you, two principles can help you overcome this amnesia:

- *Remember* the little things you said and did when your relationship was new and growing.
- *Repeat* those words and patterns by intentionally saying and doing what came so naturally during your courtship.

Almost without exception, what we are looking for in conversations with our husbands is to *know their hearts.* For many of us, it was the fact that our husbands allowed us glimpses into their hearts and told us things they had never told anyone else that gave us such certainty that "this is the one."

It may not be an overstatement to say that a wife longs to know her husband's soul with the same intensity that a husband longs to know his wife's body. And just as there are certain things your husband can do that are huge sexual turnoffs to you, the words you speak can either swing open or slam shut your husband's spirit.

Can Openers to Your Husband's Soul

To help you open the door to your groom's heart, we've developed what we call "Can Openers to Your Husband's Soul."

Can Opener #1: Conversational Clarity

In the dialogue on pages 69–70, the husband and wife both wound up frustrated—unable to communicate what they were really trying to say. Of course, in the wife's mind, it was absolutely clear what the husband should have done. He should have "figured it out" and just held her when she heard the news about her mom.

Though you may naturally expect your husband to understand what you need without obvious communication from you, my advice is, *Don't count on it!* A woman who waits around for her husband to figure out what it is that she needs from him will likely be waiting a very long time.

Early in our marriage, Mark learned that I didn't want to "be fixed" when I went to him with a problem. Sometimes I simply needed him to listen. And so he learned to listen and seldom offered his opinion. But we discovered—the hard way—that Mark's listening-only response wasn't always what I really wanted. Sometimes I *did* want Mark to come up with a few ideas, and still other times I really did want him to make a decision. But, Murphy's Law being what it is, Mark almost always guessed wrong—he advised when he should have listened; he listened when I really wanted his input; he gave options when I really just needed a decision.

Recognizing that I don't always need the same kind of response from him every time, one day Mark tried out a solution to our "translation frustration." He said something like this: "Is this one of those times when you want my advice, or do you need me to make a decision, or do you just want me to listen?" His question helped me clarify for myself what I needed from him.

Take a typical conversation about where I wanted to go for dinner:

Mark: "Where would you like to go out for dinner this weekend?"

Me: "I don't know. Where do you want to go?"

Now, remember—at this point, Mark is simply wanting to make me happy, to take me to a place I would enjoy. He really doesn't care where

we go to dinner. But he's in a quandary as to how to respond. He could say, "I don't care," but I might be tired of making decisions and just want him to pick a place. He could simply choose a restaurant, but he really wants to go somewhere that I will enjoy. He could give me a list of options. He could plan the whole date on his own and completely surprise me. So now Mark has learned that, before he responds to this very simple question, he needs help with the translation.

> *Mark:* "Babe, is this one of those times when you want me just to plan the whole date so you don't have to worry about it, or is it one of those times you've got a special place in mind where you'd really like to go, or is this one of those times when you want me to give you a list of options and let you pick the place you'd like to go?"
>
> *Me:* "Actually, this is one of those times when . . ."

As simple—or absurd—as it may sound, these seven words ("this is one of those times when . . .") can do wonders for the translation frustration and lead to open and productive conversation with your husband.

Many men stop being conversationalists with their wives because too many conversations end with the husband feeling as though he just didn't get it right. As a result he begins to say such things as "I'm just not good at mind reading" or "communication is just not my thing."

Mark plays golf the same way a lot of men communicate. Early in his golfing career, he decided—with the help of a few overly honest friends—that he stunk at the game. Once he made that decision—after just five games—guess how often he played. Though he is surrounded by good friends who love to play golf, he hasn't picked up a club in ten years.

When a man becomes convinced that he is "no good at talking" with his wife, he stops playing the conversation game altogether. Practicing the "Can Opener of Conversational Clarity" can help your husband feel like a success and can go a long way toward keeping him in the game.

Can Opener #2: Third-Object Conversation

Think about how men typically build friendships: by *doing something*—on the athletic field, around a poker table, in a foxhole, in front

of a television, on a mission trip. Women, on the other hand, are quite content to build friendships just by talking. Take a stroll through a coffee shop and you'll see what I mean. Two women sitting together—nothing but coffee and conversation between them. But two men will usually have something there—their newspapers, their Day-Timers, their Palm Pilots, sometimes just a napkin on which they are graphing their ideas. When men talk, there is almost always a third object.

Mark has a close friend who is a pastor. They meet together at least once a week for an hour and a half or so. They have incredible conversations about family, work, fears, and failures. They pray together and challenge each other, and they also have comfortable times of silence. And they do all of this *while they're running.*

Here's what you can learn: Talking with each other during a shared activity can be the doorway for your husband to begin to tell you what really matters to him. Because good conversation is important to you, make it your job to find opportunities for third-object conversations. For example, when he's headed out the door on Saturday morning to go to his favorite home improvement store, offer to go along. Your conversation in the car and as you wander the aisles will come naturally.

While she was in her seventies, Bobbie's mother-in-law found a way to create conversations with her often quiet husband by leasing a small garden plot. Twice a week they rode their bikes from their condominium to their tiny vegetable farm. And for her, the results were more wonderful than basketfuls of plump tomatoes or fresh green snap peas.

You and I often get to substantive conversation through nondirected—what our husbands might consider "pointless"—conversation. Let me explain what I mean. Your husband might think, *Why would my wife care about the boring details of my day? She's just being kind by asking, so I'll do her the favor of not wasting her time with a lot of useless trivia.*

And so when you ask about his day, he gives you the "Cliffs Notes" version, which usually lasts no more than fifteen seconds. You feel hurt, wondering why he doesn't want to share his life with you. Your husband thinks he's being kind by not boring you with the details. But he must learn that meandering conversation—sharing what he may see as pointless detail—is the most direct route to opening your heart to him.

Can Opener #3: Pillow Talk

The application of this third can opener—pillow talk—takes place in a specific place and at a specific time, namely, in your bedroom in the few moments you have together just before you go to sleep at night.

Mark is a morning person, and I'm a night owl, but we're together on this idea. Pillow talk doesn't require the same schedule every night, but it does require that, at least once a week, you both make a point of heading to bed at the same time.

First, let me be clear about what you don't want to talk about during pillow talk. It's not the time to bring up potentially contentious topics or ones that require the expenditure of a good deal of energy. As a matter of fact, as a general rule we recommend that couples avoid difficult topics after 7:00 P.M. I've never seen any studies on this, but I'm sure most couples have their worst conflicts late in the evenings when they are exhausted and easily frustrated. So be careful not to push your husband to resolve a conflict when both of you are potentially at your worst. On those occasions when you must deal with a specific source of frustration, do it with both feet on the floor, eyeball to eyeball.

Pillow talk is also *not* the time for the kind of romantic exchange that demands a response. This is a for-free gift that you give your husband, not expecting anything in return. You can ruin perfect pillow talk by saying, "I love you so much," then pausing to wait for a response and going on to say, "Well—don't you have anything to say?!" That's *not* a for-free gift.

Pillow talk is, however, a way to seal the end of your day with kind, flirtatious, and encouraging words that remind your husband of your love for him. Your husband can even fall asleep while you're in the middle of pillow talk. That's okay. What you are doing is creating a context for conversation with your husband that is pleasantly intimate because he *cannot fail.*

During pillow talk, he can enjoy listening without worrying that he may say something stupid. As your husband ends his day hearing such things as, "Have I told you lately how much I love you?" or "I loved it when you called me in the middle of your day today," he will see conversation with you as a safe and delightful place to be. This is the time for unqualified encouraging words. So be careful not to ruin perfectly good pillow talk by taking a statement such as "You are so

compassionate to strangers" and then adding, "Why don't you ever treat me that well?"

Here's the important principle: When you want to get close to your husband, you only set yourself up for frustration by expecting him to do the talking. Comments like "You never talk to me" only push him away. But when you take the initiative to offer "for-free" conversation—a safe place where he cannot fail—he is much more likely to feel close to you and be willing to risk talking more in the future.

Your husband's heart can be opened if you will help him succeed at conversation with you. A woman who gives her husband the gift of conversational clarity, third-object conversation, and pillow talk builds a bridge to her husband's heart that she can cross comfortably and safely for decades to come.

7

Friendship: The Secret Ingredient

This is my lover, this my friend.
SONG OF SONGS 5:16

———◆※◆———

ven on the answering machine, I could hear the quiver in her voice. Something was very wrong. "Susan," Jessica said, "we really need to talk to you and Mark as soon as possible. Please call me?"

We returned the call immediately. "We just got your message. We're both on the phone. What's up?"

She responded with characteristic kindness: "I'm so sorry to bother you. I know how busy you are. How was your anniversary?"

"It was fine," I answered. Then, quickly changing the topic, I said, "We could tell by your message that something's really wrong. What's going on?"

Through quiet sobs, she explained, "I knew something hasn't been right for months. Then tonight I found this folder of letters from a woman Jeff works with. He's admitted to everything, but he says he wants to change. What are we going to do?"

It was a long night—and a long year—as these two battled *together* to rebuild their marriage. There was no question they were willing to do whatever it took to get their marriage back on track. In addition to meeting with us, they attended a marriage enrichment retreat. They read books. They had double dates with other couples whose marriages they admired. But if you ask them today what saved their marriage, they'd say there was one decision that kept them hanging in there when they might otherwise have given up. What was it? It was the choice to build back *their friendship.*

I know. It sounds so unromantic, so simplistic. *What does rebuilding a friendship have to do with rescuing a marriage as troubled as Jessica and Jeff's?* you might be wondering.

The answer is *everything*.

Friendship: The Marriage-Saving Vaccine

University of Washington researcher John Gottman is what we call "a marriage inoculation specialist." He has brought a rigorous scientific approach to understanding what makes marriages work and what makes them fail. After years of observation and analysis, Gottman claims to be able to predict the future success or failure of the marriages he has observed with an accuracy rate of over *90 percent*. And usually, he says, he can make this determination within just a few minutes of observing a couple.

How does he do it? Gottman has discovered certain basic patterns that are marriage destroyers and others that are marriage protectors. And, far and away, the most significant marriage protector he has discovered is (are you ready to be underwhelmed?)—a couple's ability to be friends with each other:

> The determining factor in whether wives feel satisfied with sex, romance, and passion in their marriage is, by 70 percent, the quality of the couple's friendship. For men, the determining factor is, by the same 70 percent, the quality of the couple's friendship. So men and women come from the same planet after all.... Friendship fuels the flames of romance because it offers the best protection against feeling adversarial toward your spouse.[23]

In many ways building a friendship with your spouse is not a matter of learning new skills but simply accessing the ones you already have. Think back to our phone conversation with Jessica. Despite the fact that she was caught up in the emotions of anger and disappointment, she was able to put a hedge around those emotions and address us with her typical kindness and respect.

When it comes to conflicts between husbands and wives, we often assume that we *can't help* speaking to our spouses with disrespect and unkindness. Because I know my friend Jessica's personality well, I'm sure that the voice she was using with us ("I'm sorry to bother you. How was your anniversary?") was a voice long ago removed from her

tone with her husband. She knew how to speak to us as friends but had forgotten how to do the same with Jeff.

The secret to healing this marriage was not to be found in an extravagant romantic getaway or in some revolutionary marriage-restoration breakthrough. It was going to be found in Jeff and Jessica relearning the principles of friendship that had come so naturally in the early years of courtship.

Friends Give Time: A Prescription for the Time-Starved Marriage

Check out any cereal box (or most packaged food items, for that matter), and you'll read about "minimum daily requirements"—amounts of certain vitamins, minerals, or fibers we need if we hope to stay healthy. Without these requirements being met, our bodies become anemic, weak, unable to fight off even a small infection.

If you want to keep your marriage healthy, if you want to develop the kind of friendship that can protect your marriage, it will take time. Time together. Without it, your marriage's immune system can become dangerously weak. And the little irritations that are a normal part of life will all too quickly become unmanageable.

Creating time to be together seldom comes without a fight—not against each other but against your schedules. The demands of work, volunteer opportunities, friends, extended family, even church can all pull you away from each other with a powerful force. Couples who simply go with the flow of their schedules may find that the underlying current does anything but draw them together. If there's any area of your marriage in which you'll need to be aggressive and intentional, it's in this area of ensuring that you make time to be together.

Creating time to be together seldom comes without a fight—not against each other but against your schedules.

The Slot System

If Mark and I were sitting alongside you right now, he would pull out his Day-Timer and flip through the monthly calendar pages. You would find, on almost every week, little circled numbers scattered throughout; some days have three numbers circled; many days have none.

Mark perfected this practice after a series of very difficult conversations with me. When we were in our mid-twenties, I was painfully

aware of my husband's tendency to jam-pack his schedule. I knew we could easily settle into a dangerous pattern of his saying yes to more and more opportunities and becoming less and less available for our marriage. Mark used to say, "It'll all work out. Don't worry about it." But I needed the security of a plan—a plan we could agree on *before* we drifted apart.

That's when we came up with the *slot system,* a process we've taught to hundreds of couples—a single strategy that has done more for keeping our marriage healthy than almost anything else we have done. It may sound a bit calculated and unromantic, but, like many recommendations for the first year of marriage, great marriages are built on the little choices normal couples tend to overlook.

Here's how the plan works: We look at our time together in one-week blocks, dividing each day into three distinct slots—morning, afternoon, and evening. Each slot has a meal, and each slot involves a block of time. A morning slot, for example, begins with waking up and ends around noontime. The afternoon slot begins with lunch and ends around 5:00 P.M. The evening slot begins around 5:30 or 6:00 and ends at bedtime.

Over the years, we've learned that keeping our marriage healthy required a minimum of six slots together in a normal week. And the more unpredictable our schedules become, the more rigidly we need to practice the slot system. With this system, *you* get to rule your schedule and make your marriage a priority; without it, *your schedule* rules you, and your marriage loses by default. And that's exactly what was happening to Todd and Melanie.

Todd and Melanie had entered marriage with their eyes wide open to the challenges they would face. They were willing to do "whatever it takes" to make their marriage thrive. In fact, one of the agreements they had made in their premarital counseling two years earlier was that if their relationship ever got below "excellent," they would come in and talk with us—and that's why they were now sitting in Mark's office.

Melanie began. "Something's missing," she said. Todd nodded in agreement. "We entered marriage intending to dance together, but it feels like we're just plodding along, trying to make our marriage work."

Todd added, "It's like our car isn't running on all cylinders—like our wheels are turning without the bearings."

When we asked Todd and Melanie how they were doing in making time to be together, they both laughed—almost always a good sign in marriage counseling.

"What's so funny?" Mark asked.

"It's just nuts right now," Todd said. "What with starting a new business, I'm working late most nights. I typically get home around 8:00, and I'm exhausted. And that's when we get into our worst fights."

We asked about weekends. Melanie explained that Todd was working nearly every Saturday. She said they tried to grab some time together whenever they could. Most Sundays Melanie led the children's choir at church and Todd helped out with the youth group in the afternoon. "We've been good about having our date night on Saturday nights," Melanie added. "But lately, there's just been a lot of tension, even when we're doing something fun."

In a typical week, Todd and Melanie had only two slots together. Their schedule looked something like this:

Sunday	Monday	Tuesday	Wednesday	Thursday	Friday	Saturday
1. Church together	**W**	**O**	**R**	**K**	**!**	Todd works until 4:00 Mel and Todd Lunch
Youth Group 3:00– 6:30 P.M.	**W**	**O**	**R**	**K**	**!**	Todd golfs with the guys
7:00 Mel's Junior League	Dinner at 8:30 after work	Dinner at 9:45—after church mtg.	Dinner with Mel's parents at 7:00 (w/ or w/o Todd)	Dinner at 8:30 after work	Meet at the game for dinner	2. Date night

Todd and Melanie had forgotten the one thing this "newborn baby" marriage of theirs needed most: Time. *Quantity time* together does for marriage what an oil change does for a car. Of course, a car can go for a good while without an oil change before any problems become evident, but eventually the car starts to run sluggishly and unpredictably.

We asked Todd and Melanie to take a look at the upcoming week and select six slots when they could be together. Mark encouraged them *not* to think of these times simply in terms of one-on-one romantic getaways.

These slots could be taken up with running errands together, watching TV, taking a nap, having dinner together with friends, or even just hanging around the house. The idea is that a couple carves out a basic number of no-pressure times to be available to be with each other.

As Mark explained the process, they swallowed hard. They knew their schedule would not easily yield to this kind of discipline. We suggested that if Todd had to work late, he could consolidate his times, so that he'd work until 10:00 o'clock one night and then come home by 5:30 the next evening. Or, instead of working 10:00 A.M. to 4:00 P.M. on Saturday, Todd could go in early and work 6:00 to 12:00, leaving two full slots for Todd and Melanie to be together.

Surprisingly, after only ten minutes of negotiating, Todd and Melanie came up with a plan for the week. Once they had picked their six slots, I drew five circles in their schedule. "These circles are a bonus," I said with a smile. "The beauty of the slot system."

Here's what their calendar looked like:

Sunday	Monday	Tuesday	Wednesday	Thursday	Friday	Saturday
1. Breakfast & church together	**W**	**O**	**R**	**K**	**!**	◯
◯	**W**	**O**	**R**	**K**	**!**	5. Home improvement projects
2. Youth Group at our house	◯	3. Dinner at home	◯	◯	4. Dinner with John and Louise	6. Date night

Every circle represents a slot when each partner is free to do something else—together or apart—without feeling the need to ask permission from the other. For example, with his circle times, Todd is free to work late, play golf, or watch a game with a group of friends. And he now has five slots outside of regular work hours in which to handle the extra workload that results from his new business. But he doesn't have to choose any longer between his business and his marriage. And with her circle times, Melanie is free to be purposeful about joining an investment club, writing a novel, or teaching an aerobics class—or, of course, the two of them might just wind up spending time just being together.

When Mark and I introduced this concept to our couples' group, they were startled by the idea that we were encouraging them to create

these pockets of freedom throughout the week. They had assumed that, if they weren't spending every spare minute together, they were neglecting their marriages. Truth be told, couples who carve out *only* six slots a week actually tend to spend *more time* together than couples who say they spend all their discretionary time together. They are no longer giving each other the spare minutes—the leftovers—squeezed between their other activities. In reality, they're giving each other the *first* of their time and giving their work, hobbies, church, and friends what is leftover. Couples who put their six "together" slots in first—and then build the rest of their schedule around those slots—treat each other like million dollar clients, those people whose appointments with us we wouldn't dream of breaking.

Of course, this structure doesn't mean you no longer spend spare minutes, random lunches, or late-night dinners together. These unscheduled rendezvous can spice up your marriage, but with the slot system you no longer need to depend on them to provide the basic nutrients for your marriage.

Whenever Mark and I teach about the slot system, the question always seems to come up, "What about the times when six slots a week are simply impossible?" Given our erratic traveling schedule, we have more than a passing familiarity with this situation. Here's how it works for us: We "set the default button" at six slots per week. But when we have a week in which our time together dips below the normal level, we do our best to give ourselves *more* than six the next week. We realize that the health of our marriage requires it.

It's crucial to have this kind of system in place in the first year, especially before children come along. If you don't, it will be easy for you as a mother to shift the focus from your marriage to your children and to your other responsibilities. As one wife confessed to me, "I was married to my job, to my children, to my volunteer work—anything but to my husband." It will be during the seasons of your life when you feel as though you have the *least* time to carve out time for your marriage that you will need it the most.

Friends Give Attention: It's Easier Than You Think

Both Mark and I grew up feeling at home in theater and music. But the dancing required in these shows sometimes pushed Mark out of his comfort zone. Many of the shows he was in would be professionally

choreographed, and he would be expected to dance. The choreographer would stand in the front of this group of double-left-footed guys and say such encouraging things as, "It's simple. All you have to do is . . ." And with all the grace of startled frogs, they would attempt to follow the "simple" steps being taught—simple for the rhythmically gifted, of course; but for this pile of guys, it was anything but simple.

All too often, advice about marriage comes garbed in a false promise of simplicity. "The six easy steps" and "the seven simple secrets" are never nearly as easy and simple in real life as they are in the books. But we have stumbled upon a marriage-building process that is so simple, so boring, in fact, that almost anyone who can talk can succeed at it. You and your husband can use this no-brainer conversation method every time you are together.

Imagine this scene: You come into the kitchen for breakfast on an October Saturday morning, and your husband is engaged in his typical Saturday morning behavior—reading the paper, drinking his first cup of coffee. You exchange "good mornings," and he continues with what he's been doing. You also grab a cup of coffee. On your way to the kitchen table, you look out the kitchen window.

> *You:* "Would you look at those leaves? They're incredible!"
>
> *Your husband (glancing over the paper and out the window):* "Wow. They sure are." (He follows his comment with an affirmative "hmmm" sound.)
>
> *You:* "I love this month." (Before you move to the table, you putter around the kitchen for a few minutes.)
>
> *Your husband:* "Did you see that the Johnsons are selling their store?"
>
> *You (turning toward him momentarily and then back to puttering):* "No kidding?"
>
> *Your husband:* "Yeah."
>
> *You:* "Hey, do you want to run to the hardware store with me after breakfast?"
>
> *Your husband:* "Uh-huh."

Did you catch the drama, the tension, the passion? You're right, there isn't any. But when you read through the words of this conver-

sation, I'll bet the one thing you *weren't* thinking was, "My husband and I could never do *that!*"

As unromantic as it may seem, this kind of dialogue, practiced on a regular basis, can make a huge difference in your marriage. No kidding. In fact, couples who talk like this regularly, who simply "turn toward each other," as Dr. Gottman puts it—with nods, glances, and even the affirmative grunts ("uh-huh")—are the ones who also report the strongest levels of romantic satisfaction.[24]

Believe it or not, these kinds of no-brainer conversations are the building blocks of friendship in marriage. More than the infrequent "deep talk," these simple, low-skilled exchanges, practiced thousands of times throughout your marriage, can build an ease with regard to being together. And with them you create a comfortable friendship that can protect your marriage against the things that could easily destroy it.

Friends Protect Their Friendship: The Destructive Power of Secrets

Six months into her marriage, Belinda discovered, quite by accident, that five years before she and Ralph were married, he had had an affair with a married woman, a colleague at work. Though the relationship had been over long before she and Ralph had ever met, Belinda simply couldn't let it go.

Finding no appropriate outlet for her fury, she found herself pushing him away, contemptuously punishing him by removing her affection, chastising him for not sharing this awful secret with her before the wedding, disrespecting him for his moral failure. Within six months, Ralph had given up. But after he filed for divorce, she changed her mind, begging Ralph to return to the negotiating table. He refused, and they were divorced less than a year after they had made their solemn vows.

As I watched their marriage unravel, I had to wonder. *Would things have been different if the secret had come out before the wedding?* I have to think so. I believe one of two things would have happened: Either the revelation of this past relationship would have driven such a wedge between them that they would never have gotten married, or she would have made the decision that she loved him enough to get past his past. Either way, they would have saved themselves the financial and emotional expense of a divorce. A broken engagement, though horrible, is not nearly as painful as a broken marriage.

> I can think of very few situations in which anything is gained by deep secrets being kept from each other.

I can think of very few situations in which anything is gained by deep secrets being kept from each other. Consequently—apart from confidential information related to your job (as a pastor, a lawyer, or a CIA agent) and apart from a situation in which you are married to someone who would threaten to harm you physically if they learned the truth about you (a much larger problem than your secret)—we urge couples to adopt a zero-secrets policy as they begin their marriages.

Friends Give Feedback: Four Sentences He'll Love to Hear

Sherri desperately wanted to build a lasting friendship with her husband, Bob. But every time she made a suggestion, Bob seemed to respond defensively—taking every comment as a personal attack, as though he was being judged a failure. Even though she'd often begin her comments with such words as "Why don't you just . . ." or "Have you ever thought about . . . ," she seemed to get nowhere.

It was clear from Bob's consistently negative reaction that Sherri had to try another approach. What she needed was a way to initiate nonthreatening conversations with her husband—the kind that comes naturally with friends. With the stealth of Sherlock Holmes and the dogged determination of Winston Churchill, she began asking friends and coworkers for ideas. Then she subjected each idea to the scientific method, taking each one home and trying it out on Bob.

Sherri discovered a couple things: First, she learned that it *was* possible to give marriage-building feedback to Bob without stirring up defensiveness in him, and second, she realized that when she found a sentence that worked, not only would Bob respond to her positively, but within a few weeks he would begin to use the very same sentence on her!

I was so fascinated by Sherri's story that I asked her for the list of sentences that actually worked with Bob. After learning her four "friendly feedback" sentences, it didn't take long for these to become a part of my regular vocabulary with Mark as well:

1. *"I like that!"* When your husband knows that he has brought you pleasure, he will become more confident,

more playful, more likely to try out new ideas for bringing you happiness. A common frustration men voice about their marriages is that their wives are never satisfied, no matter what they do. "I like that!" will let him know that he has brought you satisfaction.

2. *"I don't know how you do it!"* With these words, you're presenting your husband with "the man of the year" trophy—communicating that you think he's an amazing person in all his pursuits, not just in what he does for you. When you notice that he's done something—anything—well, these words seal your membership in his fan club.

3. *"That counts."* These words give recognition that this man of yours has gone above and beyond the call of duty in order to show his love for you. When you catch him in the act of doing something ordinary or extraordinary—making the coffee in the morning, unloading the dishwasher, stopping by the bookstore and buying that novel you can't stop talking about—celebrate it with this affirmation. "That counts" will motivate him to think of more ways to demonstrate his love for you.

4. *"You know what I would just love?"* When you ask your husband for something in the language of pleasure rather than in the language of complaint, you are much more likely to get a pleasurable response. Using phrases such as "Can't you just once . . . ?" or "Why don't you ever . . . ?" always invites resistance and defensiveness. "You know what I would just love?" sets him up for an instant win.

Nothing can ensure the success of your marriage like simply knowing how to be friends with your husband. And friends, especially *best* friends, do a few simple things well. They spend time together, they pay attention to each other, they tell the truth, and they give encouraging feedback. Now, of course, you want something more than "just friendship" in your marriage. But it is only in the fields of friendship that the long-term passion and intimacy you long for can grow and flourish.

> Nothing can ensure the success of your marriage like simply knowing how to be friends with your husband.

8

Conflict: Close Enough for Sparks to Fly

Despite what many therapists will tell you, you don't have to resolve your major marital conflicts for your marriage to thrive.
JOHN GOTTMAN, *THE SEVEN PRINCIPLES FOR MAKING MARRIAGE WORK*

———◆———

We had been married for less than forty-eight hours. It was the first morning in our mountain honeymoon cottage. We had a leisurely breakfast, lounging around in the kind of plush bathrobes reserved only for honeymooners and movie stars. Looking out the window at the surrounding mountains, an aura of absolute contentment settled over us.

We sat comfortably close together, listening to the crackling of the fire. Eventually I got up to take a shower, while Mark stayed behind to tinker with the fire. But as I was singing under the stream of warm water, the thoughts running through my sweet husband's mind were far different from mine. Evidently the thought of his new bride in the shower awakened in Mark a creative idea he was sure we would never forget (I know *I* haven't!).

I was reveling in this luxurious, steaming shower, smiling over what a wonderful man I had married. I was singing songs—"Our Love Is Here to Stay" and "Can't Help Lovin' That Man of Mine." Awe and wonder enveloped me in the thought that this incredible man chose *me* to spend the rest of his life with. But everything changed in a split second.

Mark silently tiptoed into the bathroom to "make his memory." Out of nowhere, I received "the gift"—the result of his creative ruminations: a very large, very full, very icy pitcher of water dumped over me!

Forget the fact that one of the most popular movies that year was *Psycho*, featuring a terrifying attack on a woman in the shower. Forget

the fact that I grew up with an older brother who took great joy in carrying out pranks like this one. Forget the fact that I *thought* that, now that I was married, I'd be safe from surprise attacks like "The Claw" (my brother Rick used to love watching Saturday night wrestling, and I was his favorite opponent). Oh, how naive I was!

Thoughts of honeymoon joy were quickly replaced by *"Who is this jerk anyway? He was so kind, so spiritual. How could I have not seen that this man is a psychopath? Aaaah!"*

I didn't laugh. I didn't chase him around the cottage in my shower suit. I didn't say anything. I just slumped down in the shower, ice cubes melting around my backside, and cried. When Mark leaned in to try to comfort me, he found a completely brokenhearted bride. "Leave me *alone!*" I snapped.

He had expected good-natured laughter, or a "very funny," or a "just you wait until *you* take a shower!" or maybe just a "hee-hee-hee; that was a good one."

As a college student, Mark and his roommates had played this kind of prank on each other all the time. It always gave them a good laugh and created some of that "male bonding" we've heard so much about. And since it bonded Mark so well to the guys, he just *knew* it was going to be a great hit with me as well.

Bad idea.

After I thawed out and regained my composure and got dressed, we sat for a long time. Groveling and saying how sorry he was, Mark listened as I told him how terrified and hurt I felt. We learned a lot that day about the inevitability of conflict in marriage. We learned that, though conflict may come accidentally and carelessly, resolution only comes through purposeful hard work.

When you dream about marriage, I doubt very much that disappointment, disagreements, and shower-terror make it into your dreams. You aren't thinking about the ways this man you love will conspire to irritate you. Know this, though: he will. And if you want the kind of intimacy with your husband you've always longed for, it will only come from knowing how to handle conflict together.

Welcome to the Roller Coaster

Our family loves roller coasters. Let me take that back. Everyone in our family loves roller coasters—except Mark. He's the guy who steps

off Mr. Toad's Wild Ride with a face as green as asparagus. But because he likes to hang out with the people in our family, he frequently finds himself stepping into clanking little cars on greasy, twisting tracks and traveling at speeds and angles that leave his stomach wishing it were somewhere else.

These rides always include the familiar triple and quadruple safety checks. Of course, the wilder the ride, the more harnesses and straps there are and the more snugly your head is held in place. After my first roller-coaster ride, I never questioned why those people dressed in spacesuits spend so much time making sure everyone is locked in. They know that without safety harnesses, someone could die.

Marriage may just be the wildest ride you'll ever take. The turns are unpredictable; the spins can be incredibly uncomfortable. And at times, the only thing you may be able to think about is *when can I get off this thing?* So before you begin the ride, check to make sure all safety mechanisms are in place and working. The time to discover that your seat belt doesn't work isn't when you're dangling upside down a hundred feet off the ground.

> Before you begin the ride, check to make sure all safety mechanisms are in place and working.

We've found three safety checks you can use to protect your marriage from the dangerous twists and turns of disappointment, discouragement, and hurt. If you're strapped in securely, you may discover that conflict actually becomes an invitation to deeper intimacy—and can even be fun as well.

Safety Check #1: Conflict Will Happen

There is only one surefire way to guarantee you will never fight with your husband: Don't get married.

Go ahead, strive for the marriage you've always dreamed of. Strive for an exceptional, uncommon life together. Strive to love each other more deeply each year. But give up on the expectation that if you somehow "do it right" you will "get out of jail free" and never have to face the irritation, disappointment, and discouragement over the way your husband has handled a particular situation or failed to do what he promised to do when you got married.

Conflict *will* happen—guaranteed. You will not be able to predict what the specific nature of the conflict will be, but you *can* be prepared for the disagreements that are sure to come.

Maybe your husband is a morning person, and you're a night person. He goes to bed early and calls for you to join him. You say you'll be there in a minute but spend the next thirty minutes putzing around the kitchen, and his frustration begins to boil. And by the time you finally make it upstairs to join him, the fuse on the powder keg has already been lit. The spontaneous combustion catches you off guard.

Maybe your husband is the king of spontaneity, and you are a neat freak. His drinking glasses will, before long, make permanent rings on your coffee table. You've asked him again and again to use coasters. For the first few weeks of your marriage, you didn't mind cleaning up after him, but now the more of his messes you clean up, the more frustrated you become. One day he walks in the door and discovers that your tolerance has just come to a fiery end.

I can't predict where the hair trigger will be on your conflicts, but I know the conflicts will come.

Safety Check #2: Prepare to Forgive

To some people, forgiveness sounds so easy—so, well, nice. But forgiveness is tough. It isn't for cowards. There is nothing effortless about it. It can, in fact, present the most demanding challenge of your entire marriage.

> When you do not forgive your husband for the hurt or disappointment he has caused you, you lock yourself in a prison and wait for your husband to find the key.

But when you do not forgive your husband for the hurt or disappointment he has caused you, you lock yourself in a prison and wait for your husband to find the key. Creating a list of demands he must meet before he can be forgiven will only keep *you* behind bars. I have seen women who stay "locked up"—emotionally, sexually, vocationally, spiritually—burning with bitterness for years. Ironically, you're the one who has the most power to bring healing. Your forgiveness can neutralize the corrosive effects of your husband's blunders.

If you want a safe ride on this wild adventure, be prepared to forgive this man.

Safety Check #3: Do You Have Your Fire Extinguishers Handy?

Now let's get practical. You've resigned yourself to the fact that conflict in your marriage is inevitable; you're prepared to forgive this man

who won't always get it right. We want you armed with the most powerful strategies available for reducing and overcoming the conflicts.

These secrets—"fire extinguishers," so to speak—have been proven to snuff out the fires of conflict—those burning, painful, thoughtlessly spoken words and reactions that have the potential to explode like a stick of dynamite. Where do these secrets come from?

Once again we turn to Dr. Gottman. What I love about his approach is that these strategies for overcoming conflicts are more than just good ideas; they are the very ones used by couples who *have* built happy and satisfying marriages. One of his most significant findings was that focusing on communication skills and on active listening—techniques recommended by most marriage counselors—are seldom helpful in handling conflict. These techniques quickly get forgotten once a couple becomes embroiled in an emotional conflict.

So get ready. You just may be surprised at how simple these "fire extinguishers" are.

Complain; Don't Criticize

Dr. Gottman makes this observation: "There is no such thing as constructive criticism. All criticism is painful. Unlike complaints—specific requests for change—criticism doesn't make marriage better. It inevitably makes it worse."[25] A complaint is focused on a specific issue—a *specific request* for change. Raising a concern typically will not have any adverse effect on the happiness of a marriage. Criticism, on the other hand, converts a concern into an attack.

Here are a few examples:

- *Complaint:* "I wish you would take out the trash!"
  Criticism: "How many times do I have to ask you to do something as simple as taking out the trash? Why can't you remember to help out around here?"

- *Complaint:* "Don't you think we need to carve out some time for us? It's been a long time since we went on a date."
  Criticism: "You seem to have *plenty* of time for your buddies. What about me? When do I get some of that attention? No more nights out for you until we have a date."

- *Complaint:* "It hurts me when you don't hold my hand in public. It makes me think you're ashamed of me."

  Criticism: "Why won't you show me any affection in public? All you care about is keeping up your image. What's the matter? Are you afraid people will think that you love me?"

In the heat of the moment, when your emotions have percolated to the surface because of genuine frustration, it's difficult to say the right thing every time. But you *can* keep from globalizing your concern into a criticism. Stick to the infraction.

When the Flood Comes, Take a Break

Watch a tennis match on television sometime. What happens when a player disagrees with a call? Go to a baseball game and see what happens when the manager argues with the umpire—two grown men screaming at the top of their lungs, their noses no more than three inches apart.

Their anger is like a flood. As they become consumed by the emotions of conflict, they can no longer deal with it in a productive way. When a man "gets flooded" during a conflict, he may just shut down to a sullen silence, grunting out a "fine," a "who cares," or a "whatever." Or he may go into an attack mode and shout out with defensiveness and contempt, "I said it was fine! What more do you want from me?"

No, it's not your imagination. According to the research, "It's a biological fact that men are more easily overwhelmed by marital conflict than their wives are. It is harder for a man's body to calm down after an argument than a woman's."[26] Many wives, though, make a critical mistake by *continuing* their complaint even after their husbands have become flooded. Because women are the ones who will bring up problems—more than 80 percent of the time—their tendency is to be unwilling to let them go.[27] And because women feel a greater ownership of the problem, they also tend to have more tolerance for enduring the conflict.

When you or your husband gets flooded in a conflict, the best thing to do is to recognize that you're wasting your time and simply take a break. In one love lab experiment, researchers interrupted couples in the heat of conflict, explaining that the staff needed to make some adjustments to the microphones. The researchers simply asked the couples to wait for twenty minutes before returning to their previous

conversation. And in *every* case, heart rates had gone down, "floods" had subsided, and couples were able to deal with the conflict more productively.[28]

Start Arguments Softly

- *Soft Start-Up:* "Can we talk for a minute about the trip we're about to take to my mother's house?"

  Harsh Start-Up: "Every time we visit my mom, you act like such a spoiled brat."

- *Soft Start-Up:* "What's the possibility that we could renegotiate the chores around the house?"

  Harsh Start-Up: "Let me tell you something. I'm not your mother. I'm not your slave. And I'm tired of waiting on you hand and foot!"

The research is absolutely conclusive that the introductory moments of a conflict have everything to do with its outcome. If you begin every confrontation with thoughtful words and a pleasant face, your chances for a satisfying outcome are wonderfully improved. If you charge into conflicts with your head down and your nostrils flaring, your matador will respond the only way he knows how.

When Bobbie's friend Peg was first married, she and Grant held "fireside chats" every Friday evening. They asked each other, "Is there anything I did this week that bothered you?" The setting was calm and serene. Emotions were completely in check.

"It really bugs me when you drive over the reflectors in the middle of the road on purpose," Peg admitted. Grant did this just for the fun of it and had no idea it was a sore spot, and he thanked her for letting him know.

Peg could have attacked him while his tires were thumping their annoying cadence. "That noise is driving me crazy. Can't you stay in your lane like everyone else?" Because Peg practiced a soft start-up, a conflict was avoided; a problem was solved.

> The research is absolutely conclusive that the introductory moments of a conflict have everything to do with its outcome.

Don't Expect to Resolve Every Conflict

There are two very different kinds of conflict in a marriage—solvable and perpetual. And you may be surprised—or disappointed—to

learn that almost 70 percent of conflicts fall into the *perpetual* category.[29] These are usually personality tendencies and quirky habits that are not threatening to your marriage. The majority of perpetual issues we argue about in our marriage will simply not be solved, issues such as these:

- Dana loves parties and wishes that Walter wasn't so shy and quiet in a group.
- Donald is a strict disciplinarian and wants Rena to be firmer with their son; Rena thinks Donald should lighten up.
- Anita is extremely frugal and likes to have plenty of cash in reserve; Cliff thinks nothing of spending money, especially on risky ventures.
- Jim loves to work out and won't miss a day of exercise; Sally hates the thought of breaking a sweat and doesn't understand his obsession.
- Bobbie is a free spirit who sometimes leaves the dish towel lying haphazardly on the counter; Robert can't walk through the kitchen without straightening it out.
- Mark hates the television and believes that it will turn our children's brains to broccoli; I enjoy watching television and wish Mark would slow down and watch it with me.

I was amazed to discover that couples can actually live happily together with unresolved conflicts. In fact, in our work with couples, we used to spend an inordinate amount of effort trying to get couples to resolve all their conflicts, usually with minimal success.

The next time you're talking to a veteran couple—one you consider to be happily married—ask them if they're dealing with some perpetual conflict that has been an issue for them for their whole marriage. I have little doubt that they will say yes. Satisfied couples have simply found ways to dance with the conflict issues that don't seem to budge.

When it comes to television in our home, I doubt that Mark and I will ever agree. He would be happy to see all televisions donated to science—definitely not given away to the poor, because no one should have to endure the "brain-rotting effects of this spawn of Satan." I, on the other hand, grew up with the television on almost perpetually. And though our family watches only a fraction of what I did growing up, I do love it when our family spends an occasional evening together watching TV. When we're sitting in the nursing home forty years from

now, Mark will probably still think we're wasting our time in front of the television. I'll still be saying, "Shhhh! This is the best part!"

Do the Patch Work

A strategically placed patch can salvage an otherwise useless thing. A dress, a pair of jeans, or a punctured tire can be restored with this kind of simple repair. When your conflict with your husband spirals into a negative or destructive place, you can patch it with a statement or gesture that deescalates the battle and restores your relationship.

When things got a little tense between my parents, my dad used to smile and say to my redheaded mom, "I love it when your face gets the color of your hair." Mark and I have come up with our own patch that seems to resolve at least most of our petty conflicts: I get to be right on the odd days of the month, and Mark gets to be right on the even days. When we are arguing about directions or about what time Mark said he'd be home, one of us will interrupt the fight with "what's the date today?" We let the calendar decide who's right.

But patches don't all need to be silly. It can be a simple statement such as "I can see your point" or "Wow! I've been completely missing what you were saying." The key to successful patching is the receiving spouse. When your husband offers a patch, even if it's not perfect, you have a choice. You can either keep pounding your point, which may result in your husband becoming flooded and increasingly resistant. Or you can join him with some patch work of your own.

I'll never forget the story our friends Rusty and Betty told us about a car trip they had taken. After an erupting conflict, they settled into an uncomfortable, icy silence. Ten minutes into the silence, Rusty decided to play. He didn't realize at the time that it was a patch, but it clearly was. As they passed an unusually large pack of mules, he said brightly, "Relatives of yours?" At this point Betty had a choice. She could maintain the tension (and perpetuate the misery of their trip) or she could match her husband's levity. She chose the latter and said, "Why, yes. On my husband's side, of course." A willingness to risk this kind of playfulness *and to receive it* from each other has a delightful way of keeping us majoring on our love and minoring on our conflict.

And just in case you're keeping score: Over the past twenty-three years, I've had the chance to bless my husband with enough of my own "good morning, camper!" pitchers of ice water in the shower. Hee-hee-hee.

I know I'm right—it's an odd-numbered day!

9

Money: The Other Lover

Money is a wonderful thing, but it's possible to pay too high a price for it.

ANONYMOUS

———◆×◆———

A group of men had finished their workout and were talking in the locker room. A cell phone interrupted their conversation. One of the guys picked it up and checked the caller I.D. The preprogrammed message read "Your Wife." Glancing around the locker room, he flipped it open and said hello.

The woman's voice on the other end of the phone was enthusiastic. She didn't waste any time with pleasantries. "Honey," she said, "you know how we've been looking at cars?"

With a skeptical hesitation, he answered slowly, "Uh-huh."

"Well, I think I've found the perfect one. It's a little more than what we wanted to spend, but you are going to love it!" Her words were ecstatic, punctuated by rapid breaths as she continued, "It's a little red Mercedes convertible. The sticker price is $53,000, but I think they can do better than that, don't you?"

He paused for a moment. "That sounds like a fair price to me. I'd go ahead and give them what they're asking. I just want you to be happy."

He could tell she was beaming as she answered, "I'll buy it right now."

"Sounds great. Have a great day!" He closed the flap on the phone and looked around the locker room.

With a mischievous grin he called out, "Hey, anybody know whose phone this is?"

When It's *Your* Money, It's Not That Funny

I've learned a good general rule: When conversations about money come this easily in my marriage, I want to be sure it's really my husband I'm talking to! In real life, dealing with money can present some of the greatest challenges that your marriage will ever face.

According to research, nearly 70 percent of married women list money as the number one stressor in their families.[30] And the Gallup organization has documented that financial pressure is, hands down, the number one problem faced by families. Not particularly surprising. What *is* surprising is that there isn't even a close second. While most respondents agreed that financial stress was the biggest challenge, the second-place answer (health and health care concerns) received only 6 percent of the votes.

In the light of the pressure put on the normal marriage by finances, it is surprising how many couples are not prepared for the challenges they are certain to face. In fact, only about 1 out of every 10 of the couples we work with has even begun a budget. Before saying "I do," most couples treat the warnings about future financial challenges in the same way they may treat a flight attendant's safety instructions.

I wonder, *What if all airplane passengers knew there was a better than 50 percent chance that they would actually be using the floatation devices beneath them or the oxygen masks neatly concealed above them?* I don't know about you, but I'd be listening pretty carefully to the preflight instructions.

The Single-Mind Principle

> Few issues can eat away at the fabric of a marriage like a husband and a wife who have different unspoken expectations about finances.

There are all kinds of reasons couples avoid financial preparation. The idealist says, "Money problems will take care of themselves if we love each other enough." The passive-aggressive spouse says, "When it comes to money, I just smile and nod and buy whatever I want." The avoidance specialist says, "Money always makes us fight, so we just don't talk about it anymore."

More often than not, couples who don't talk about finances slip into quiet standoffs that keep everybody unhappy. Few issues can eat away at the fabric of a marriage like a husband and a wife who have

different unspoken expectations about finances. What you need are a few steps to help you and your husband structure your finances in a way that keeps both of you on the same side of the table.

Our Money

Start with the agreement that, after the marriage, all of your income will go into a single pot called "our money." Moving 100 percent of your income into a single pile prevents a number of unnecessary and potentially explosive conflicts:

- You avoid arguments over who is responsible to pay which bills.
- You no longer have "his and her" funds and bills that can easily lead to patterns of blaming and finger-pointing.
- It puts you together on the same side of the table as you creatively address the many financial challenges of your marriage.
- Your egos will be less threatened in the event that one of you makes a lot more money than the other.

The Marriage Insurance Premium

So far, so good. But what happens when one of you takes some of "our money" and spends it on something that the spouse would see as foolish? You may be convinced that a new $350 juicer is an absolute necessity; your husband may be equally convinced that paying $500 for a new set of golf clubs is a much higher priority. As crazy as it sounds, issues of no less consequence have unraveled the trust of many marriages.

To prevent this kind of predicament, we've developed a secret we like to call the *Marriage Insurance Premium* (or MIP). It works like this: At the beginning of each month, one of the first bills you pay out of "our money" is your MIP. There are no commissions, no agencies; in fact, you pay the money to yourselves, giving each of you absolute power over a bit of money each month.

The MIP need not be the same for each of you. For example, you and your husband may agree that you will receive $100 a month and he will receive $50 a month. You can take your money and put it in a mutual fund or save it up and buy the juicer; your husband can put his toward a new Nike driver. The only rule is that neither of you can criticize the MIP expenditures of the other.

With this arrangement, each of you gets to make a few unilateral decisions without creating a conflict. We call it marriage *insurance,* because it protects you from potentially destructive conflicts over money—and it's much cheaper than marriage counseling or a divorce.

The Spending Plan

Once you've allowed the MIP to create enough space for your financial idiosyncrasies, you're ready to develop your spending plan. I like the term *spending plan*—what you *can* spend money on—much better than *budget*—what you *can't* spend money on.

The secret cannot be reduced to making more money. The insurance industry tells us that large sums of money paid out to beneficiaries are typically gone in *six months.* The same is true for lottery winners.

As we've watched couples who become wealthy, nearly all of them shaped their spending plan with the same two priorities in view: giving and saving. Couples who agree on these two priorities often find that the process of determining the rest of their spending plan comes much more easily. Though your circumstances may require different percentages, the simplest strategy is summed up in this formula:

- Give 10 percent.
- Save 10 percent for the long haul (retirement and children's college expenses).
- Save 10 percent for the short haul (purchasing cars or furniture or carrying out major home improvements).
- Allot 70 percent for "Our Money"—including the Marriage Insurance Premiums, out of which bills are paid.

We picture the total process like this:

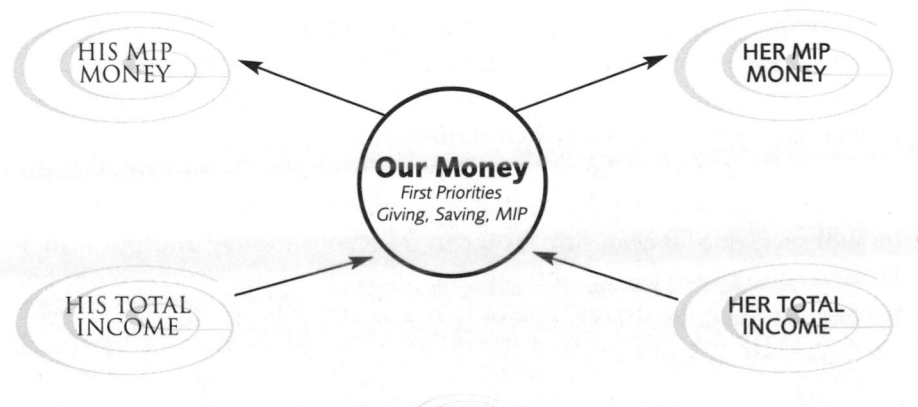

As you build your spending plan, start by listing, month by month, all your sources of income, including your paycheck, your husband's paycheck, gifts, and your investment income. Then make a list of all the expenses you can think of and put them into categories: giving, savings, MIPs, housing (rent or mortgage), utilities, car expenses, clothing, groceries, travel, telephone, donations, magazine subscriptions, personal (haircuts, dry cleaning), insurance, home decor, gifts, and miscellaneous expenditures.

From this point, you have both moved to the same side of the table in determining how much to allot for each spending category.

Money Attitudes That Murder Marriages

Money itself never causes conflict in marriage. What escalates into money fights are the unspoken *attitudes* you and your groom bring into your marriage. As a wife, there are two mind-sets that will hurt you every time:

"Money Is My Husband's Department"

Albert and Jennifer were financially comfortable when they first got married. Both had high-profile jobs that provided generous incomes. In fact, Jennifer had been so successful that she had over $100,000 in savings when they got married. After the wedding, Albert took care of everything related to the money—the insurance, the investments, the bill-paying. He made almost every financial decision, and she experienced great comfort in not having to worry about it.

When their first child was born, Jennifer wanted to stay at home. Albert agreed that they could swing it financially, and they continued in their familiar lifestyle. Then Albert lost his job. Through it all, he assured Jennifer that they would be fine. Asking no questions, she kept her spending at her normal level.

Albert was able to land a few short-term consulting jobs, but as he moved into the third year without employment, trouble began. He began putting restrictions on Jennifer's spending, and she began asking questions. What she discovered shocked and terrified her: Over the course of the past two years, they had spent their entire savings. And they were currently living on loans.

Jennifer had thought she was being a good wife, supporting her husband and not asking questions. Albert had tried to protect Jennifer by

Couples who wait to talk about finances until there's a problem set themselves up for conflict from which they may never recover.

keeping the bad news at bay in hopes of a turnabout. Both were trying to do the right thing—trying to show love for each other. But this arrangement left Albert carrying a heavy weight he was never supposed to carry alone and left his wife with the devastation of feeling betrayed.

Couples who wait to talk about finances until there's a problem set themselves up for conflict from which they may never recover. As much as you may think it's preventing discomfort early in your marriage, it's never helpful to abdicate the responsibility for decisions about what to do with "our money."

"It's Easier to Ask for Forgiveness Than Permission"

Bobbie has a friend who lives by the shopping motto "Never leave a paper trail." As often as possible, Jeri avoids using checks or credit cards so that her husband will never know where she's been spending her money.

The crazy thing is that Jeri really has very little to hide. She's not running a drug-smuggling ring; she's not gambling on the side. She's only buying a few extra things for herself, for the house, and even a few surprises for her husband. She loves the freedom of being able to buy these things without "asking for permission." Her small consulting practice provides enough of "her own money" to do this undetected.

Jeri has a legitimate need to have this freedom to make some discretionary financial decisions herself. She wants to be treated like an adult. But the naked truth is that she doesn't trust her husband enough to come openly to the table to talk about what she's doing. Her "ask for forgiveness rather than permission" approach sets the stage for secrets, for distrust, and for hiding—a pattern that can easily find its way into other areas of their relationship.

Wise Woman's Words

I've done an informal survey of married women about the subject of money. I asked them, "If you could say just one thing to new brides about how to build the right kind of pattern for dealing with money, what would it be?" Consider these tips as sage advice from the front lines:

"It's Not Unromantic or Unspiritual to Pay Attention to Money"

You don't have to read far into the New Testament to discover that God cares deeply about your attitudes related to money. There are five times more references in the New Testament to money than to prayer. You can add up the Bible's every reference to heaven or hell, and you'll still wind up with less material than you'll find related to money. And you may be surprised to know that, of Jesus' thirty-eight parables, sixteen relate to money in some way.

You may think that spending a romantic evening together or sharing a deep conversation about spiritual things will lead to satisfying intimacy. But neglecting conversation with your husband about money often puts up an obstacle to this intimacy. The earlier and clearer your conversations about money, the freer you'll be to pursue the things that matter most.

"There's Nothing You Need Badly Enough Right Now to Go into Debt for It"

By recent estimates, the typical household in America has $23,000 in nonmortgage debt. If we assume a moderate interest rate of 10 percent for that debt, the average couple is paying about $2,300 a year in interest alone. If a young couple would choose to avoid nonmortgage debt and put the $2,300 a year into savings, they could have, after twenty years of marriage, a nest egg in the neighborhood of $100,000, depending on the interest rate. Without spending a penny more than the average couple already spends on interest alone, you and your husband could have the many options this kind of money brings.

Too many couples leverage their future in order to buy a few more things they just have to have right now. The strain that a high debt load places on a marriage can be immense. Particularly during this first year, it's very important to live free from nonmortgage debt.

Asim and Colleen employ what they call their "walk-away principle." They agree to go home and leave any item over $200 in the store for twenty-four hours. If one of them "just loved it" the day before, it may not be as enticing the next day. With the passion removed, the couple can decide if the item is a "need" or a "want."

"If You Want to Live on One Income Someday, Live on One Income Now"

Anna and Andrew got married in their mid-twenties, knowing that one day they'd want to start a family. Early in their relationship they

decided that Anna would not work outside the home once the children came. As a two-career couple, they lived at the level at which they could afford to live. Before the children arrived, they grew accustomed to new cars, a house with a large mortgage, frequently eating out, and annual high-dollar vacations.

Midway through their fourth year of marriage Anna became pregnant, and they realized the rough ride they had set themselves up for. When they looked at what their spending plan would be, based on only one salary, they were shocked at what it was going to cost to have a baby *and* to be a stay-at-home mom. Faced with the decision of vastly decreasing their standard of living or abandoning the decision for Anna to stay home with the baby, they made the difficult choice and severely cut back on their lifestyle. Putting a for-sale sign in their front yard was a painful reminder of their poor planning.

It would have been far easier if Anna and Andrew had learned to live on one income during the first few years of their marriage. They would have had three years of Anna's salary in savings—a cushion that could have *increased* their standard of living when the baby came.

So Where Do We Begin?

We met with Mike and Lynn several times before their wedding. In addition to regularly scheduled premarital sessions, they asked for special help in overcoming their frustrating pattern of tension with regard to money matters. They were wise enough to see that this pattern would set them up for a lifetime of frustration. And so, even before their wedding, these two resolved to build a different set of patterns. They knew that the marriage they've dreamed of would never be possible as long as they couldn't talk about money without becoming resentful.

One of the things we loved about working with this couple was their willingness to keep trying until they found a strategy that worked. In the first place, they did the kinds of things you've read about in this chapter—like creating a budget and establishing a monthly MIP. They even took a class on financial planning. They also tried some wild ideas—their own patented money dance they agreed to do every time they felt tension creeping into their ordinary money talks, and the special song—complete with motions—that they could never get through completely without laughing. And for a while they agreed to wear clown noses every time they talked about money. (I'm not kidding you.)

Now, ten years into their marriage, they would tell you that no single money strategy "worked." What did work was their uncompromising commitment to work a plan together, their absolute willingness to rid themselves of the corrosive oppositional patterns that elevated money above their marriage.

So where do *you* begin? How about resolving during this year to establish a pattern that allows the two of you to talk and negotiate about money without the tension and self-destructive seriousness that so often accompanies couples' financial conversations? Begin by agreeing that you will stay on the same team, sit on the same side of the table, and make your first priority not just solving a particular money issue but doing so in such a way that money never drives a wedge between you and your husband.

10

Sex: Better Than Chocolate

*Marital sex can never prove enduringly successful for a man
until his wife gets her most central needs satisfied.*

NEIL CLARK WARREN, *CATCHING THE RHYTHM OF LOVE*

---

*I*t started out like most days for Nick. He was out the door
and on his way to work an hour or two before Cathy woke
up. As he dressed for the day, his desire to climb back under
the covers with his newlywed bride was intense, but he thought better of
it. Cathy had been exhausted lately from her new job. Nick reasoned that
the last thing she needed was to wake up to her overly amorous husband
pawing all over her. Taking care not to disturb her, he left and focused his
thinking on the night they'd spend together when he got home.

Throughout the day, Nick had many sexual thoughts. These were
brought on by a glance at an attractive woman, suggestive clothing, or
even a kind and encouraging word from a female coworker. It didn't
take much. Sometimes just a magazine cover, a billboard, or a random
song on the radio was enough. At times he found himself thinking
about sex for no apparent reason at all.

Nick was not a sex addict. He was a man committed to living with
integrity. He was deeply in love with his wife and committed to "fidelity
of the mind." And so he had made the decision that, instead of letting
his mind linger on a person or image that might have prompted sexual
thoughts, he would always seek to redirect those thoughts exclusively
toward his bride.

At 6:00 P.M. he begins his drive home. He imagines a night of lovemaking with his bride. Out of faithfulness to his wife, he may have

daydreamed about this scene ten times or more throughout the day. But the second he walks through the door, he realizes that his mind's trip to Fantasy Island is over.

Cathy greets him at the door with an unemotional hello and an immediate reminder that he had forgotten to take the trash out. "We missed the garbage man, and our trash cans are full." As they walk toward the living room, she lets him know that his sweaty jogging clothes are still right where he left them—in the middle of the walk-in closet.

Despite her obvious frustration with him, he goes ahead and hugs her, attempting a brief but sincere kiss. She pulls away, shoots him a disapproving look, and says, "Don't start getting any ideas."

Nick is thinking, "Start *getting any ideas? I've been having these ideas since 5:00 this morning!*" He gives up and trudges into the den, slumps into his chair, picks up the remote, and sits in stony silence.

It doesn't have to be this way. A woman who seeks to understand her husband sexually, who sees his sexual interest in her as a marker of faithfulness rather than of selfishness, is far more likely to experience full and satisfying intimacy. But sustaining this kind of incredible, mutually satisfying sex life will most likely not come naturally.

Without question, moments of sexual ecstasy are normal in any marriage. But you want more than a few moments. You want a sexual *lifestyle* with your husband that is consistently, even increasingly, satisfying for both of you. And it all begins with understanding yourself.

The Whiplash Effect

For a young woman who has guarded her heart and her bed and who enters marriage with the gift of no experience, to make the change from being the virgin bride to being her husband's sexual playmate can be more than a little challenging. Happily, we know far more about how to get ready for sex than Queen Victoria, who passed on this bit of wedding-night wisdom to all of her soon-to-be-married daughters: "Close your eyes, grit your teeth, and pray for the Empire."[31]

For years, turning *off* your sexual desires may have been the way you demonstrated faithfulness to God and to your future husband. But now, this same faithfulness invites the exact opposite response. So don't be surprised if you experience an unsettling whiplash effect during this first year, as you move from a habit of saying "no. No! NO!" into a pattern of "yes. Yes! YES!"

Sex is not simply about satisfying your *husband's* needs. It is a free-falling, rollicking, best-friend fun that can invite the childlike nature of you and your husband to "come out and play"—the most natural form of holy play a couple can experience together. Couples who have the richest intimacy, the greatest resilience, the most contagious sense of joy, are those who have learned light-heartedness at a *child to child* level.

In premarital counseling, we say to couples that if there isn't plenty of play in their lovemaking, they're missing the point. Great sex in marriage is not primarily about "getting it right"; it's more about fumbling and bumbling around together until you laughingly stumble upon those things that bring the greatest satisfaction and joy.

Learning early in your marriage to see sex as a no-pressure playground can prepare you for those times when sex may feel more like work than play. If you don't cultivate a spirit of playfulness in your marriage, the typical encounters with your overly amorous husband can easily lead to resentment and anger. When I see my husband's advances not as demands for performance but as affirming invitations to laugh together, I am free to say, as one tired, disheveled bride said to her husband on a day when she felt anything but attractive, "You've *obviously* got incredible taste in women."

I love to watch animal shows on television. Whether it's the guy with the crocodiles or someone talking about out-of-control adolescent elephants, these shows always capture my attention. Not long ago, I was watching a special on otters and monkeys, and there was one sentence I heard that will always stick with me: *It is always the most intelligent animals that know how to play.* The same is true for us. We are at our best, our most intelligent—in marriage, at work, in life—when we have learned how to play. And in marriage, sex is the grand playground.

Now, when I describe sex as play, some women assume that I am talking about "slap and tickle" games or jumping raucously on the bed. Uhhh—not necessarily. Truth be told, when it comes to this very vulnerable area of our lives, women like you and me want to be taken seriously; we want to be spoken to with quiet words of romance and cherishing respect.

> Sex is not simply about satisfying your *husband's* needs. It is a free-falling, rollicking, best-friend fun that can invite the childlike nature of you and your husband to "come out and play."

One warning: Women who have been sexually abused will undoubtedly experience difficulty stepping into this kind of holy play. These women can carry a grave resistance to their husband's sexual invitations. A woman with this kind of history may struggle sexually with her husband because *she's* dealing with something that is beyond his control. If this describes you, don't let your past prevent you from enjoying the sexual intimacy with your husband you were made to enjoy. By seeking the help of a qualified Christian counselor early in your marriage, you can experience healing and move on to satisfying intimacy with your husband.[32]

> It is always the most intelligent animals that know how to play.

Getting to What *You* Want: You Are His Only Teacher

Even though we aren't stuck with Queen Victoria's attitude, far too many women resign to endure sex rather than enjoy it. I saw this resignation in the young bride who asked me, "I'm just wondering—how often am I really going to have to do this?"

Maybe you have no trouble affirming the goodness of sex—and maybe the whiplash effect will have a limited effect on you. Perhaps you'll struggle with a different problem. You may have difficulty finding sex consistently satisfying.

I've got some good news and some bad news for you:

- The good news is that your husband *can* learn to bring you great pleasure in sex.
- The bad news is that *you* have to be the one to teach him.

And here's a little more good news and bad news:

- The good news is that you will have little difficulty finding out what satisfies him.
- The bad news is that it will take your husband a lot of effort to understand and practice the things that bring you pleasure.

During our engagement, Mark and I read a Christian book about sex. One of the chapters promised to give "The Key to Feminine Sexual Response." Soon after we were married, I discovered two things about sex: (1) My husband was determined to master that "key" and use it with monotonous frequency, and (2) on my excitement scale,

that technique ranked just below watching oatmeal boil—in spite of what the book said!

Maybe this picture from the world of sports will help you understand your husband a little better. When it comes to sex, the only game your husband may know how to play well is baseball. And unless you teach him otherwise, his game will look something like this:

- He will touch the same three bases as quickly as possible— in the same predictable order,
- then he will rush for home.

Running the bases may come naturally to your Babe Ruth, but it won't feel much like a home run to you.

Men—the sexually predictable gender—have the ironic ability to think about *sex* all the time but seldom ever *think* about sex. Many husbands simply assume that their wives have the same approach to sex that they do—but we wives can be anything but predictable.

What is even more confusing for your husband is that you may want such different things at different times. I know there are times when I want my back massaged or my feet rubbed or my hair brushed. Sometimes I want a long gourmet encounter; at other times, the last thing I want is a forty-five minute WWF (World Wrestling Federation) main event, and a quick romp is more the order of the day. Although I happen to be married to one of the most loving and creative men in the world, I'm pretty sure he'd get it wrong almost every time without clear signals from me.

So be prepared to teach your husband *your* version of baseball— with rules that go something like this:

Start out in the batter's box and take a nice slow jog to first base. Once you get there, just touch it for an instant, turn around and head back to the batter's box for a few practice swings. Then jog out to left field, pick some flowers, and come back to the batter's box again and just sit and talk about the game for a few minutes. Take a few more pitches, and head straight for second base as fast as you can—but don't stay there long. Take a jog over the pitcher's mound right back to the batter's box one more time. Once you get there, swing as hard as you can, and when you make contact, run directly to third base. I'll be your third base coach. You'll just have to watch for my

signals—I may want you to stay on base, head back to first, or run for home like there's no tomorrow! If you'll listen to me, you will score. But more important than that, the next time you invite me to play, I'll be humming the tune to "Take me out to the ball game!"

Trust me on this one: The chances of your husband just "figuring you out" sexually are about as likely as him figuring out what you want him to pick up at the grocery store without a list.

So, during this first year, your mission is to teach your husband how to please you and how to satisfy you. Help him become an expert on helping *you* enjoy sex. But, of course, teaching him how to satisfy you sexually requires that you become aware of what pleases you—a process that may feel like sailing uncharted waters. Just relax. The first year of marriage ought to be the worst year of sex you'll ever have. Don't stress out over having great sex during this year; you've got the rest of your life to work on it. You wouldn't expect to pick up a new language after your first conversation in a foreign land. Let this be a year of experimenting and learning about each other. God has designed human sexual intimacy in such a way that you can successfully bring each other pleasure—even if you don't quite know what you are doing yet.

> The first year of marriage ought to be the worst year of sex you'll ever have. You've got the rest of your life to work on it.

In this first year, you may need to ask your husband to begin with a time of nonsexual touching before moving into foreplay. You need to specifically tell him exactly where to touch you or move his hand to a particular spot while gently encouraging, "Try this." You've been designed to enjoy a deeply erotic, completely exclusive physical love with your husband. And you are invited into the joyful journey of exploring with your husband how he can best bring *you* pleasure.

You're in the Driver's Seat

Permit me a crude comparison (I'm sorry, Mom): Have you ever been on a long car trip and needed to go to the bathroom? Have you ever noticed how easily the person driving is able to underestimate the urgency of your need? Can you relate to the frustration when the driver accidentally "forgets" that you mentioned you needed to stop about thirty minutes earlier?

Of course, great sex is about so much more than "getting relief" from a biological urge. But I believe that if you truly understand the intensity of your husband's desire for you, if you have a clear picture of what it feels like for him to sit uncomfortably forgotten in the backseat, you'll come to realize how often you are in the driver's seat.

So far in this chapter I've portrayed the husband as the initiator of sex and the wife as the resisting one. However, in the healthiest couples these roles change—with both the husband and wife initiating sex at different times. Regardless of who is pursuing and who is being pursued, though, the principle is the same: The one who has the ability to fulfill or to deny the request for intimacy is holding the power. The person in the marriage with the most power in this situation is never the one pursuing; the pursuer is, after all, the one who is risking rejection.

When you are in the driver's seat, you can make the choice to allow the sexual invitations of your husband to draw you into a mutually satisfying responsiveness. As one bride put it, "Even when I'm not in the mood, sex with my husband is almost always a good idea."

Consider one more parable: Your husband is frustrated because you constantly nag him to help out in the kitchen. The conflict over this issue gets so heated that the two of you come to talk to us. When Mark suggests that your husband may want to do a little more housework, your husband is indignant: "You're not suggesting that I need to clean the kitchen even when I don't feel like it, are you?"

By now, you probably know us well enough to know that we would say, "Yes, friend, that is *exactly* what we are suggesting."

He might argue, "But I'm just not good at kitchen cleaning. I have this built-in resistance to cleaning kitchens—particularly when my wife seems to want me to do it all the time!"

How would you want us to respond? How about something like this: "If it matters so much to your wife that you clean the kitchen, don't make a constitutional amendment out of it. Just go clean the kitchen. In reality, by avoiding the kitchen work, you're creating much more frustration in the long run than if you simply headed straight for the sink."

Are You in the Mood?

There's a single question we pose to every couple before they get married: "Once you're married, what do you plan to do when one of you is in the mood for lovemaking and the other is not?"

If you can't come up with an answer, you're setting yourself up for a cycle in which one of you will feel pressured and the other rejected. Of course, there's no perfect strategy, no "one size fits all" answer for every couple. But our experience is that almost *any* plan works better than the all too common "Gee-whiz, I hope this works out, knock on wood" approach.

Some couples successfully use what we call the "never say no" agreement, summarized as, "If you're in the mood, I can get there." Others have an amendment to the agreement in which the pursuing partner lovingly agrees to accept a "not tonight" answer, with the understanding that it is given on a clearly limited basis. When a husband knows in advance that his wife's answer will ordinarily be yes, he's much more willing to respond with understanding than if he has the sense that "not tonight" has become the default answer.

You and your husband can come up with your own creative solutions to the pressure/rejection cycle. You may say, "This is one of those nights when I need for us to make love"; or you may ask, "Are you feeling amorous?" The key is to intentionally clarify your expectations or needs, and then agree on a plan before you end up wounding the heart of the other.

The issue is not about who gets what they want. The issue is how to use healthy sexual interest—even when it's not timed perfectly—as an opportunity for responsive intimacy rather than as a frustration that leads to resentment.

11

In-Laws: Outlaws, In-Laws, and Other Unmentionables

As far as it depends on you, live at peace with everyone.
ROMANS 12:18

───◆·✦·◆───

I met Mark when I was just fifteen years old. He was seventeen. It was 1976, and the whole country was caught up in celebrating our nation's two hundredth birthday. Our hometown of Waco, Texas, had decided to celebrate the bicentennial with a citywide production of *The Music Man*, with a cast of students from all the public schools in the city.

With a head crammed with dreams about being on stage and singing, I was, along with hundreds of others, jammed into a strange high school choir room, auditioning for roles in the musical. I could only dream of playing the part of Marion, the leading lady. Since I was only five-feet-one-inch tall, I was more likely to be cast as one of the children or as a short townsperson in the chorus.

My nervousness that night didn't prevent me from looking around the room to see how others were doing in their auditions. There was one young man who caught my eye. I thought he would be the perfect Harold Hill—the male lead. *And wouldn't it be fun,* I imagined, *to play Marion and have to kiss him for eight slow bars of music!* Little did I know that my young Harold Hill had been watching me as well.

Mark got the lead role, and, as I suspected, I got to sing in the chorus—with a one-line solo, I'm proud to say. As weeks of rehearsal

turned into months, I got to know "the music man" quite well and enjoyed his rides home from rehearsal almost every night. Our routine went something like this: Go to rehearsal, take other kids home from rehearsal (did you know you can fit eight teenagers in a 1962 Volkswagen Bug?), drive to my house, sit in the car and talk—and it *was* only talk, much to my chagrin.

One night, after hours of listening to the radio with the motor turned off, Mark tried to start the car—but nothing happened. The battery was completely dead. It was after midnight, but I knew just who to call. The man who always saved me from catastrophes: my daddy. Dad was the automotive manager at the Sears store and knew more about cars than *anyone* in town. I told Mark I would just go in the house and ask Daddy to come out and help. No problem. So I did.

And did Daddy *ever* come out, looking just like, well, just like a daddy at midnight. His hair was disheveled, and he was wearing one of his vee-neck T-shirts. Topping off the look was a pair of polyester shorts. Mark got out of the car to greet him. Daddy took one disapproving look at the teenage boy who had spent the last couple hours "talking" in the dark with his daughter and asked him to get back in the car. Mark obeyed without a word. Daddy's mission was to get the car started and get his daughter into the house. Small talk with this boy was not a priority.

The plan was for Dad to push, and once the car had a little speed, Mark would pop the clutch. The engine would start, and Mark would be on his merry way. And that's exactly what happened. We lived on a hill, so Daddy didn't have to push much. The car started right up. I was beaming. The two most important men in my life had finally met, and now they had succeeded in their first project together.

I don't know how parents know these things, but a few years later, when Mark asked to marry me, Daddy told Mark that he knew—on the night of the dead battery—that Mark was going to be "the one." Three-and-a-half years later, I walked down the aisle of First United Methodist Church on my daddy's arm. When we got to the front of the church, one of the ministers popped the big question: "Who gives this woman to be married to this man?"

My father, who ordinarily kept his faith to himself, surprised us all with these words: "The Lord Jesus who gave her to us, her mother, and I do." That day he, along with our other parents, added a new title to his resume: "In-law."

In-Laws

They can be intimidating, infuriating, and intrusive, but they can also bring an incredible, incomparable stability to a marriage. In fact, in some European cultures, the low divorce rate is due, at least in part, to the presence of a supportive extended family surrounding the marriage. In-laws can be wonderful. That's the good news. But do beware: The relationship between you and your in-laws can be less than smooth and supportive. Overly involved or, conversely, overly detached parents can put stress on a marriage.

> It's imperative that *you and your husband*—not your parents—set the guidelines and boundaries that will be most supportive of your marriage in the long run.

As you're getting started in your new life, it's imperative that *you and your husband*—not your parents—set the guidelines and boundaries that will be most supportive of your marriage in the long run. But get ready. Making these adjustments will most likely be more challenging for you than it will be for your husband.

A New Hero

Scott and Joan were having trouble communicating and needed an objective third party to help them sort things out. The conversation turned to the subject of her father. Her eyes lit up as she described his strength, his kindness, and his availability to them as a couple. She talked affectionately about how he had come over to trim the bushes recently—without even being asked—and how he had bought her a plane ticket so she could attend her high school reunion.

She was animated, and her voice was lively and engaging. But Scott's face revealed a different story. The more she talked in glowing terms about her father, the more Scott's countenance dropped.

"My dad is my hero," Joan said with a flourish as she finished her remarks.

At that moment, Joan might as well have pounded the mat and declared Scott down for the count. Instead of motivating her husband, her unqualified admiration for her father demoralized Scott and moved him toward nonresponsiveness and apathy.

After Bobbie and Robert were married, Bobbie and her mother talked frequently on the phone. Bobbie had grown up in a home where

the act of spending money was celebrated. Now, as a newlywed, she was facing an austerity she hadn't known. The phone conversations with her mom often turned—predictably—to the subject of money. Bobbie was open about what she and Robert couldn't afford, and Bobbie's mother frequently offered to "help."

Even though you'd think Robert would have been delighted with the extra cash in the account, he wasn't. In fact, Bobbie's appreciation for "her mother's generosity" became unfair competition for her new husband. It was when Robert finally asked Bobbie to stop talking about finances with her mother that Bobbie began to realize how insecure these gifts made him feel. And as painful as it was for her to give up the goodies, Bobbie agreed.

The lesson to be learned here is this: When you compare your husband—directly or subtly—to either of your parents, your marriage loses.

With nothing but the best intentions, parents can sabotage the stability of a young marriage. When a mom or dad says to an adult daughter—with or without words—"Honey, if things don't work out, you can always come back home," seeds of marital insecurity are planted. The message is this: "You may be married to this man, but deep down we all know that you're really still ours."

> When you compare your husband— directly or subtly—to either of your parents, your marriage loses.

More often than not, in-law challenges are caused by the good things they offer—gifts, trips, meals, babysitting. Unintentionally, though, these gifts can leave residual guilt and instill pressure to "perform"—to show up for the family reunion, to come for Christmas dinner, to take or not take a particular job. So naturally there will be times when you feel torn between disappointing your husband or disappointing your parents—or his.

When a choice is required, couples in the strongest marriages *choose to disappoint their parents*. They do it lovingly and respectfully. They may have to set boundaries repeatedly in order to affirm that their loyalty is to each other and that their love for and loyalty to their parents come second.

You and Your Mother-in-Law

Dealing with in-laws can be a *huge* issue, especially in the first year of marriage. And it's not a new problem. The first book of the Bible—the

book of Genesis—counsels the man to step away from parents as a foundational step in building the right kind of marriage: "A man will leave his father and mother and be united to his wife, and they will become one flesh."[33]

Like many wives, you may find that your most acute in-law difficulties take place between you and your mother-in-law. Here's why: Tensions can result when both of you are vying—even subconsciously—for the affection of the same man. And if he doesn't intentionally choose to "leave," he forces his wife to compete with his mother for the rest of their lives.

This unresolved situation can hinder the building of a strong marriage:

- There is the daughter-in-law who chronically feels that, in her mother-in-law's eyes, she'll never be good enough for her son.
- There is the mother-in-law who is "concerned" that her son has changed since his marriage, and she's worried that she has "lost her son."
- There are the daughter-in-law's hypersensitive feelings—feelings so raw that anything her mother-in-law does is wrong: if she gives a gift, it's the wrong kind; if she doesn't call, she doesn't care; if she does call, she's being intrusive; if she gives money, she's being controlling; if she doesn't give money, she's being selfish.

Jason and Lynn's Nonnegotiables

By the time she and Jason decided to get married, Lynn had seen too many friends entangled in trivial, exhausting tensions with their mothers-in-law. She determined that her marriage would be different. And so, before the wedding, she and Jason developed one of the most helpful strategies for preventing in-law tension we've ever seen. After hours of discussion, they came up with these five nonnegotiables:

1. We will always speak and listen respectfully to our own parents and to each other's parents.
2. When holidays come, we will decide, without feeling guilty, where it's best for the two of us to be. Once we've decided, we'll let our parents know.

3. We will put a fair limit on our time and conversation with our parents, so that when they call or visit, we can welcome them with open arms rather than treat them as intrusive interrupters. (We don't, for example, have to answer the phone every time they call or say yes to every invitation they give.)

4. We will each agree happily to attend three in-law "command performances" each year. (Lynn might say, "Jase, if it's important to you that I go with you and your parents to the polka festival, I'll be the first one on the dance floor." And when the dancing is over, Jason recognizes that he's used up one of Lynn's command performances.)

5. We will choose our attitudes rather than blame others for our responses. (Lynn recognized that for her to grow bitter over her relationship with her mother-in-law would never help her marriage. She determined that *she* would be the one to decide how she would respond to her mother-in-law. She told me, "I will never say to my husband, 'Your mother *made* me so angry!' I always want to be the one to *choose* my response to her.")

Jason and Lynn's strategy is a starting point. Did this plan keep Lynn from ever getting irritated with her mother-in-law? Of course not. But it did help keep her from reacting negatively or childishly when her mother-in-law hurt her feelings in some way.

If you move into your marriage without the protection of your own in-law agreement—similar to the one Lynn and Jason established—you may be setting yourselves up for years of conflict and frustration. Whether or not you think you'll ever need them, you and your husband must begin to make nonnegotiable rules of your own so that you have a plan to deal with the future. If you lay the groundwork in the first year of your life as Mr. and Mrs., it will give you a wonderful resource when and if both sets of your parents become Grandpa and Grandma.

The Tension of Time

To give couples a perspective on healthy relationships with in-laws, Mark and I try to help them gain a clear sense of *normal*—what they can expect from each other when it comes to the amount of time they'll

be spending with their own families and with their in-laws. We do this by inviting couples to play a little game.

We explain that we're going to ask two questions, each of which requires a specific number for an answer. We ask them not to share their answers out loud until we signal them. When we're sure they understand the process, we ask about the bride's family: "How many days—with or without her husband—will this bride need to spend with her family (parents, grandparents, siblings, extended family) in a given year?" As they begin calculating their answers, we remind them not to speak until we give the signal. Once they have their number, we count to three, and they call out their—sometimes very different—numbers in unison. Then we ask the question about the groom's family: "How many days—with or without his wife—will this groom need to spend with his family in a given year?"

The answers are often fascinating and often quite entertaining. When, for example, the husband guesses that his bride-to-be will need to see her family twenty-four days a year, and her answer is 240 days, we know we've got something to talk about.

There is no hard-and-fast rule here. There may be times—when a parent is sick, or you or your husband work in the family business, for example—that time with parents could be unusually lengthy. Regardless of your situation, though, remember the basic principle for relating to in-laws: Decide early on to protect your marriage by disappointing your parents rather than jeopardize your marriage.

Stay Connected with Your Husband First

Sharon had a low-grade frustration about her marriage. She couldn't identify the specific problem, so she spoke in generalities about a sense of "being disconnected" from her husband. I asked questions—about time together, about their conversations, and then I asked about in-laws. Her voice danced as she talked about how well she and her husband get along with her parents. "In fact," she said, "I talk to them three or four times a day."

"Three or four times a day?" I wondered out loud.

After moving to a city hours away from her parents, Sharon had naturally made up for the infrequent face-to-face contact by multiplying phone time with them. "My mom is really my best friend," she boasted. "You don't think there's anything wrong with us talking as much as we do, do you?"

I offered, "I wonder what would happen if, for the next thirty days, you limited your conversations with your parents to four times a week." She was skeptical but agreed to try it.

Without telling her husband what she was doing, Sharon informed her parents of her decision. Her mom and dad were confused and a little hurt, but they trusted their daughter and respected her perspective.

A little over a month later, Sharon and I met again, and I was eager to hear how the experiment had gone. Ever meticulous, Sharon showed up with a couple of pages of written reflections. She wrote the following:

> The first two weeks were horrible. I was so angry with you for suggesting this assignment that several times I thought about calling you just to tell you that I was calling the whole thing off. But I stuck it out, and I learned a few things I never expected to learn—about myself, my parents, and my marriage.
>
> I kept hoping that a lightbulb would go off for Chuck—that somehow during this month he would start to understand what I really needed from him. But, steady and true as always, Chuck wasn't changing. He continued his typical—but sometimes boring—style of communicating. And the longer I moved into this experiment, the angrier I got at him. I realized how much I was missing him. I realized how far apart I felt from him. Finally, I admitted to myself how dishonest I had been for not telling him how lonely I felt.
>
> By the third week, I knew I had to say something to Chuck. I told him that I needed to talk. We turned off the TV. I told him how much I loved him and how much I missed him and how badly I needed something to change in our marriage.
>
> He was dumbfounded. He had no idea I was feeling this way. Then he asked that classic "guy question": "So what do you want me to do?"
>
> I knew I had to have something specific, so I was ready. I said, "Could we take a walk and talk for twenty minutes on the nights we're home together?" He said, "Sure," but it was that whimsical smile of his that let me know that he wanted to love me even if he didn't understand me.
>
> I believe that *not* having the emotional security blanket of talking to my parents three or four times a day stirred up a lone-

liness in me that I didn't have words for before. We're not out of the woods yet, but I've decided to continue to limit my phone time with my folks to give Chuck a chance to meet some of those needs.

One of your primary tasks during the first year of your marriage is to establish a new "culture" of what is normal for the two of you. Sharon had settled into a pattern of *normal* in which her most emotionally connected conversations were with her mother and father and not with her husband. And because those conversations felt safer and much more natural, she avoided taking the risk of asking Chuck for the emotional intimacy she longed to have with him.

But, of course, in-laws aren't the only potential interruptions to your new marriage.

The Delightful Interruption: Children

Denise and Eric were more than a little excited about the arrival of their first baby. Even though it was early in their marriage, they were ready. They prepared everything they could think of—everything, that is, except their relationship.

After Denise became pregnant, Eric began to miss the "carefree" Denise. For months she suffered from a morning sickness that seemed to last twenty-four hours a day. And the thought of lovemaking only seemed to nauseate her more. On those rare days when she did feel better, her face seemed to be buried in a magazine or parenting book. From Eric's perspective, she seemed to have time and energy to do things that didn't include him—paint the nursery, keep the house immaculate, pick out curtains, shop with her mom, and watch parenting videos—but little time for him and no interest in romance.

Though he was excited about the baby, Eric began to pull back, protecting himself from feeling rejected by his bride. At times, he became defensive and harsh. Not being comfortable asking for what he needed, Eric became resigned to the notion that he had lost Denise.

"Don't get me wrong," Eric told Mark after the baby came. "I love this kid. But something is definitely missing between Denise and me. She used to be my partner, my best friend, my lover—the one I wanted to do everything with. But now, it's like she's found another best friend. I just can't compete with a newborn!"

Let's face it. With a baby in the house, you may as well throw out the idea of "balance" in your life. Nothing can upset your equilibrium quite like having a new twenty-four-hour-a-day responsibility that refuses to fit neatly into *your* schedule.

So take care of yourself, and don't stop taking care of your marriage. If the love of your life and the vitality of your relationship are not nurtured, well, your baby won't be either. Taking care of your marriage *is* taking care of your baby. There is no single more important investment you can make in your child's future than to invest in your marriage. It is not an either/or proposition. You don't have to choose between loving your children or loving your husband. The reality is this: Kids do best in homes where the marriage is put first. Like little satellites, children orbit around the marriage. If it's unstable, the kids will spin out of orbit.

> Taking care of your marriage *is* taking care of your baby. There is no single more important investment you can make in your child's future than to invest in your marriage.

Children always change a marriage. A baby will either bring you much closer to your husband or drive a wedge between the two of you. Because of the new bond that Denise experienced with her baby, Eric got the message loud and clear: "Love is in short supply around here, and you are standing outside the circle where the real love is."

Let me tell you what your husband will be wondering when the baby comes: *Will it ever be the same between us?* The answer, of course, is "No, it never will." But it doesn't mean it has to be worse.

If the time comes for you to have children, the most powerful thing you can do is to be intentional about expressing affection and attentiveness to your husband. When he senses that there is more than enough love to go around, he will be much more attentive to you and a much happier partner with you in parenting.

A Word About Exes

Betsy and William were in our weekly marriage group. This was a second marriage for Betsy, and because she had two boys from her first marriage, she had to make regular arrangements with their father. Though she had, for the most part, gotten over her anger and

hurt about the divorce, nearly every time she had to talk with her ex-husband, the familiar emotions of shame and sadness were stirred up again.

As our group talked about principles for building healthy relationships with in-laws, Betsy made an insightful observation: "You know, it seems that a lot of the same principles we've been talking about for dealing with in-laws also work for a relationship with an ex-husband." Initially, the group laughed. But we could tell from the expression on her face that Betsy wasn't kidding. You could see the question marks on the faces around the group. Mark asked, "Betsy, can you say a little more about what you mean?"

Betsy was quick to answer: "Well, first of all, the big idea we've been talking about is that we've got to be careful to make our marriage central, right? To put our best emotional energy there. With me, it's not that I feel attached to my ex-husband, it's that I can easily get caught up in such frustrating conversations with him that by the time William gets home, I'm emotionally exhausted. Sometimes I have very little patience for this man I love."

"Another thing," she went on, "is that if I can't forgive my ex for what he's done to me, I hold myself hostage to resentment and bitterness. It's just like not being able to forgive parents or in-laws. Bitterness keeps us attached to the very person we're trying to pull away from."

Not only did our group begin to see how these principles applied to in-laws and other interruptions, but Betsy's comments shed light on how forgiveness can set us free.

12

Help: The Iceberg Cometh

We seem to have focused so much on exuberant beginnings and victorious endings that we've forgotten about the slow, sometimes torturous, unraveling of God's grace that takes place in the "middle places."

SUE MONK KIDD, *WHERE THE HEART WAITS*

———◆❖◆———

Mark and I could hear the shouting. From a distance we couldn't tell what was going on. But as we rounded the corner and saw cars in the parking lot, the situation became frighteningly obvious. We realized that in order to get to our car we had to walk directly toward the commotion. A tall, angry man was standing outside the passenger door of a red Volvo, screaming into the window. We couldn't help but overhear pieces of the conversation—at least enough to realize that it was his wife who was receiving the full force of his rage.

The man's anger escalated out of control, and he slammed his fist into the side of the car. Oblivious to the fact that he had an audience, he raged on at his wife, working himself into a frenzy. In a final act of desperate frustration, he began kicking the door. By this time his wife had had enough. The car began slowly moving out of the parking lot as he commanded her to stop: "Mary, don't you drive away! Mary!"

We were dumbfounded as we watched this man in a suit and fancy dress shoes chasing the car the length of the parking lot, screaming all the while, "Mary! Mary!"

What to Do When You Need to Rebuild

In some marriages—this one, for example—the need for help is painfully and publicly obvious. But more often, marriages go flat because of long, slow leaks—not because of sudden blowouts. Sadly, couples often come for counseling only after years of inattentiveness and apathy have resulted in a crisis. Deeply ingrained levels of defensiveness and contempt are often so high that any help seems too late.

Our hope is that you will put into practice a few habits that can keep your marriage so strong that you'll never get to a point of desperation. Paying attention to the cues, knowing when you need help, and making the necessary adjustments can stop the little irritants from posing any real threat to your marriage.

> No matter how deeply you love each other right now, there will be times in your marriage when you'll look at this man you've married and you will simply not like him.

But no matter how deeply you love each other right now, no matter how much you have in common, there will be times in your marriage when you'll look at this man you've married and you will simply not like him. This feeling may last for a moment, a week, or a month, but you *will* experience it. At those times you will need a rebuilding strategy, a blueprint for what to do when your marriage feels as though it's wandering down the wrong path. The advice we give to couples is this: "If at any point either one of you feels that your marriage is below the 'A' level (that's 90 percent at most schools), *that's* the time to get help."

Let's start with the good news: Rebuilding is almost always possible. But it doesn't happen accidentally, any more than my kitchen *accidentally* gets clean. Marriages are restored when couples give focused attention to a few key rebuilding strategies.

Circle the Wagons

In the nineteenth century, those who traveled west across the American frontier were prepared for danger. Whether from hostile thieves or wild animals or bad weather, wagon-train travelers had one rallying cry when facing danger: "Circle the wagons."

Single-file lines were the most efficient way to travel in a wagon train, but it was also the most vulnerable. A totally different formation was required when danger was detected. Survival depended on stopping all forward progress and moving quickly into a formation that would best

protect them. In your marriage, you need to learn—and learn quickly—how to circle the wagons when the need arises. The threat may be intense and obvious—such as the discovery of an addictive behavior. Or it may be slow and subtle—a gnawing feeling that something is not right. In either case you'll need a clear, agreed-upon process for circling the wagons—a willingness to do inconvenient things for the sake of survival.

It's what Nathan and Diane did. These two outstanding young adults were both strong Christians. Early in their marriage they made a simple promise: If our marriage ever hits a crisis level, we will give first priority to restoring and protecting our marriage. Little did they know how soon that promise would be put to the test.

> In your marriage, you need to learn—and learn quickly—how to circle the wagons when the need arises.

They had been married for a little over a year when their world fell apart. Their problems seemed ordinary, but Diane was concerned about Nathan's long work hours and his inattentiveness to her. She signed them up for a weekend marriage conference.[34]

They checked into the hotel on Friday night, enjoyed dinner together, and went to the first session. They enjoyed the speaker and took notes so they could remember the key points. Before going to bed, they eagerly reviewed some things they agreed they'd be able to do to improve their own marriage.

But it was the Saturday morning session that turned the slow leak of Diane's concern into an explosion. In talking about the challenges faced by men, the morning speaker mentioned the threat to intimacy in marriage that Internet pornography provided. Nathan held his breath, desperately hoping that Diane wouldn't take note of the comment. But he had underestimated his wife. Back in their room, Diane asked a simple question: "Have you ever looked at pornography on your computer?"

"Uh, well, yeah, I did—once."

"Once?" she pressed, the look on Nathan's face exposing his attempt to conceal the truth.

Over the next two-and-a-half hours Nathan made a full confession of his deep involvement in cyberporn. The exposure of his mind's unfaithfulness broke Diane's heart. And her tears devastated Nathan.

"I've been trapped and unable to overcome this," Nathan poured out to his bride. "But I was more afraid of losing you if you found out, so I just kept it to myself."

This could have been the beginning of the end for their marriage, but Diane and Nathan knew what to do. Because they had a plan, they circled the wagons. Nathan drastically reduced his work responsibilities for the next few weeks. They called and made an immediate appointment with a marriage counselor. They spent the week talking about what had happened. No amount of tears or contrition from Nathan could stop Diane from expressing her hurt, her anger, and her raw feelings about the situation and about him. She didn't hold back. "You have betrayed me, and I don't *feel* like staying married to you right now," she said. "But I made a 'for better or worse" commitment—and we will work this through."

On Thursday the counselor helped Nathan and Diane to continue sorting through their crisis. He showed them how to begin the process of restoring trust and intimacy to their marriage.

The time to decide how to circle the wagons—to have a plan for what to do in a crisis—is *not* when the arrows are flying. If you and your groom have never faced a crisis, you may find it hard to believe that you will one day need help in your marriage. But right now is exactly the time for you to build your plan.

Agree right now that if there's ever a time when either of you senses the need for help, the other will agree *without question* to enter the "circle the wagons" mode. This is not a time to debate whether things are really bad enough to take this step. The fact that one of you declares the need to circle the wagons is enough.

Protect your Marriage, Bury the Weapons

Regardless of the seriousness of the issue, a crisis in your marriage can only be resolved if you are willing to lay down any weapons of destruction you may be tempted to use. The *crisis* is the enemy, not your husband.

The research evidence is conclusive: There are four specific responses that will never help your marriage.[35] So commit to protecting your marriage by burying forever these weapons that only bring destruction and never bring healing:

1. defensiveness—"Oh, so it's all *my* fault now?"
2. contempt—name-calling, cutting humor, eye-rolling that accompanies such comments as, "So what are you going to do about it, sue me?"

3. withholding of attention—the passive, nonresponsive stone wall that seeks to move to a position of power by shutting down and not responding at all

4. personal attacks—"Could you pick up your socks before you go upstairs?" becomes "You don't care about anyone but yourself, do you?"

Healthy marriages play by the rules. When you're in a conflict, negative responses only escalate the problem—and someone will get hurt. Using destructive weapons may be effective in taking your partner down and winning an argument, but the first casualty is going to be your marriage.

Feed Your Marriage

Before a crisis pays a visit to your marriage, you can fill your pantry with good things. The idea is not to seek heroic—and often unrealistic—measures, such as taking a two-week trip to Hawaii. Instead, focus on simple, doable actions that can give your marriage exactly what it needs in order to grow. These are healthy staples that are marriage-nurturing activities. You can keep them on the shelves and pick one whenever you want to strengthen and rekindle your love for each other:

- Agree to take walks together.
- Establish a date night.
- Rent a movie and snuggle on the sofa.
- When you think about your husband during the day, call him or e-mail him. Tell him how much you love him.
- Leave an "I'm thinking of you" surprise gift in his closet.

Especially during a season of healing, you'll want to focus on giving a wholehearted yes to each other as much as is humanly possible. Whether the request is for you to give your husband a warm greeting at the door or for him to pick up his dirty socks in the family room, the idea is simply to feed the marriage by intentionally and warmly responding to each other's needs.

One of the best things you can do to revitalize your relationship is to attend a marriage enrichment weekend.[36] When couples tell us, "We can't afford it," we are reminded of a divorced friend whose husband spent over $25,000 on the proceedings. While he was married, this man had been rigid and unwilling to "waste" his money on a weekend getaway with his wife once a year. In comparison, a $300

weekend is a fraction of the cost you'll pay emotionally and financially if your marriage gets off course.

Build a Support Team

If you're stuck in a negative pattern—the nagging wife/unresponsive husband; the pressured wife/rejected husband; the angry wife/passive husband; the childish wife/scornful husband—identify what you're doing. And then agree that it's something you both want to stop. And once you've stopped, you'll want to have a support team in place.

Long before the fires of frustration ever threaten to engulf your marriage, make sure you have at your fingertips more than enough resources to extinguish them. So right here and right now, in your first year of marriage, put together a team of people who will promise to stand with you on the side of your marriage—a marriage mentor couple, the pastor who married you, maybe even a professional counselor you both trust. Invite them today to be a part of your support team.

> Right now, in your first year of marriage, put together a team of people who will promise to stand with you on the side of your marriage.

You're not looking for a group of people to be your therapists and to solve your problems. You are simply looking for people whom you trust and who can create an environment of hopefulness for you—those who will encourage you to hold on to all the right reasons you married each other in the first place.

Recognize Your Power to Change Your Husband

Three weeks after our wedding, at the ripe old ages of nineteen and twenty-one, Mark and I visited a friend's church one Sunday evening for worship. To illustrate a point—a point long since forgotten—the pastor asked a question of all the married couples in the room.

"How many of you," he asked, "can honestly say that there is nothing about your husband or wife that you would like to change?"

No one raised a hand—no one, that is, except us.

All eyes turned toward us as the pastor made his way down the aisle, carrying his microphone. Walking directly up to me, he asked, "And how long have the two of *you* been married?"

"Almost three weeks," I proudly answered. The congregation, as if on cue, erupted with laughter. We were dumbfounded and angry. *Just because so many people have accepted mediocrity in marriage,* we reasoned, *doesn't mean that we have to.*

But our anger subsided long before our first anniversary, when I began to discover "one or two" habits of Mark's that I would really like to change. What that laughing congregation knew clearly we learned slowly: Every wife, no matter how much she loves the man she has married, will, sooner or later, develop a wish list of changes she'd like to make in her husband:

> Every wife, no matter how much she loves the man she has married, will, sooner or later, develop a wish list of changes she'd like to make in her husband.

- Maybe you married your husband because you loved his stability, but now there are times when you sure would like to loosen him up.
- Maybe you married him because you loved his spontaneity, but now you wish he would be more predictable and better organized.
- Maybe you were attracted to him because of his athletic physique, but now you wish he'd give up the gym more often and focus on you.
- Maybe you loved his sense of humor, but now you long for conversations that don't have a punch line.

I was wrong when I assumed that an excellent marriage meant that I'd never want to change Mark. Marriage *can* be God's most effective life-shaping force for change in a person's life. And you have the ability to be an agent of change in your husband's life. But to do so, you have to come to two paradoxical realizations:

- I *cannot* change my husband.
- I really *can* change my husband.

It *is* a strange paradox. If you focus on changing your husband, you have virtually no chance of changing him. Here's why: When a husband becomes his wife's number one home improvement project, she winds up with a man who feels powerless ever to satisfy her. He assumes that, no matter what he does, no matter how hard he tries, his wife will always be able to find one more thing about him that needs changing.

At this point, you may be thinking, *Wait just a second. I thought you told me my husband was never going to get it on his own—that I need to learn to ask for what I need from him.* Don't be confused: asking for what you need is very different from giving advice. Overloading your husband with advice and suggestions *will* be perceived as criticism, and criticism robs him of the adventure and fun he experiences in his choosing to do the noble thing—not because he was forced to do it, but because he loves you. But if he feels emasculated and dependent, it's highly unlikely that he'll make the changes you desire.

> If you focus on changing your husband, you have virtually no chance of changing him.

What Time Is It?

There was something I was determined to change in Mark. He had one habitual pattern that, more than any other, had irritated and angered me. More evenings than not, he was late getting home. For years I tried to change the pattern. I tried confronting him, withholding affection, scowling through dinners—all the things we've just told you not to do—but nothing seemed to work, until I ambushed him.

For the sake of fairness, I'll let Mark tell the story:

> I had tried. I really had. I set my watch ahead. I said I'd be home later than I expected to be, just to give myself some wiggle room. I got up from my chair to leave early. But my best-laid plans fell victim to the apparent conspiracy of people who just *had* to talk to me—urgently—just before I walked out the office door. I would usually make the obligatory "I'm going to be late, honey," call and then head to the car, spending the ten-minute drive home preparing my defense.
>
> I would say to myself. *Hey, I'm not all that bad. I'm just fifteen minutes late. I know I'm not perfect, but I'm a heck of a lot better husband than a lot of guys. And besides, this person really needed my help. His marriage was in trouble!*
>
> By the time I got home, dinner was not the only thing that was boiling in the kitchen. I would give a halfhearted apology—an explanation, really, of whose fault it was this time. My bride would let me know how it felt not to be able to trust her husband's

word; I would call a foul, and we'd have a side order of tension with our dinner.

After ten years of dealing with my habitual lateness, my wife had had it. She was tired of making the same speeches week in and week out. She was tired of trying to change my behavior. She was *really* tired of my excuses. So, like a desperate woman, she took action. Without consulting me, she decided to try something very, very different the next time I came home late—of course, she didn't have to wait long. I walked in as usual, with my rationalizations fully prepared. But I was stepping into an ambush.

Instead of the usual quiet but tense "you're late!" reception I'd grown accustomed to, I was mauled at the door by my bride. She wrapped me in a bear hug and gave a promising kiss on the lips. As she held me, she whispered in my ear, "I'm so glad you're home. I missed you so much!"

That was eight or ten years ago, I don't quite remember. What I *do* remember, though, are the changes that took place in our marriage because of the changes my bride made:

1. I don't prepare speeches or rationalizations when I *am* late.
2. I can't wait to get home.
3. When we eat together after I'm late, we still enjoy ourselves.

Does Mark still arrive home late on occasion? Sure. But there's no longer a scolding "mother" waiting for him. Now he's been motivated to change—not because of my speeches, but because he was wooed, even seduced, into change. Guess which approach he likes best.

The change happened, not just in Mark's behavior but in our marriage, when I took the focus off what I couldn't control—his lateness—and put it into what I could—my *response*.

Changing your response doesn't *guarantee* a changed husband, of course, any more than planting seeds in the ground and watering them guarantees a healthy garden. But it greatly improves your chances for a bountiful harvest. You really *can* change your husband. It happens when you go first and create an atmosphere in which transformation can happen—first in yourself, and then in your husband.

MEET IN
the Middle

Welcome to the middle. As you've already realized, the whole point of this book is to get you and your husband talking—both to help him become an expert on knowing and loving you and to help you learn to know his heart and respond well to his attempts at loving you. We've designed the questions here explicitly to help you take the ideas you're reading about and let them impact you and your marriage.

But even before you dive into the questions, you'll likely want to take a minute or two after each chapter to ask your husband about something you've read. Starting out with questions like "Are you really like this?" or "If I tried something like the book suggests here, would you like it?" will only help you become more of an expert on this man you have married.

After each chapter, we encourage you to discuss together the questions called "Touchpoint" and "Crossing Over." "Touchpoint" questions are meant to talk over with your husband, while "Crossing Over" questions will draw out his response to something he just read or give you opportunity to share something you learned in your chapter.

We've laid out the "Meet in the Middle" questions in a way that provides maximum flexibility for you and your husband. You may choose to answer them on your own, with your husband, or with a group of close friends. It's your call. You may even choose different approaches to different chapters—with some chapters, you may answer all the questions, with others, you may pick a few or just one. However you approach this process, we invite you to invest the kind of focused attention in your marriage that will make this year the most important year in your life.

Introduction

1. How did you get this book? What prompted you to read it?

2. What do you hope to learn or understand better about marriage? About yourself? About your husband?

3. Is there anything about the topic of this book that makes you a little nervous about reading these pages? Why or why not?

Touchpoint

Think about couples you know. What qualities do you most admire and appreciate about other people's marriages?

Chapter 1: The Most Important Year: Reality Check

1. To what degree, if any, have you experienced "the princess crisis"? Put differently, what has been most surprising for you about the abrupt transition from being a bride to being a wife?

2. Embedded in Deuteronomy 24:5 are some interesting principles that can make your first year of marriage the most important year of your life.

- The *"Wet Cement Year" Principle:* Problems not dealt with in the first year simply become larger and more paralyzing as the years go by. In what areas and about what issues are you trying not to make waves? What little irritants and which of your husband's insensitivities are you hoping will simply go away?

- The *Slow Learner Principle:* What things have you been surprised to see your husband not figure out more quickly? What do you need to identify as things that please you?

- The *Responsive Feedback Principle:* What good things does your husband do that make you happy—things you need to respond to better? Be specific about these things, as well as about the response you'd like to have.

Touchpoint

What one thing did the two of you do together naturally during the peak of your courtship and romance that you want to make sure you continue to do throughout your marriage, even when it may be inconvenient?

Crossing OVER

Your husband is being encouraged to invest this year in learning to bring you happiness. Find out from him how you can best communicate when he has done just that.

Chapter 2: Needs: Dare to Dream the Impossible

1. In a healthy marriage a husband finds great joy in bringing pleasure to his wife. To help him succeed, you'll need to develop three specific skills. First, you need to know your own needs—whether it relates to sex or to sandwiches—well enough that you know clearly what your husband can do to bring you pleasure. Start making your list right now. After all, being out of touch with your own needs will prevent your husband from doing the very thing you long for him to do, namely, to cherish you.

   Second, you need to be able to ask your husband clearly, specifically, and winsomely for what you need and, like Cathryn (page 28), even what you want.

   - What vague complaints can you rephrase as expressions of specific needs?
   - What issue or desire or need of yours is your husband just not getting? Restate it as a specific request and give him another chance.

2. The *Yes Spiral* begins with a willingness to say yes to the request—spoken or unspoken—to meet the needs of your spouse. It's characterized by the choice to demonstrate love—even when you don't feel like it. Review the *Yes Spiral* and the *No Spiral* conversations (pages 32–34). Make it your own experiment this week to say yes to your husband. Note the results—and keep in mind that, since you are, in reality, "one flesh" with your husband, when you meet his needs, in some mysterious way you are meeting your own needs as well.

Touchpoint

You need to know and meet your husband's needs with the same playful intentionality you hope he seeks in trying to meet yours. Just what does your husband desire from you? Ask him. The playful questions on page 31 may help get your conversation started.

*Crossing*OVER

Find out from your husband what one thing he would ask of you if he knew you would not turn him down.

Chapter 3: Spiritual Unity: More Than Meets the Eye

1. What "transcendent thirds" exist in your marriage (similar likes and dislikes, passions, and hobbies)? What are you or could you be—individually and as a couple—doing to move toward "The Transcendent Third"?

2. Wherever your husband is in his relationship with God, what can you do to encourage his spiritual growth? What can you do to woo him? Which one of these ideas will you act on this week?

3. To which specific characteristics in you and your husband does the statement on page 40, "Spiritual unity does not mean spiritual uniformity," speak? What can you affirm about your husband's style of living out his faith?

Touchpoint

Mark and I encourage engaged couples to keep things simple when it comes to building the right kind of spiritual habits in their marriage.

- What is one spiritual practice you can choose to do as a couple?
- With what imperfect community of faith—church—will you two connect?

Find out from your husband what things you can do that would most encourage him to grow in his faith. And while you're at it, find out the things you could do or say that would be the biggest turnoffs to spiritual intimacy.

Chapter 4: Family of Origin: White-Water Wedding Guide

1. All of us enter into marriage with our own set of "command-ments" about what is normal. Remember Robert and Bobbie's car trips? What *normals* of yours are different from your husband's *normals*?

2. There are only two kinds of couples preparing for marriage: those who seek to be honest about the nature of their issues, and those who pretend they have none. To which category do you belong? How about your husband? What warning, if any, do your answers to that two-part question contain?

3. Think back to a recent argument. What was the topic or content (money, sex, in-laws, a messy kitchen)? What might the real issue—a genogram issue—have been (a pattern of anger and reac-tion, dominance and subservience, or power and helplessness)? Be aware that these *patterns*, not the subject matter of your dis-agreements, are the most destructive to marriages.

   What are some of the most important "new normals" that you want to establish in your marriage?

Touchpoint

A marvelous tool to help you and your husband recognize your rules of *normal* in a nonthreatening way starts with a genogram (see pages 45–50). Begin by drawing a family tree. It will help you identify pat-terns of *normal* in the family.

Give a brief description of each person you named. Giving partic-ular attention to your parents' and grandparents' marriages,

- describe their marriages, good and bad.
- describe how each seemed to deal with conflict in marriage.
- describe the spiritual life that each couple shared.

Look throughout the system and see if there are any marriages you admire. Why? Then see how you do writing your own "Normal Report." Answer these five questions:

- What would someone growing up in this family system see as a normal husband?
- What would someone growing up in this family system see as a normal wife?
- What would someone growing up in this family system see as a normal marriage?
- What would someone growing up in this family system see as a normal way to deal with conflict?
- What would someone growing up in this family system see as a normal spiritual life for a married couple?

What insight(s) about yourself have you gained from this exercise? What areas of potential conflict and danger have you identified?

What did you learn from reading the analysis of Greg and Carrie, their genograms, and where *normal* might take them in five years?

*Crossing*OVER

Show your "Normal Report" to your husband and ask for his input on what *normals* you might have missed from the family you grew up in.

Chapter 5: Roles: Welcome to My World

The Bible does something much more profound than prescribe specific tasks for husbands and other tasks for wives. It gives three clear directives for women about their role in marriage—describing roles that Christian wives are called to play in their husbands' lives. But these roles can never successfully be forced on a wife; in fact, they only work when you freely choose them.

- *Image-Conscious:* What was your reaction to the chapter's reflections on the Genesis account of creation and the conclusion about the pinnacle of God's efforts? What does it mean to you that you are God's gift to your husband, that you are God's image bearer?
- *Help Me!* What new understanding or appreciation of "helper" did this section give you? Even though your husband may not

admit it or even know it, he needs you as a helper. What specific help does he need these days? What things could you be doing to help him that you aren't yet doing?

- What things does the analogy between marriage and a waltz say to you about submission? About your role and your husband's role in marriage? About leadership?

Touchpoint

Is *submission* really a dirty word? In the Bible, submission is mutual and voluntary. It is the willing choice of a wife to submit freely to her husband and his willingness to lovingly submit to her. It is having as a marital guideline "If we ever get stuck and we're unable to agree on what to do, I want you to win." In what ways has the issue of submission surfaced in your marriage? Talk together about whether or not you agree with the ideas of submission presented in this chapter and about how the whole idea of submission feels to the two of you in your marriage.

*Crossing*OVER

In your husband's chapter, he was told that his three primary roles in your life are as a leader, a warrior, and a lover. Find out from him which of these three roles he likes the best and which gives him the most discomfort.

Chapter 6: Talk: Did Someone Hit the Mute Button?

1. When have you realized that you and your husband speak different languages? Give an example or two. Also, what have you noticed about your husband's deafness? Be specific about some situations. (And don't forget to laugh!)

2. Tell of a time or two when your husband's default settings kicked in and, when you expressed a concern, he assumed either that you wanted him to fix the problem or that you were attacking him.

3. It may not be an overstatement to say that a wife longs to know her husband's soul with the same intensity that a husband longs to know his wife's body. To pry open the door to your groom's

heart, be clear about whether you want advice, a decision, or a listening ear ("this is one of those times when . . ."); look for an activity you can share (third-object conversations); and keep up the pillow talk (kind, flirtatious, and encouraging words that end your husband's day by reminding him of your love for him). Look for opportunities this week to use these three "can openers."

Touchpoint

"Relational amnesia" is forgetting the ways we used to talk before we got married. Back then, your husband may have allowed you glimpses into his heart and told you things he had never told anyone else. Talk about the little things you used to say and do when your relationship was new and growing and your conversations were incredible. Select at least one conversation pattern that you want to ensure becomes a habit in your marriage.

*Crossing*OVER

Tell your husband about the "can openers," and find out which ones he would prefer you use and which ones he would prefer you avoid.

Chapter 7: Friendship: The Secret Ingredient

1. What dimensions of your friendship with your husband do you especially value? Be specific and make as long a list as you like. You'll want to refer back to this when the principles of friendship with your husband do not come so naturally.

2. We suggest that couples adopt a zero-secrets policy.

   • What secret from your husband (if any) are you carrying around? When will you tell him?

   • When your husband tells you his secrets, what words of assurance, forgiveness, and affection will you offer instead of judgment? Practice now so you're ready with the words when you need them.

3. Which "friendly feedback" sentences—"I like that!"; "I don't know how you do it!"; "You know what I would just love?"; and "That counts"—will you consciously add to your vocabulary this week?

Touchpoint

Talk together about how you can form the habit of making your first sixty seconds together warm and welcoming. Decide what you will do to ensure that the first minute with your husband is filled with welcoming expressions of love.

CrossingOVER

Keeping your marriage healthy—developing the kind of friendship that can protect your marriage—takes time. Review the description of the slot system on pages 79–83. This week, carve out six slots of time to be together.

Chapter 8: Conflict: Close Enough for Sparks to Fly

1. Three safety checks can help protect your marriage from the dangerous twists and turns of disappointment, discouragement, and hurt.

 Safety Check #1: *Conflict will happen.* Can you discern a normal pattern for how conflicts happen in your marriage? Think about the last conflict you had. Were you surprised?

 Safety Check #2: *Prepare to forgive.* For what do you need to forgive your husband? Whether the incident happened five seconds ago or five years ago, just do it!

 Safety Check #3: *Do you have your fire extinguishers handy?* Arm yourself with these powerful strategies for reducing and overcoming conflicts. Which of the following strategies do you think will be the most important in your marriage? Which ones will be the hardest for you to use?

- Complain (make a specific request for change); don't criticize.
- When the flood comes, take a break.
- Start arguments softly.
- Don't expect to resolve every conflict.
- Do the patch work.

Intimacy with your husband will come only from knowing how to handle conflict together.

- What did you learn about how to handle conflict from the family in which you grew up?
- What do you know about your husband, his family of origin, and his upbringing that suggests how he handles conflict?
- What guidelines for handling conflict would you like to establish in your marriage?

*Crossing*OVER

Ask your husband about the four fire safety instructions from his chapter. Talk together about which of these are most challenging for the two of you.

Chapter 9: Money: The Other Lover

1. If you and your husband tend to avoid financial preparedness, what do you think is behind this tendency—idealism, passive-aggressiveness, avoidance, something else? You might also consider what your genograms suggest about how each of you deals with money.

2. When in your marriage, if ever, have you lapsed into "Money is my husband's department" or "It's easier to ask for forgiveness than permission" thoughts or actions? What can you remind yourself of in order to avoid these pitfalls?

3. Which of these wise women's words is most important to you? Which is most difficult?

   - "It's not unromantic or unspiritual to pay attention to the ways you'll handle money in your marriage."
   - "There's nothing you need badly enough right now to go into debt for it."
   - "If you want to live on one income someday, live on one income now."

- "Agree to stay on the same team, sit on the same side of the table, and make your first priority not just solving a particular money issue but doing so in such a way that money never drives a wedge between you and your husband."

Touchpoint

Here are a few steps to help you and your husband structure your finances in a way that keeps both of you on the same side of the table.

- *Our Money*: Why is it important to have "our money" rather than "his money" and "my money"? Have you agreed to this arrangement? If not, why not?

- *The Marriage Insurance Premium*: Ask your husband what he thinks of the idea of an MIP. Talk to your husband about establishing one.

- *Spending Plan*: Focus on what you can spend rather than on what you can't spend. Work with your husband to develop (if you haven't already) a spending plan. The guidelines on page 102 can be helpful.

*Crossing*OVER

Ask your husband what money and tigers have in common, and find out what one action or attitude you can take related to money that will best demonstrate your love and respect for him.

Chapter 10: Sex: Better Than Chocolate

1. Making the change from the virgin bride to your husband's sexual playmate can be more than a little challenging. To what degree have you experienced "the whiplash effect"? What benefits come from defining and approaching sex as "the most natural form of holy play a couple can experience together"?

2. Far too many women are resigned to endure sex rather than enjoy it. What would you like to teach your husband about what gives you sexual pleasure? Be as specific as possible. What, if anything, is keeping you from sharing this information with him—and what will you do to get beyond that barrier?

3. Where do you see yourself—and where do you see your husband—in this chapter's discussion of sex, particularly in the section "Getting to What *You* Want" and the two very different versions of baseball played by husbands and wives (pages 112–14)? If you haven't already, read "your version of baseball" to your husband. Comment, too, on the parables of the long car ride and the dirty kitchen in "You're in the Driver's Seat." What messages do these two stories have for you?

Touchpoint

What plan do you have for those times when one of you is in the mood for lovemaking and the other is not? If you don't yet have a plan, see the suggestions on page 116. The goal is to see healthy sexual interest—even when it's not timed perfectly—as an opportunity for responsive intimacy rather than as a frustration that leads to resentment.

*Crossing*OVER

Ask your husband to read to you any one of the following sections from his chapter: "Pressure and Rejection: Turning Off the Spin Cycle" (page 119), "Made for Each Other" (page 121), "Spoiling Your Appetite" (page 123), and "All the Marbles" (page 125). After listening to what he reads, talk to him about anything that surprised you or that you wonder about.

Chapter 11: In-Laws: Outlaws, In-Laws, and Other Unmentionables

1. In-laws can be intimidating, infuriating, and intrusive, but they can also bring an incredible, incomparable stability to a marriage. In what way, if any, either directly or subtly, are you comparing your husband to either of your parents? In what ways, if any, has a parent (yours or his) sabotaged the stability of your marriage by offering "good" things that come with strings attached? When, so far, have you had to choose between disappointing your spouse and disappointing your parents? Which did you choose? In retrospect, would you say it was the better choice?

2. Stay connected with your husband first and foremost. Are regular, too frequent conversations with your parent(s) keeping you from being as emotionally connected to your husband as you'd like and as would be healthy? Who can help you answer this question and, if the answer is yes, who will hold you accountable for changing?

3. Imagine being pregnant with your first child. Plan now what you will do to take care of yourself and what you might do to take care of your marriage. (Hint: Be intentional about expressing affection and attentiveness to your husband.) Remember that taking care of your marriage *is* taking care of your baby.

Touchpoint

Answer the following question about your family and your husband's family: How many days do each of us (with or without each other) need to spend with our families (parents, grandparents, siblings, extended family) in a given year? Talk together about what your answers tell you about yourselves.

*Crossing*OVER

Read Jason and Lynn's in-law nonnegotiables (page 121) to your husband and see what he thinks of these suggestions. Work together to make your own boundaries and plans for dealing with the two sets of parents.

Chapter 12: Help: The Iceberg Cometh

1. No matter how deeply you love each other right now, no matter how much you have in common, there will be times in your marriage when you'll look at this man you've married and you will simply not like him. Why is it good for you to know this fact right now?

2. Be sure to feed your marriage. Which of these marriage-nurturing staples is part of your diet: taking walks together, a regular date night, a movie rental so you can snuggle on the sofa, telephone calls or e-mails telling your husband you love him, "I'm thinking

of you" surprise gifts, regular weekend getaways, or something else? Which of these items is the next you'll add to your diet?

3. Don't forget to build a support team. Who can help you hold on to all the right reasons you married each other? Start putting this team together today.

4. Marriage can be God's most effective life-shaping force for change in a person's life. When have you seen this truth lived out in marriage? What hint of this power, if any, have you already noticed in your own marriage? In what ways, for instance, do you sense iron sharpening iron?

5. Change happened, not just in Mark's behavior but in our marriage, when I took the focus off what I couldn't control—his lateness—and put it into what I could—my response. What response to one of your husband's behaviors that's bugging you can you work on changing?

Touchpoint

Rebuilding a marriage is almost always possible, but it doesn't happen accidentally. How prepared are you and your husband to give focused attention to key rebuilding strategies?

- *Have a plan:* What will you and your husband do to circle the wagons? The time to decide is now, before the arrows start flying.

- *Know the signals:* Why should the fact that one of you declares the need to circle the wagons be reason enough to do so?

- *Protect your marriage:* Commit to burying forever the destructive weapons of defensiveness, contempt, the withholding of attention, and personal attacks.

Crossing OVER

Find out from your husband how he would most like you to respond if you sense a warning light going off in your marriage that he seems to be ignoring.

Notes

1. "What Happens after the Wedding?" Interview with Pamela Paul, Sheryl Nissinen, and Terry Real (*The Oprah Winfrey Show,* air date: 28 October 2002).

2. Leah Heidenrich, in her master's research project titled "Bride Illusion: Depression in Newlywed Women," cited in Sheryl Nissinen, *The Conscious Bride* (Oakland, Calif.: New Harbinger, 2000), 176.

3. Reported in John M. Gottman, *The Seven Principles for Making Marriage Work* (Three Rivers, Michigan: Three Rivers Press, 2000), 5.

4. Reported in Linda J. Waite and Maggie Gallagher, *The Case for Marriage: Why Married People Are Happier, Healthier, and Better-Off Financially* (New York: Doubleday, 2000), 67.

5. Waite and Gallagher, *The Case for Marriage,* 67.

6. Reported in Philip Yancey, *Finding God in Unexpected Places* (Nashville: Moorings, 1995), 82.

7. Neil Clark Warren, *Catching the Rhythm of Love* (Nashville: Nelson, 2000), 16–17.

8. Willard F. Harley, *His Needs, Her Needs* (Grand Rapids: Revell, 1993; revised edition 2001), 7.

9. See the real-life examples in Les and Leslie Parrott, *Becoming Soul Mates* (Grand Rapids: Zondervan, 1995).

10. "The Good Wife's Guide," *Housekeeping Monthly,* 13 May 1955; can be viewed on the Internet at www.lucaschristian.com/wifeguide.htm.

11. Research cited in *CBMW News,* vol. 1, no. 3 (June 1996), 1.

12. Genesis 2:18.

13. Many of the foundational principles in this chapter have been inspired by John Eldredge's treatment of this topic in *Wild at Heart* (Nashville: Nelson, 2001).

14. Genesis 1:1, emphasis added.

15. Psalm 27:9, emphasis added.

16. See John 14:16, 26; 15:26; 16:7.

17. The National Domestic Violence Hotline (1-800-799-SAFE [7233]) is staffed twenty-four hours a day to provide crisis assistance and information related to spouse abuse.

18. C. S. Lewis, *That Hideous Strength* (New York: Macmillan, 1946), 76.

19. Quentin Schultze, *Winning Your Kids Back From the Media* (Downers Grove, Ill.: InterVarsity Press, 1994), 30.

20. Jane Austen, *Sense and Sensibility* (New York: Bantam Books, 1983), 316.

21. Story adapted from Gary Smalley, *The Hidden Value of a Man* (Colorado Springs: Focus on the Family, 1992), 106.

22. Dialogue adapted from Jeff Van Vonderen, *Families Where Grace Is in Place* (Minneapolis: Bethany House, 1992), 49–50.

23. Gottman, *The Seven Principles for Making Marriage Work*, 17, 20.

24. Gottman, *The Seven Principles for Making Marriage Work*, 79.

25. Gottman, *The Seven Principles for Making Marriage Work*, 264.

26. Gottman, *The Seven Principles for Making Marriage Work*, 177.

27. Gottman, *The Seven Principles for Making Marriage Work*, 114.

28. Gottman, *The Seven Principles for Making Marriage Work*, 179.

29. Gottman, *The Seven Principles for Making Marriage Work*, 130.

30. Richard Swenson, *Margin* (Colorado Springs: NavPress, 1995), 168.

31. Cited in Mary Pipher, *The Shelter of Each Other* (New York: Ballantine, 1996), 38.

32. For more information about healing from sexual abuse, see Lynn Heitritter and Jeanette Vought, *Helping Victims of Sexual Abuse* (Minneapolis: Bethany House, 1989); also visit www.joshuachildrensfoundation.org.

33. Genesis 2:24.

34. Diane signed up for a "Family Life Today" conference. Find out more about this organization on the Internet at www.familylife.com.

35. See Gottman, *The Seven Principles for Making Marriage Work*, 27.

36. Marriage Encounter (1-800-795-LOVE); Marriage Enrichment (1-800-634-8325); A Weekend to Remember (501-223-8663).